SHEEPDOG TRIALS

SHEEPDOG TRIALS

Eric Halsall

Commentator of BBC TV's `ONE MAN & HIS DOG´

 Patrick Stephens, Cambridge

Dedication
This book is dedicated to the sheepdogs of Britain, in particular Rhaq, Meg and Gael whose friendship gave me so much pleasure.

First published 1982

British Library Cataloguing in Publication Data

Halsall, Eric
  Sheepdog trials
  1. Sheep dogs—Trials
  I. Title
  636.7'3   SF428.6

  ISBN 0-85059-565-7

Produced for the publishers, Patrick Stephens Limited, Bar Hill, Cambridge, CB3 8EL, England, by Book Production Consultants, Cambridge.

Text photoset in 11 on 12 pt Baskerville by Manuset Limited, Baldock Herts. Printed in Great Britain on 115 gsm Fineblade coated cartridge, and bound, by Biddles Ltd, Guildford, for the publishers Patrick Stephens Limited, Bar Hill, Cambridge, CB3 8EL, England.

Frontispiece *Course director Eric Halsall explains a point to Irishman Tim Flood at the 1979 Stranraer International.*

Contents

Sincere acknowledgement for the use of pictures is made to BBC on pages 8, 167, 174, 184, 185, 188, 189 *bottom*, 194, 195, 197, 201, 205; Bee Photographs, 162; Steve Benbow, 119 *top*; Burnley Express, 34, 155 *right*; Paul Carlton, 83; Denbighshire Free Press, 175; Evening Standard, 98, 153 *top*; Farmers Guardian, 15, 33, 39, 137; Richard Fawcett, 22, 23, 28, 52, 53, 56, 57, 60, 65, 151; J. Hardman, 133; R. Hawksbee, 142; Mary Heaton, 181 *left*; Marc Henrie, 29 *bottom*, 59, 61, 77, 108 *right*, 109, 112 *bottom*, 115, 116, 117 *left*, 118, 129, 138, 140, 143, 150, 155 *left*; R.J. Hickson, 53 *bottom*; K. & J. Jelley, 11, 13; Derek Johnson, 45, 161, 163, 165, 170; Lancashire Evening Post, 108 *left*; Lancashire Life, 51; Birthe Lundman, 38; Frank H. Moyes, 29 *top*, 35, 46, 62, 76, 87, 100 *left*, 112 *top*, 113, 200; Matt Mundell, 93, 99; Oxford Times, 119 *bottom*, 213; Glyn Roberts, 189 *top*; T. Roberts, 121; Scottish Farmer, 43, 96 *left*, 106, 134 *top*, 134 *bottom*, 135, 183; F. Sirett, 88; Les Wilson, 181 *right*, 191, 193; Margaret Wood, 26; and Yorkshire Evening Press, 187 *left*.

Acknowledgement and sincere thanks to the photographers of the pictures on other pages, the sources of which are either doubtful or not known.

Preface

I write this introduction whilst I sit on the rocks high above the Cliviger Gorge in Lancashire. Gael lies by my side in the lee of a grey boulder, her eyes watching a Gritstone ewe which grazes the rough bents close by. Rhaq and Meg are now dead, their friendship, the happy hours we spent together, but fond and lasting memories.

Most of those recollections are associated with the dogs and sheep on the hills of the Pennines; they stir the memory further to all the collie dogs I have known and whose doings on the hill and at sheepdog trials I have had the pleasure of recording for the farming Press. I think that we who have known the thrills of trials competition for so many years have been very selfish. We have kept the pleasure to ourselves, and it was only when television came along that we grudgingly allowed others to join us.

In my book *Sheepdogs, My faithful friends* I wrote of the skills and of the illustrious heritage of the collie dog and of its valuable role in the management of farmstock. Such has been the response and interest to the 'discovery' of sheepdog trials as a spectator-sport that this book is written to add the extra pleasure of knowledge and purpose, organisation, judging, and running of trials.

The book is the product of a lifetime's friendship with sheepdogs—and from the friendship of farming folk down the years, folk who have tolerated my journalistic quizzings with so much good nature. They have helped to compile the unique fixture-list of trials at the end of the book and to contribute the fine array of pictures. Wherever I have been able, I have acknowledged and credited such pictures. Where I have been unable to locate the exact source, I now say 'thank you'. I say thank you to photographers Marc Henrie, Frank H. Moyes, Richard Fawcett and Derek Johnson who have gone out into the field to take special pictures.

I have written of sheepdog trials as a source of entertainment and sport whilst never forgetting their very practical purpose of improving the skills of the collie for its prime purpose of herding farmstock efficiently. Without the expertise of the collie dog so much of the world's surface would be barren and unproductive. The diligence of such dogs has stirred me to record their qualities—measured in this book through competition, for it is on the trials field that most people will meet them. Perhaps I am wrong in this assumption, for millions of people have become enthralled by the magic of the sheepdog in their own homes—in the BBC2

Glyn Jones and Eric Halsall with Bracken and Gel at Rannerdale.

television series 'One Man and His Dog'. Because of the popularity of this programme I have detailed the action and results.

In this respect I thank producers Philip Gilbert and Ian Smith for their schooling of a television amateur; I thank my colleague on the programme Phil Drabble for his ever-constructive criticism and unstinted support; and I thank all the field staff and competitors whose confidence in success has brought success.

I appreciate the encouragement of my professional colleagues, to the Editors and staffs of the *Farmers Guardian, The Scottish Farmer*, and the *Burnley Express*.

Writing as a spare-time activity makes immense demands on others closely involved, so that my most sincere thanks go to my wife for putting up with the inconveniences, and to my sister and brother-in-law for carrying out the out-of-doors 'heavy work' which I dodged. Even to Gael who on occasion has also 'missed out'.

Eric Halsall
Cliviger, 1982

Chapter 1

Master of his craft

I watch Kyle win the world's greatest Shepherds' competition over the storm-tossed field of Kilmartin in Argyll, consider the collie's real value to the shepherding of his home fells in Yorkshire, and thrill to the unexpected and ofttimes disastrous acts in trials competition.

Buffeted by driven rainstorm, the hairs of his long black and white coat curled with water and wind-cut to a knife-edge parting across his flank, Kyle raced away over the soaking ground of Kilmartin.

Three and a half years old, a working collie dog in the prime of life, the stamina of his muscular body and the courage of his spirit holding scant respect for the cussedness of the weather, Kyle was away to gather sheep. Fast over the rough grass so that water flew from his racing feet, belly to earth in his streamed crouch over level ground, tail held out to balance his stance when he leaped burn and ditch, he speedily covered the half-mile of rough terrain to start the herding of twenty Blackface sheep.

Though he went daily to gather Swaledale sheep on the high windswept fells of his home in the Yorkshire Dales, that Blackface gather in September 1970 in Argyll was special—for it was carried out as an examination to assess his ability in a demanding craft. In partnership with his master, Michael Perrings, whose role was to guide and help him, it was the most severe examination of his prowess which Kyle had ever faced. It was the highest competitive shepherding test that he had ever undergone; the probing and revealing tests of gathering, driving, shedding and penning sheep for the Shepherds' Championship of the International Sheep Dog Society (ISDS), the most coveted of all shepherds' trials honours.

Watched by the knowledgeable eyes of three judges and under the critical gaze of a packed grandstand of spectators, he carried England's hopes in one of the greatest shepherding contests in the world. And Kyle knew it. Born with intelligence of the very highest, he knew that day's work was special. There was the general hubbub of activity about the place, more than he had ever seen before in his life, and he had been to many sheepdog trials. There was the tension of the human throng which his keen and acute senses could read like a book, there were the clipped and precise instructions of his master which meant that Michael was a little tense, and there was the gathering of the most illustrious of his contemporaries, the wisest dogs in the world.

Though the weather conditions could not have been worse for the dogs to show their immaculate skills, they were conditions which were so often their daily lot on the sheepruns of Britain. Used to the vilest of weather in his home shepherding on the high slopes of Whernside in Upper Wharfedale, Kyle ran out for his sheep on that testing day like the practical dog he was, a strong, lithesome, clever working collie whose skills had already won other trials championships. Of the finest breeding—his mother, Thomson McKnight's Gael had won the Supreme Championship of the International Sheep Dog Society the year he was born in 1967—and taught by his master to use his inbred intelligence in the toughest of schoolrooms on the high hills, the rigours of Kilmartin held no qualms and, like all experts, he delighted in displaying his craft. For him the test was less demanding than his daily job on the home fells though it would demand all his concentration and test all his energy and will-power in a compact examination of every aspect of sheep herding of half an hour's duration.

In this major trial the collie's ability was tested on gathering ten sheep at half a mile distance, bringing them a quarter-mile towards the handler, returning to pick up another ten sheep, bringing the two flocks together, and driving the twenty sheep for 600 yards through gated obstacles into a shedding ring where five marked sheep had to be separated from the rest and then penned.

Yet, though this championship test of the International Sheep Dog Society was the stiffest, such trials were really Kyle's recreation for they were only a potted version of his homework. In one major aspect was Kilmartin's test different to daily herding work. Kyle's every move and mood, his partnership link with his master, their resultant teamwork, was scrutinised and analysed, applauded and criticised by experienced judges whose standard was perfection. Only one yardstick measured a collie's worth and that was its ability to work. That was the standard against which Kyle was measured.

Perfection was not possible under the adverse conditions of the day. Though Kyle, as a strong hill-dog, made light of the rough terrain and shrugged away the discomfort of the weather, the sheep were loath to move over the waterlogged ground and ill at ease in the buffeting rainstorm so that they were wilful and unusually difficult to herd. Wind noise and bluster stretched communication to the utmost so that Michael had much to leave to Kyle's own initiative, particularly at the vital half-mile gathering points where the rustled swaying and tossing of trees distorted Michael's whistled commands.

The handsome black and white collie did not fail his master. He ran out without a falter to meet the twenty Blackface ewes which were held in two separate flocks at each distant rushy corner of the big field and though they were screened by the vegetation of the terrain and unseen through the storm at his eye-level, he found them without trouble. Knowing that it was essential to show his authority and prove that he intended to be boss at the very start, he spread his pads into the yielding ground to steady his stance and walked purposefully up to the ewes. One ewe, truculent and resentful of being disturbed at her grazing of

Right *A paw of affection from Kyle to his master, Michael Perrings.*

the wiry grass, turned on the dog and stamped her forefoot in annoyance and defiance.

Kyle did not hesitate. His eyes unflinching and commanding, he measured his stride to face her. She hesitated, bleated, and turned away. And so Kyle showed her that he was to be obeyed and, leading her companions, she walked willingly away before him. Having bossed the dominant ewe, a sturdy sheep, fit and well-grown and the leader of the flock, he would have little trouble with the rest. A quick shake to cast the water from his coat, and Kyle geared the pace of his charges to his own steady lope. Eyes slit against the prick of the heavy raindrops but never for a second leaving the sheep, his ears slightly lifted to take his master's commands, he walked them round the course, never letting them stop to question his authority, bunching the twenty ewes before him, lining them to pass between the gated obstacles of the 600 yards driving test with balanced precision.

When the outfield work was completed and he brought the sheep into the shedding-ring, his mood changed. From the watchful and mindful, though almost relaxed mood of flowing mastery his attitude became one of concentrated tension. Here within the sawdust-marked ring of forty yards diameter his partnership with his master became dependent on half-second decisions. Of the twenty ewes he had

Pedigree of KYLE (47050) 1970 International and English Shepherds' Champion with Michael Perrings

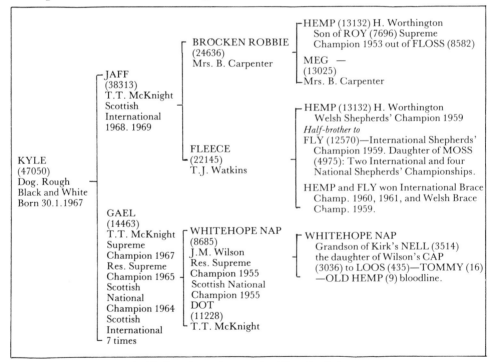

The numbers in brackets are the Stud Book numbers of the International Sheep Dog Society.

Hope, son of Kyle and sire of many top class collies.

taken round the field five wore red-collar markings. In the shedding-ring these five had to be isolated and the other fifteen drive off.

It was the test of patience, temperament, courage and steadiness and more than ever a test of partnership between dog and man, and so often it was the test which decided the competition honours.

Michael, feeling that victory was within their grasp, knew it was the vital test for him and Kyle. They were the final pair to contest the championship and of the eight which had gone before, seven had failed to complete the trial. Only John Bathgate's 5½-years-old black and white Nim from a Blackface herding in the Southern Uplands of Scotland had finished the tests with challenging points and his outfield work had been below Kyle's standard—and he had lost a third of the shedding points. So Michael felt it was the time for bold decisions. He could trust Kyle to play his part and hold back or let depart whichever sheep he ordered. With nothing in mind but the job, neither dog nor handler was aware of the teeming rain as the grandstand crowd stilled in anticipation.

Kyle, his muscles tense as coiled spring, lay stretched flat on the ground, holding the twenty sheep by the strength of his eye, an almost baleful glare which dared any sheep to doubt his authority. Michael, not allowed to touch the sheep in competition, eased three non-ribboned sheep to the side of the ring and as a narrow space opened between the rest of the flock, called in Kyle.

Released from his tension, the dog sprang between the sheep, and three of the fifteen were driven off outside the ring. Leaving them just beyond the perimeter of the ring so as to attract and draw off the other sheep, man and dog played the tense game of tag.

Sheep that were unmarked were allowed to run, but when a marked sheep attempted to follow Kyle was immediately called in to turn it back. So the shedding game was run, unmarked sheep released, marked sheep held, Michael depending absolutely on Kyle's power of character and speed of reaction to his instructions to stay out or come in—for should a red-ribboned sheep be allowed to break away the whole test would have to be re-started and the failure so heavily penalised by the judges that victory would certainly be lost. One false move could lose it. Should Michael fail to call Kyle in time, should Kyle fail to respond in time, and the coveted championship would be gone.

The situation was tense, further pressurised by the time factor. The whole trial from outrun to finish had to be completed within thirty minutes. Done well, the shedding of the sheep was a joy to watch, man and dog absolutely together in their thoughts and actions, sheep not unduly harried and consequently not frightened.

Within six minutes and with twelve minutes of the allotted thirty minutes total time left the shedding was completed and Kyle drove the fifteen unwanted sheep well away in case any should be inclined to try to rejoin the remaining five.

Perhaps it was reaction after the intense pressure of the shedding, perhaps it was the sudden strong squall of rain which almost bowled Kyle off his feet, perhaps the five sheep had hopes of rejoining their brethren, but trouble suddenly loomed at the final test of penning. There was a gasp of dismay from the watchers as the five sheep shied away from the open gate of the pen and milled round in sudden panic. Would the championship be lost at the last test?

Quickly Michael, who was holding the rope attached ready to close the gate of the pen, stepped back. Kyle, on the opposite side, dropped flat to the ground. Momentarily the pressure was off the sheep. They quietened—and seizing the opportunity before they could grasp the initiative, Kyle slipped to his feet, stepped forward in a slinking feline approach and the sheep turned to walk into the pen. Michael banged shut the gate, and the test was over.

Michael gave Kyle a quick pat on the head, Kyle gave a flip of his tail, the International Shepherds' Championship was won for England by a convincing 33 aggregate points from three judges, and Kyle could take his place among the great collies of the land. His success was akin to and comparable with a racehorse winning the Derby.

I watched Kyle earn his championship with his litter-sister Gael stretched half asleep across my knees. A lovely natured smooth-coated bitch, she took little notice of her brother's finest hour though occasionally lifting a lazy ear to her master's well-known whistles, but she played an important role in the event.

Brought up together, Kyle and Gael had lived and worked together all their lives and had rarely been separated. Gael went to Kilmartin for the ride just so that Kyle would not miss her when it mattered most. When he came off the trials field, she was his first thought and he greeted her with a flip of his tongue over her nose. With typical feminine aloofness she had not bothered to leave her rest

Kyle's litter-sister Gael, on the extreme left of the picture, was included in the Yorkshire Sheepdog Society's nursery-championship team in March 1969. From left to right, Michael Perrings with Gael, John Chapman with Spot, Adrian Bancroft with Anne who was to win England's Shepherd's championship in 1973 and 1975, Douglas Fisher with Moss and Herbert Hargreaves with Pip.

place across my knees, though she did recognise Kyle's greeting with a flick of her tail.

Kyle's greeting was almost an invitation to play, for even after his testing work he was relaxed and in no way spent. He lolled the exertion from his lungs but, had he been asked, he would have been readily able to do another stint of hard shepherding for, like all his breed, he had the stamina to run all day if necessary. He was mud-spattered and grimed, his long coat draining away the rainwater, but he was in no way discomforted. Strong and fit, well-coupled, compactly boned and light on his feet, Kyle was typical of today's Border Collie, tireless at work and able to run the rough screes and limestone crags of the fell without falter. A keenly handsome flop-eared dog, he was rough coated, black and white in colour, with dappled forelegs and the traditional white neck ruff. In stature around eighteen inches to the shoulder, he was lithely muscled and balanced with his tail held low. His eye was strong but flexible in his dominance over sheep. He had the blue-blooded pride of an illustrious line back to Old Hemp, foundation sire of the modern collie dog. He was the best of British collies, of a breed totally dedicated to the herding of stock and invaluable in the management of sheep.

On the extreme right of the picture, Michael Perrings and Kyle won the richest trials prize in the United Kingdom in 1974, the 3-day Texaco event watched by 1,000 people and contested by 140 dogs at Eddleston in Peebleshire. Left to right—Peter Hetherington with Hemp was fourth, Raymond MacPherson and Tweed fifth, and Tim Longton and Cap second.

Victory at Kilmartin was Kyle's finest trials achievement. He had been bred for it, he had trained for it, to prove the ultimate quality of his line in the skills of shepherding sheep. The trials victory was reflective of his supreme ability in the more mundane, yet essentially more important job of shepherding sheep on the fells of Yorkshire where he earned his daily bread. His work over Kilmartin's storm-tossed land had shown sheepmen from many parts of the world that his line was of the greatest, that it was capable of first-class stock herding with efficiency and integrity, without fuss, and with respect for sheep.

That his craftsmanship had given pleasure to all who watched was in the way of a bonus—trials have only recently been discovered as spectator sport by the public at large, and in 1982 to the extent of almost eight million viewers of television trials. The trial had reflected Kyle's inbred skill, his innate wisdom and intelligence, proved the quality of his breeding, and thrilled an admiring public— the whole purpose of a sheepdog trial. In no other way could sheepdog character be readily assessed, accepted or rejected, for the broader, more essential purpose of stock management.

Ever since his birth on 30 January 1967 in the byre at Glencartholm on the banks of the River Esk on the Scottish borderland, Kyle's whole upbringing had been geared to that crowning moment of acclaim at Kilmartin. That proof that he could shepherd sheep better than most enhanced the reputation of an illustrious line of sheepdogs which had taken the excellence of British shepherding skills to the sheepruns of the world and which in competition had won 49 of 65 Supreme International Championships. Kyle had a good start in life for he inherited the skills of his mother, Thomson McKnight's Gael, winner of seven successive Scottish International caps, five National titles, and the 1967 Supreme Championship. She was a daughter of Scotland's power dog, Whitehope Nap.

Kyle's father was Jaff, a strong Welsh-blooded black, white and tan dog who also represented Scotland at international level with Thomson McKnight. He was a smooth-coated son of Mrs Barbara Carpenter's Brocken Robbie out of T. J. Watkins' Fleece, the litter-sister of Worthington's Juno, the 1963 Supreme Champion.

Kyle, and his sister Gael, spent their early puppyhood at Glencartholm nurtured by the greatest sheep bitch of modern times in the love and warmth of the McKnight household, one of the most hospitable places in Scotland for man or beast. Soon they moved to an equally caring home in Yorkshire, to Throstle Nest Farm in Wharfedale, and there began to find their vocation in life under the watchful eyes of Michael Perrings.

Gael moved to Yorkshire first—soon after she was weaned—but Kyle had his introduction to the rudiments of shepherding on the Blackfaces of Glencartholm before he joined his sister at the age of seven months. Together again, they played and learned their craft on the high sheep pastures between the limestone crags which rise from the green banks of the Wharfe to the 1,700 feet heights of Conistone Moor towards Whernside. There, where the wind rules and grass grows lushfully low, where the snow often lingers till long after the curlews have returned to the hill, and where lambs gambol in cold sunshine, they took their first tentative steps at the craft of shepherding. There, they met the Swaledales, 600 tough, hardy hill ewes which could wrest a living and produce and succour their lambs from the five square miles of hard ground.

The most popular hill breed in Northern England, the Swaledale is an independent and capable sheep, yet amenable to the herding instructions of dogs it can rely upon and trust. One of the 47 pure breeds of sheep in Britain—many of which Kyle and Gael were to meet on the trials field—the Swaledale gives a steady return in meat and wool to the Northern sheepman. Working with such active, alert and fast sheep fashioned both Kyle's and Gael's strength and temperament, and taught them to be decisive and masterful in their ways. Gael was the most forward in learning her lessons, indeed Kyle was sent for a change of tuition and environment to spend a few weeks on the hills of the Cliviger Gorge close by my home where he came to know the curly-horned Lonk and the good-natured Gritstone breeds of sheep.

True skill is hard-earned and the natural crafts of a collie dog take their own time to mature and so it was with Kyle. Shepherding sheep was his purpose in life. He had character from birth and his individual traits were developed by patient and respectful teaching to form the ideal shepherding partner for Michael

Perrings. He was taught how to use his inbred skills, to understand the intelligent power he possessed and not to abuse it, so that he developed into a reasoning and trustworthy dog. He was not 'broken' to work—a term of imposition so often heard in dog training—so that he remained an individual and not an unthinking robot.

Having learned the basics Kyle developed quickly, becoming indispensible to Michael in the management of the sheep on the fell. It was his authoritative manner, it was his speedy legs which brought every sheep within Michael's reach. He became the extension of his master's arm in reaching the scattered flock. He became dependable at every shepherding job. Wind-plucked and feathering streaming, he ran the vastness of the moor and raced down the wind to gather the fleetest of sheep in the sheer exhilaration of supple fitness.

In springtime he was kind and gentle in his herding of the lambs. He licked milk-froth from their tiny noses with a flip of his tongue. He was tolerant with their mothers who suddenly became intolerant of his interference with their babies. In the extreme heat of the summer sun he respected the lethargy of sheep which sought shade, and refreshed his own spirits in the dampness of the bogs. When the fieldfares flew down the dale and wet cloud settled over the hilltop with clinging greyness, his knowledge of the land and sense of direction brought Michael home safely from the tops. His long coat frozen and matted white, he

Well-bred and able to transfer his own quiet authority to his sons and daughters, Mrs Barbara Carpenter's Brocken Robbie was Kyle's grand-sire.

ruthlessly drove laggard sheep to the safety of lower ground when snow blizzards raged the heights.

On the trials field Kyle's shepherding qualities came out for all to see in the short space of two years. He started his competitive life right at the bottom of the ladder on the nursery fields of the Pennines; and he was just over two years old when he won his first novice victory at Cautley, near Sedbergh in North Yorkshire in May 1969. Leading an entry of 69 collies on Swaledale hoggs, he scored 42½ of 45 points to beat his half-brother, George Hutton's Kep from Threlkeld, also sired by McKnight's Jaff.

Three months later Kyle won his first open honour, beating some International collies at the Royal Lancashire Show trials at Blackpool. Before he went to the Kilmartin International to represent England he added another Open Championship, dropping only one point at Todmorden; and at the English National trials in 1970, remembered for their dour shepherding, at Houghend on the fringe of Manchester he won the Shepherds' title and was reserve National Champion, only two aggregate points below Tim Longton's three-years-old Glen from Quernmore.

Kyle's trials experience, blended to the rigours of his work on the home fell in Wharfedale, made him a specialist at his craft at the early age of three and a half years. A delight to see on the trials field, Kyle's skills in the successful management of his master's sheep flock were vital to the economy of the business of farming—for ingenious though man may be, he has yet to build a machine to replace the role of the collie dog in agriculture. The year after his International Championship success Kyle won Yorkshire's most coveted honour and he took his tenth top trials victory before he was six years old. He won further honour for England and competed with success in the BBC television trials. Trials put his skills on the market to the general benefit of the breed. He had that touch of genius in his method of handling sheep and his particular qualities of outrunning, quick and easy action, power in close work, and initiative were noted by all who saw him work.

In demand as a sire, he extended his own illustrious line of proven and skilled herding dogs which made light of hard work on the hill and which won honour and prestige in competitive shepherding. His best-known son was Hope, one of the bonniest collie dogs I have ever seen. Hope's brain matched his beauty, though he was never very successful on the trials field and his fame lies in his ability to father top-class workers.

Hope enjoyed the satisfaction of his skills at home and never was there a happier, more placid, friendlier dog in the world. He would work with anyone, with Michael's wife Margaret, with either of the three children, Alison, Isobel, or Jill, and I have fetched the milk-cows from the far field and down the dales road with him. What impressed me when I herded the cows was the way Hope separated the cows from the sheep which were also grazing in the field.

Hope, who was mothered by Adrian Bancroft's Anne, the clever bitch who twice won England's Shepherds' Championship, came to join his father when Michael and his family had moved to farm Field Gate at Giggleswick in

Ribblesdale, and it was here among less exacting shepherding conditions that Kyle spent his later years.

Kyle's sister, Gael, who lazed through the Kilmartin International on my knees, also proved the value of sound breeding though her story was tragically short. Trim and gentle, clever and thorough in handling sheep, she demonstrated her quality even earlier than her brother, winning the Trawden Sheepdog Society's nursery Championship in Lancashire when she was barely two years old. She partnered her brother in running third in the English Brace Championship in 1970 and won the Holme Association's Driving Championship later in the year, but her particular limelight was the winning of the Fylde Society's Open Championship, one of the top trials of the year, in the spring of 1971.

Sickness troubled her and I remember how she overcame it to concentrate on the herding of hill hoggs to a standard of near-perfection, losing only half a point in the face of wild and stormy conditions to lead the best in the land—127 collies which included 31 Internationals. Her work was intelligent, controlled, and easy paced, and showed what a great little bitch she was. She died later in the year and was sadly missed by Kyle and by all who knew her.

Kyle and Gael were typical of the modern British working collie, renowned throughout the world's sheepruns for power, strength, and temperament, an honest to goodness working dog which is master of its craft. It has been shaped by blending the wisdom and stamina required for the hard graft of day-to-day shepherding in harsh places with the expertise and finesse needed to meet the high standards of the trials field. This display of expertise and finesse, coupled with the thrills of competition, has given sheepdog trials their great appeal. There is drama in the way trials championships are won and lost, especially at international level.

Each year in September when the top collies from England, Scotland, Wales and Ireland meet to test their strengths this drama of International Championship unfolds. The most coveted awards in the world are won on the single inspired action of an intelligent dog, on the steady unflinching stare of a dog's eye, on the precise step of a forceful dog, almost on the flick of a dog's tail. The most coveted awards in the world are lost on a moment's loss of concentration, on the sudden panic of nerves, on the wrong command of a handler, on the despairing lack of patience.

By his quick knowledge of the ways of sheep at the final penning Kyle won his Shepherds' Championship at Kilmartin in 1970. By the simple yet supremely clever act of shifting his balance to counter a wilful Mountain ewe at Tywyn in 1980 the sixteen-months-old Bwlch Taff, son of television stars Glen and Bwlch Bracken, won the Welsh National Championship for Glyn Jones of Bodfari.

By deceptively placid work in shedding, penning, and final singling which was unfaulted by all three judges Martin O'Neill's Risp won an outstanding victory for Ireland by a mere half-point in the International Farmers' Championship at Lockerbie in 1976; and by a quick forward step of authority on Brecknock Cheviot ewes at Libanus in the Brecon Beacons in 1977 John Thomas' 7½-years-old rough coated Craig penned them for a Supreme victory which was slipping away.

Old Hemp, foundation sire of the modern working collie.

Harry Huddleston's great-hearted Bett from North Lancashire moved Welsh Mountain ewes with such authority that they never seriously contested her right to the Supreme title at Chester in 1969; and it was the truly expert understanding by another bitch, the 4½-years-old Jen, with her master Tom Watson in the shedding ring on a blustery Saturday morning at Bala which clinched the 1980 Supreme Championship for Scotland.

Recall the quick and willing response of Glen on the command to return for the second batch of sheep at Edinburgh in 1946 during his winning of Jim Wilson's sixth Supreme Championship; and the decisive pressure of eye which turned Pat's sheep into the pen to win the 1937 English Championship at Keswick for Mark Hayton.

Read of the cool and calm manner by which James Scott's Kep found affinity with his sheep to win both the 1908 and 1909 International Championships; the anticipation of William Wallace's Loos—best remembered as a brood bitch—in countering a truculent ewe by the drive-gate when she won the International

Farmers' Championship at Criccieth in 1925; and the faultless control of John Bagshaw's two-years-old Roy to score maximum points to win the 1931 Longshaw Championship.

It is easier to recall the qualities which brought success, it is often painful to recall incidents of failure.

There was Jim Gilchrist's mistakenly given command, when raindrops bleared his spectacles, to send the clever and doubting Spot, Scotland's champion, on wrong instructions during the International contest at Chester in 1966; there was June's brave but disastrous shedding grip to dash her International hopes in 1973 after she had won Scotland's National title for William Cormack; there was the uncharacteristic lack of concentration from Jim Cropper's Clyde during his worst-ever fetch in the centenary Supreme at Bala to drop him to Reserve Champion; and there was the almost nervous lack of authority in the shedding ring by David Brady's most reliable Meg when the Television Championship was within her grasp at Cilycwm in 1980.

It is that air of uncertainty, the very real possibility of the unexpected happening which causes the pulse to suddenly quicken and adds the spice to turn an interesting competition into a totally absorbing event. And more than ever since television brought trials contest to the notice of millions of people through

Left *Sheep and lambs seek shelter by the wall and are quickly covered by sudden wind-blown snowfall.*

Right *Then a collie—Richard Fawcett's Zeus—is invaluable in scenting them out for rescue.*

the BBC 'One Man and His Dog' programmes have the simple excitements of sheepdog trials appealed. Here is a spectator sport developed from an ancient and basic craft which has honest competition, the ultimate in skill, and when watched in the beautiful places of Britain full participation without the fears of hooliganism. And also without the pampered prima-donna acts one sees in so many other sports today. The reward for victory is a pat on the head and a responding tail twitch—not the hugging and kissing that denotes success elsewhere on the sports field.

The trials' suggestion of mystery—their dialect of 'lifting' and 'wearing' sheep, of 'away to me's, 'come by's, 'that'll do's—excites the imagination and now that the old-world mystique, once only understood by a select band, has been dispelled by modern-world television techniques, an even more intriguing contest has been revealed. Since the basic, and even the more technical requirements of sheepdog trials were explained, the watcher has been taken from the cold aloofness of the pure spectator to the warm inner circle of a participant.

Born on the high fells, the wild mountainsides, the lovely dales of this land, sheepdog trials provide contest which retains freshness for mental relaxation and commands the spellbound attention of droves of town and city dwellers. 'Drawn by the magic that lies in the sheepdog's eyes,' to quote J. Wentworth-Day, there have been 20,000 people standing enthralled to watch the trials in London's Hyde Park, and the audience for the BBC television trials of 'One Man and His Dog' has reached almost eight million.

Trials produce fascinating sport for, at whatever level of competition, be it nursery, novice, open or international, nothing is a foregone conclusion—the result is never predictable. With the conflicting temperaments of dog, sheep, and man involved, he would be a wise—or foolish—man who would forecast the outcome of a trial, and especially at international level with 53 dogs, all of which have won the competitive right to represent their country. And all this sporting excitement is generated from what is basically a piece of farming practice. But then football and rugby used to be played with a pig's bladder!

A sheepdog trial is simply a series of practical shepherding tasks designed to test the working ability of a collie dog in the management of farmstock—the tasks arranged to form a continuing series of tests in gathering, controlling, bringing, driving, shedding and penning sheep into which is introduced the competitive element. But the purpose of a sheepdog trial goes way beyond sport and entertainment. That trials provide thousands of town dwellers with the peace and relaxation of the open spaces and teach them something of the widsom of country ways is justification for their existence and popularity. That they are a prime factor in the improvement of the shepherd's dog for its vital role of shepherding the world's sheep flock is total justification.

Chapter 2

To Bala for the start

I sit on the historic course of Bala and re-create the first sheepdog trials ever to be held, and I applaud the insight of the farmers of the Borders who first used trials to examine the qualities of their dogs in order to improve their herding efficiency.
The years 1873 to 1900.

'Mine is better than yours.' This age-old claim of the braggard is probably responsible for more wagers and more black eyes than any other comment. And such a comment—uttered in a most gentlemanly fashion of course!—has been, and still is, the cause and reason why many sheepdog trials exist today. For when a man claims that he has the best dog in the village there is only one way to prove or disprove it—by the holding of a contest.

Be it racehorses, be it gun-dogs, be it running dogs, the only way to prove which is the best is to match one against the other. And so with sheepdogs. When Ernest Priestley threw out his challenge to his fellow shepherds and gamekeepers on the Rutland estate in North Derbyshire in March 1894 they ran a trial—and inadvertently started the world-famous Longshaw trials. Assessed only on their ability to work stock, sheepdogs could only be proved in a practical manner. The normal type of dog-show, the first of which was held at Newcastle in 1859, where visible appearances and type are all that count is therefore useless. Proof of a sheepdog's looks are in its deeds. Practical working tests where the dog's ability to herd sheep is assessed and explored is the only possible way to set one above the other. Whether the dog looks like a half-bred cow-hound, whether it is short or tall, whether its parentage is open to doubt does not matter one jot if it can herd stock efficiently. That almost all working collies—now usually referred to as Border Collies—are handsome and pleasing to the eye is incidental to their value and grading, though it reflects with full marks the skill and dedication of our forbears which have allied beauty with brains.

And so working sheepdog trials were evolved. It is interesting to note that the gun-dog people were of like mind for they also tossed the show-ring aside in the late 1800s in favour of field-trials. The first recorded sheepdog trials which were open to all-comers were held at Bala in North Wales in 1873 when Richard John Lloyd Price, squire of the 64,000 acre Rhiwlas Estate and a well-known breeder of gun-dogs and Old English Sheepdogs, was persuaded to organise a working test by his friend S. E. Shirley, who founded the Kennel Club in the same year.

We all saw history repeated at the Bala centenary trials organised by the International Sheep Dog Society in September 1973 when Mr Lloyd Price's grandson, Lt-Col. Price, presented the awards, and yet again the long connection of the family with sheepdog trials when the International again returned to Bala in 1980 and the founder's great-grandson, Mr Robin Price was the president.

On 6 July 1873 a letter appeared in *The Field* stating that with the assistance of the Rhiwlas Field Trial Committee—a gun-dog society—the Welsh squire was to organise 'a novelty', a sheepdog trial 'open to the world' on 9 August of that year. He stated that an 'experienced and trusty shepherd' would assist with the judging and the entry fee would be ten shillings, quite an expensive entry in those days. Things did not go exactly to plan and the event was eventually held on 9 October 1873 in the Garth Goch, the place a mile and a half outside Bala.

Reported in *The Field*, 18 October, the trials, in addition to their great historical interest, reflect the sound thinking of the organisers on the necessity to test a working dog at its basic craft. Though slightly different in procedure, the tests were for dogs to gather, drive, and pen sheep in two separate contests, and the course distances of around 500 and 800 yards on a large grassy common are close to the present International Sheep Dog Society course measurements. Present trials competitors will give a wry smile at the reference to the wild and unpredictable nature of the 'little wiry Welsh Mountain Sheep' and may perhaps have some sympathy with the comment, however unprofessional and bad shepherding,

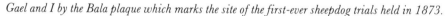

Gael and I by the Bala plaque which marks the site of the first-ever sheepdog trials held in 1873.

that the the best way to master the sheep was to chase them around and 'tire them out first'.

We have all learned from experience that it is essential to screen off the two pens where the sheep are held whilst waiting and after their turn on the course. The Bala dogs found difficulty in getting sheep away from the sides of the holding pen and the exhaust pen proved a nuisance by being in sight of the competing sheep. Instinctively sheep will be drawn to the penned flocks and make life impossible for the dog trying to herd them.

Ten dogs entered the historic contest, ranging from the big, smooth coated, black and white, prick-eared Sam, a dog of the North Tyne Ridley blood, to the local, tiny Chap with John Jones of Hafod. Some 300 people, standing on the slopes of a natural earth mound, watched the trials from just after lunchtime until half past four in the afternoon. Over 100 years later I stood on that rough grassy mound of Garth Goch. It is land with many historical connections, for relics of an old tribal battle have been found on the field, and the rock to which is now fixed a plaque commemorating the first sheepdog trial had been used in days gone by as a target for the lead bullets of the old militia. The plaque, affixed in August 1979, also reflects the far-reaching interest which that first trial created in working collies, for the idea to mark the spot was encouraged by a visiting sheepman from New Zealand.

My visit was in May and the mountain slopes were sun dappled although the clouds were moving down with rain from the tops of the Berwyns. The gorse bloomed yellow and the field over which the trial was run, now divided from the mound by a public tarmacadam road, with lush-green in the brimming light and black Welsh cows grazed its sweetness. A golden sovereign had been found whilst cultivating the field on the spot where our sheepdog forbears had sited their refreshment tent by the tree-fringed River Hirnant which bounded the course on the right. How much whisky would that sovereign have bought in 1873?

In somewhat pensive mood I tried to envisage the happenings of that day in 1873. I sat down by the rock, my collie Gael at my side. She looked into my face, wondering why I appeared so engrossed in doing nothing. Viewed from my 'handling point' the site made a good trials course. The gather was down across the road to rise at the distance to the foot of Garth Rhiwaedog and would be a good test of a dog. It would be interesting to see a trial over that ground again. Perhaps not. The tarmacadam roadway prevents it in any case, and the men of Bala have built on their unique tradition to improve their trials event. Nowadays the Bala trials, held on the second Tuesday and Wednesday in August, take place over the fields by the River Dee which have been used for the International. Two fields of National-style working eliminate all but the top six dogs from each, and these twelve contest the championship on a double-gather International-style course.

The rain from the Berwyns spattered over Gael and me as we sat on the historic site. Such had been the weather conditions those long years ago when the spectators watched Jamie Thomson win the trials with Tweed, a small, compactly built, black and tan dog with an intelligent foxy head. Thomson was a Scotsman

Harry Huddleston and his international Cap check a wayward ewe at the pen. Yorkshire open trials 1980.

working in Wales at Bwlch-yn-horeb and Tweed was Scottish-bred, so the result cannot have been the most popular. But Tweed completed all his tests, he paced well, was pliant and quiet in his work, and he obeyed the commands of his master. John Jones and Cap were placed second with J. Robson and Sam third.

Wales had to wait 100 years to redeem the Bala victory—Glyn Jones and the clever three-years-old Gel from Bodfari winning the centenary trials in 1973— though Welsh collies had long before proved their ability equal to the Scots when Thomas Roberts' little rough-coated Jaff from Corwen won the 1924 Supreme Championship of the International Sheep Dog Society at Ayr.

Started as a sport to test dog against dog at its basic craft, for even the earliest trials were pure tests of practical shepherding and Bala had the basic ingredients with no useless stunts included, trials were held for the pure satisfaction of showing off the qualities of one's dog and of proving oneself a better handler than the neighbour, for material gain was negligible. Prize-money was, and still is, of very small amount, and though wagers were probably laid on the results in the early years, they are now prohibited under the rules of the International Sheep Dog Society.

With the start of competitive trials the enthusiasm to breed a winning dog quickly grew, though wise stockmen that the farmers of the Cheviot region on the borders of England and Scotland were—from whence came the Border Collie— they had long realised that the more efficient the dog the easier it was to manage and control their stock. Efficiency, particularly in farming, leads to an easier, more relaxed and satisfying life, together with a more profitable and successful

Above *Where no machine could do the job shepherds and their dogs gather the flock. Blackfaces come off the hill at Talla Linnfoot, Tweedsmuir.* **Below** *Trials add the polish to a collie's capabilities but it is on the hill where its craft is essential. Ray Ollerenshaw's Shep above the Ladybower Reservoir in the Derbyshire Peak.*

'going on'. Farmers on both sides of the English-Scottish border had spent years and years improving their sheep to this end and had in fact turned their interest to the collie dog around the end of the eighteenth century as recorded in the writings of James Hogg, the Ettrick shepherd.

In the dusk of a grey day with darkness fast approaching and faced with the job of driving home some newly weaned and consequently very unruly Blackface lambs he had bought from a neighbour, James Hogg writes that he lost hope of mastering them. But 'Hector managed the point and we got them safe home,' he no doubt thankfully recorded. We expect no more of our dogs today.

Hector, be it said, was quite a character. He was certainly Hogg's favourite although he was not half as clever as his sire, his master's surly old Sirrah, though 'he had three times more humour and whim about him'. Both the black-coated Sirrah, whom Hogg reckoned to be 'the best dog I ever saw', and Hector were 'canine songsters'—another inherent trait in the Border Collie (for my old Rhaq would lift his muzzle to the sky and yowl in tune to any music he heard)?

Hogg's writings are the most valuable in Border Collie history, for he was a practical shepherd and not given to flowery expression and distorted truths so that his observations and comments are absolutely authentic. He shows that the collie dog was quite a character even in his day though one gets the impression that it was only certain dogs, or families of dogs, that were exceptionally intelligent and that the vast majority were in no way up to modern standards.

Whilst considering the improvement of working collies, it is interesting to note that Hogg refers to the power of the dog to control sheep with its eyes, a trait which no other breed of dog possesses and one which we tend to look upon as being a relatively modern characteristic. Of his Hector, Hogg wrote that the dog sat trembling 'with his eye still steadfastly fixed on the lambs', and again he wrote that Hector when indoors spent all his time watching and pointing the family cat.

Hogg also records that his father was aware of the collie characteristic of 'eye', taking us back to around 1750, but the trait was not common and appears to have been a characteristic of only isolated dogs, perhaps a select bloodline or family of collies. That it was a characteristic of the individual and not of the breed as a whole, though general working qualities were established, is supported by the memory of another legendary Border shepherd, James Scott of Hawick, who could not recall seeing 'eye' until 1875, two years after the first Bala trials and forty years after Hogg's death.

James Scott records seeing a little mottled bitch working at Hawick with John Crozier, a shepherd at Teviot Water, which had the creeping feline approach to sheep and 'the eye'. The dog that was placed third at Bala, the Ridley-bred Sam was reported as 'fettering the sheep with his eye'. It is interesting to note that Sam was of the Cheviot, whose farmers were the pioneers in collie improvement and from whence came the great stud dogs of the early trials era, including Old Hemp in 1893 who had everything that was ideal in a collie and who is accepted as the 'father' of the modern dog. The story of collie bloodlines is discussed more fully in *Sheepdogs, My faithful friends*.

James Scott was famous in his day as a handler of working collies and his grand dog Kep, cool and calm in temperament and reliable and unflurried with sheep, won the International Championships in 1908 and 1909. Apart from his reputation on the trials fields where he won 45 awards, Kep was one of the best of breeding sires, passing his exceptional coolness and quiet efficiency to his progeny, and he played a big part in the improvement of the breed. He widened the scope of the Old Hemp dynasty and added his own particular qualities of steady power and controlled action. Kep, brainy and broad-headed, was himself the product of the wise breeding which took place in the Borders around the turn of the century when great strides in collie improvement were made.

Prior to this 'awakened' period when the collie came to be recognised as the shepherd's greatest helpmate in the management of sheep and during the 38 years between Hogg's time and the holding of the first sheepdog trials, the breeding process had been somewhat individualistic.

Certain strains or families of working dogs were confined to localities and they were undoubtedly good at their job, though in finesse and skill not to the polished neatness or overall ability we take so much for granted today. Some strains were particularly good with sheep at hand, having the power to push sheep into confined paddocks or buildings. Some were good at shedding off sheep, others at driving sheep, others were perfect on the gather, whilst others were quick to follow command.

James Hogg wrote about the exceptional quality of hirsel-gathering of his uncle John Hoy's dogs, in particular The Tub, a snow white bitch. Whilst generally competent with sheep, these dogs were specialists at one particular facet of their craft. Our forbears, wise men that they were, started putting the bits together to form the ideal composite. Taking the qualities of outrunning from one strain, they married them to the inbye skills of another, slowly fitting the jigsaw together to form the pattern. It was a slow progress, for nature takes her time and only fools rush her.

Horizons were narrow—that good hill dog from the next dale mated to the gentle but clever bitch from down the road—so that scope was limited. In the long run this could only be good so long as the danger of in-breeding was watched; and slowly, but surely, by discriminate breeding, rejecting the weaknesses and extremes, using the desired traits of stamina and intelligence, the Border Collie emerged. Without doubt the running of sheepdog trials escalated the progress to the ideal so that by the late 1800s the collie dog of the Border country had become a clever and specialised working dog equal in many ways to the dog of today. Trials provided the 'short-cuts'. With dogs gathered together 'in one field' to show their skills the breeder did not have to go wandering the countryside to find his stock. With the finest collies of the district competing in comparison, their strengths and weaknesses became apparent, their characteristics and tempera-ments bared for knowing eyes to see. Trials focussed interest on every single characteristic which went into the make-up of the collie dog and, as today, became the shop-window from which breeding stock could be chosen. Narrow horizons were suddenly broadened, and with the desire to produce the winner at the trials, interest quickened.

The first Border trials were held at Byrness in the valley of the Rede in Northumberland in September 1876 and the records are inconclusive as to the outcome, mentioning three possible winners, Walter Telfer with his old white dog, home-bred at the Rooking; John Robson, one of the organisers, with a beautiful bitch called Maddie; and Simon Rutherford's bearded collie from Blackburnhead.

The course was a good hill test, dogs having to cross the fair-sized River Rede to go to their sheep half a mile away on the opposite hillside. Two months before the Byrness trials an attempt had been made to hold such an event in London—with dire results.

It was said that this trial, on 30 June 1876, was held as a result of a challenge made by Welsh shepherds to meet any opposition after smarting under Jamie Thomson's victory for Scotland at Bala. On the invitation of the officials of Alexandra Park, under the patronage of the Kennel Club, and organised by Richard John Lloyd Price, the entire Bala 'show' was transferred to the city and it is reported that 'the Cockney's relished the introduction immensely. Not only were they treated on a lavish scale to Welsh swear words from Welsh throats; they also got Welsh mutton for nothing'—for many of the active little Welsh wether lambs took a dislike to the city life and in spite of the cleverest of dogs broke bounds and were never again caught—officially! The remaining sheep were sold by tender.

Some reports state that show-bred collies took part because certain officials were anxious to prove that such dogs were capable of working sheep. If so it was a great flop and the desire to forget the experiment may be the reason for the lack of detailed records. The 'Official Card' of 'The Kennel Club first colley trials, Alexandra Palace' lists two sets of judges, Le Gendre Starkie, of Huntroyde near Burnley in Lancashire, and John Williams, of Gwernhefin, Bala, 'for work', and S. E. Shirley, MP, and R. J. Lloyd Price 'for appearance'. The influence of the show-bench is thus apparent, and there was a prize of a silver cup valued at £5 for the 'best-looking dog or bitch'.

When 'beauty' prizes are awarded today at sheepdog trials they are for the 'best conditioned collie', which naturally encourages dogs to be kept fit, and there is a deal of difference between working-fitness and what can only be described as 'lazy-fitness'. I have known handlers be criticised today by the unknowing for owning 'skinny dogs', but the contented work dog does not carry an ounce of unnecessary flesh.

Entry fees at Alexandra Park were 7s.6d for puppies—dogs under two years of age—with a first prize of £10; and 10s for older dogs with the first prize of £15. The overall winner from both classes, John Thomas from Cwm-yr-Aethnen, Bala, with his four-years-old red coated Maddie who was valued at £40, received a silver cup presented by R. J. Lloyd Price and a further £15. One of the trials regulations stated that the owner of any dog injuring or killing a sheep had to pay 30s for the crime.

There is also a record of Queen Victoria having seen a sheepdog trial at about the same time as the Alexandra Park event—maybe even the same one. Always

Holme's winning team at the 1974 Pennine nursery championship. Chris Winterton with Toss, David Carlton with Scott, John Squires with Rex, Bob Moore with Sally, John Heap with Moss, Tom Gumbley with Cree.

interested in dogs, the Queen was said to have seen an exhibition trial run for her special benefit.

Also a little hazy in accuracy of detail, the first trials to be held in Scotland were at the Carnwath Agricultural Society's show on the fringe of the Pentland Hill in Lanarkshire in the early 1870s. They were won by a young Pentland shepherd, James Gardner, with Sly, a pretty little black and white bitch with a strong 'eye'. Sly was particularly good in the outwork and at the shedding and she earned £1 in beating a big black dog handled by a local man, Robert Russell. Sly ran second at the West Linton trials a year or so later.

In 1876 Lord Arthur Cecil of Orchardmains, Innerleithen, a trials pioneer in the Borders, bought the winning bitch at West Linton for £10, a high price in those days.

Trials created a lot of interest in the Border country and there were twelve entries at Jedforest in 1882 led by a gentle black and white bitch of great polish with Tom Turnbull of Attonburn.

First prize money had gone up to £6 at New Cumnock in 1897 and was won by the eighteen-months-old Lock handled by John Hastings of Glenwhargen who repeated his success in 1898, the first-ever collie with two premier trials honours. Five hundred people watched 32 dogs work over the New Cumnock hillside course of 600 yards gather, in 1899, and a year later the course was snow covered for 31 entries.

Alex Millar, who subsequently became one of the most famous of Scottish

Left *A champion of the future? Eric Halsall, Herbert Todd and Bob Moore at Holme-in-Cliviger, 1977.*

Right *Remote control—a shepherd with good dogs can manage the most distant sheep.*

handlers, won the 1900 event with the five-years-old black and tan Bruce. He eventually won the 1925 International Championship with the 4½-years-old Spot, three International Farmers', three International Brace, and nine Scottish National titles.

Alex—or 'Sandy'—Millar, who believed that a good dog was born, not made, said that whilst you could make any dog of reasonable intelligence into a fairly efficient worker, you wanted something more than ordinary intelligence in a dog that was going to make a name for itself in sheepdog trials in the face of strong competition. 'There must be an inherited instinct—one cannot describe it other than as an instinct—for herding sheep,' he said.

It was Sandy Millar who made the very profound statement, 'You have got to make a friend of your dog. I talk a great deal to my dogs, try to make them feel that we're partners and pals, and there is very little I say that they don't understand.'

Border trials undoubtedly improved Border Collies—and they improved the art of handling them. At Bala in 1873 the dogs were reported as barking and yelping whilst on the course and at all the early trials voice was liberally used by handlers to command their dogs. It was William Wallace of Otterburn at the Hawick trials in 1883 who first showed that such fuss was not necessary. It is recorded that he worked his dog with a mere hiss at hand and instructed it with a low whistle at a distance. Minimum command and quiet control are now expected on today's trials fields.

William Wallace who removed much of the strain from competitive

shepherding won the second championship organised by the International Sheep Dog Society in 1907 with Moss, a most competent collie who won eleven first prizes and two seconds in fifteen trials before being re-named Border Boss on going to improve New Zealand collies. One of the best handlers in the country, Wallace repeated his International Championship victory in 1922 at Criccieth with Meg.

A contemporary of William Wallace, James Scott of Troneyhill, Ancrum, near Jedburgh in Teviotdale, was also a quietly efficient handler and he was a practical shepherd who, present at the very birth of sheepdog trials, strongly believed that trials had a great part to play in improving the shepherding of sheep. James Scott watched the growth and expansion of trials—winning two International Championships in the process—and with a lifetime's experience and knowledge said in a training article in 1929 that it was unfortunate that the majority of sheep farmers were not alive to the importance and value of a well-trained collie. 'If they were,' he wrote, 'they would encourage in every way possible all attempts to make their canine friend more valuable, serviceable and efficient. But they don't; few of them are so disposed. For instance, it is rare one meets a farmer who will give his hearty support to sheepdog trials, notwithstanding the undeniable fact that nothing in our day has tended so much to raise the collie to a higher standard of training than has sheepdog trials. And yet farmers don't believe in them nor encourage them. If they have not a whole, they have at least a half objection to them.'

Farmers contended that whilst a collie was being trained to precision it caused unnecessary disturbance of the sheep flock. James Scott simply made the obvious point that better a little disturbance during training than a continual disturbance whenever the untrained dog went to the sheep. I believe that even today there is still a lot in what James Scott wrote, but not for the same reasons. I firmly believe that a very great number of stockmen are not fully aware of the collie's intelligence and potential as a working partner. This was brought home to me by the number of surprised and complimentary remarks about the prowess of the collies taking part in 'One Man and His Dog'.

Another reason—to bring a collie to the peak of efficiency requires extra work, time and interest, for a trials competitor is simply an ordinary well-bred intelligent farm dog with the 'extra polish'—and so many farmers care not to make the effort. Those who made the extra effort at the end of the nineteenth century are the ones to whom the modern farmer should be eternally grateful. Their effort in arranging the first trials and defining the qualities required in the working collie really established the breed, and in 1893 they must have felt that they had reached their goal in producing the ideal dog.

In September 1893 Old Hemp was born and it is written that 'he flashed like a meteor across the sheepdog horizon'. No one had ever seen a dog with his qualities before. He had everything, his every characteristic was geared to the shepherding of sheep. He was an outstanding dog. Adam Telfer of Fairnley, Cambo, in Northumberland bred him from the tan-marked black and white Roy and the shy almost black-coated Meg. With wise insight, Adam Telfer softened the hard eye of Meg with the good-natured manner of Roy and strengthened her reticent self-conscious ways with the open temperament of her mate to produce the genius of their son. Hemp was a sturdy black and white dog, lithe and well-fashioned, and he became the premier stud-dog in the Borders.

And so by the year 1900 the farmers of the Borders had brought the collie dog from the 'gash and faithful tyke' of Robbie Burns' days, through the competent yet boisterous dogs of James Hogg's days, to the quiet skills of Old Hemp. With those basic skills held in the bloodline and the dangers of in-breeding wisely controlled, the genius of one dog has since been broadened to a breed so that it would be difficult to find a working collie today whose ancestry cannot be traced back to the Northumbrian dog.

This evolution of the Border Collie is one of the great success stories of British agriculture. Adaptable to differing terrain, climate, and sheep temperament, British-bred collies now shepherd one-third of the world's sheep population of over 1,000 million; their role in world agriculture is unique for they make possible the harvesting of meat and wool from the most barren places of the world.

Chapter 3

To improve the collie dog

Tells of the formation of the International Sheep Dog Society and the ambitious aims of the Border men which blossomed to success with the emphasis placed on the correct testing of their dogs over well-set courses which have stood the test of time.
The years 1901 to 1921.

Under what was undoubtedly a grand title at the time—but which has since been well-earned—the International Sheep Dog Trials Society was formed by a dozen or so sheepmen from the Border country meeting at Haddington in East Lothian in July 1906.

Trials had become popular in their locality—and were also being held in Wales, the Lake District, the Derbyshire Peak, and in Ireland—and with creditable foresight they decided to bring some standard organisation to their new-found interest. 'Let's get the basic arrangements and methods of testing a dog sorted out,' was the purpose of the gathering. That it went further to the formation of the new society is a measure of their enthusiasm. When they closed their meeting under the chairmanship of George Clark of Eaglescairnie Mains, they had appointed James Wilson of Lauder Place, East Linton as secretary, formed a committee of ten, decided on their aims, and planned an inaugural event under a sub-committee of five organisers. They were men who, whilst appreciating the fun and honest competition which trials had created, did not forget the prime purpose of their dogs, the purpose of shepherding their sheep with efficiency on the home farm. Their trials had to contribute to this purpose.

I wonder sometimes if we of the modern organisation tend on occasion to forget that purpose and put competition first. The trials 'bug' can become a disastrous infection, the desire to win a silver 'pot' over-riding all else to the detriment of shepherding for a living. The improvement of the collie dog for pure practical shepherding must always be the aim of every trials society and individual, an aim realised by the founders of the International Society when they stated that their first purpose was to 'improve the breed of the collie with a view to the better management of stock'. Untrained dogs abuse sheep, causing unnecessary stress and strain and losing meat and wool in the process.

In addition, the men who met at Haddington in 1906 decided that their purpose was to interest the public in the shepherd and his dog and to bring shepherds together for their mutual benefit. These aims have stood the test of time

Left *Now what shall I read today? Colin owned by Birthe Lundman in Sweden.*

Right *Bob Moore's Sally in quiet command of Lonk ewes on the hills above the Cliviger Gorge in Lancashire.*

and are almost identical to those as now printed in the Constitution of the International Sheep Dog Society. Nor was the new society long in putting its aims into practice and the month after its formation held the first-ever trials to be known as 'International', though the 27 competitors were either Scottish or English handlers. It was not until 1922 that Welshmen competed, and Ireland was not involved until 1961.

The dogs which were allowed to compete at Gullane Hill in East Lothian in August 1906 had to be qualified—a rule which was subsequently abandoned and, until re-considered in 1982, caused a lot of discussion and dissent in later years when ever-increasing entries at the Nationals got out of hand.

Too many entries for the prescribed time—which extended to four days at some recent Nationals—leads to hustle and bustle and incomplete testing of dogs. This applies more than ever to the many one-day trials held throughout the country and can do the collie breed more harm than good.

The first International was confined to dogs which had won a prize or commendation at a local trial. Gullane was reported as a 'red letter day for the knights of the plaid', spectators were numerous, and conditions good with 'the weather just such as to make all animate nature rejoice'. The cream of the Border dogs competed and, embarrassing though it may be today because of the human element involved, the championship was won on a re-run trial. The judges decided that after one sheep had been left on the gather, the black and white Don under Richard Sandilands deserved another chance.

A rough-coated son of James Scott's Kep and George Gilholm's Jet, Don from Dundas Mains, South Queensferry, won the first International title with sound

rather than outstanding shepherding. He ran out well to gather and it is interesting to note that his 'lift'—starting the four sheep on their journey down the field—by sweeping round without halting was criticised because he did not stop at the end of his outrun.

This is a facet of judging often argued today. I dare not say it is 'old-fashioned' because I don't agree, as many present day judges do say a dog should 'clap down' to the ground when it gets behind its sheep. Their argument is that if the dog does not conclude its outrun by stopping, you cannot test its power of moving the sheep at the 'lift'. I like nothing better than to see a dog come sweetly round on to its sheep at a sensible pace and start them away on the fetch-line in one decisive action—just as Sandiland's Don is reported to have done at Gullane. I would consider it more practical shepherding than the 'stop–start' action—and sheep don't always abide by the text-book!

Don did all the other sections of his test of fetching, shedding, driving, penning, and singling well enough, showing a particularly fine concentration of purpose at the pen. The time allowed for the completion of the work was twenty minutes and one of the most fancied dogs, Thomas Gilholm's Bill, another son of Scott's Kep, from East Fortune, Drem, got no further than the pen, though his instinctive method was 'strangely fascinating' to watch. Bill was a good-looker, his glossy coat glistening in the sunlight being a reflection on his careful upbringing by Mrs Gilholm. How well I remember the skill and devotion with which Mrs Greenwood cared for her husband Len's collies at Ramsden Farm, Walsden. Because of her knowledge and love of the dogs which won to International standing, and which were so vital to the management of their 500 sheep on the bleak Lancashire Pennines, Len could always show off their skills with pride.

Mrs Irene Mundell of Stronyaraig in Argyll always gives husband Alasdair's black and white Cap an final grooming before he goes into the public gaze. Her care was well illustrated when I borrowed the handsome Scottish International collie for my companion in the opening sequence pictures of the 1981 BBC series 'One Man and His Dog'.

Handsome is as handsome does—Cap won the Scottish heat of the trials. And if truth were out, very many farmers and shepherds entrust the care of their dogs to the women folk.

Back at Gullane, perhaps the most famous dog to compete was James Scott's Kep from Troneyhill, Ancrum. The clever collie who became almost as well known as Old Hemp for his part in the founding of the modern breed had a sound trial, showing his masterly style, his initiative to work without undue command, and his great power of control over sheep.

A handler of sheepdogs who was to become a household name, Alex Millar, then of Ballagreich, had the distinction of being the first man to compete in an International trial when he started the event with Frisk who 'acquitted himself most gallantly' under the adverse conditions of rebellious sheep.

After handing the shepherd's crook which marked the victor to Richard Sandilands at the end of the day, the Society had £9 in their funds, the satisfaction of having held a worthwhile event, and the good will of the majority of Border shepherds. There were still those, as indeed there are today, who were sceptical of the limelight the collie dog was receiving.

Expansion did not come easily. The world before World War I was still very parochial, people did not travel much, and farming news depended upon whether you could afford *The Scottish Farmer* or not. Membership at 2s.6d a time never exceeded the 100 mark and the nine one-day trials held up to 1914 never left the Border area. Seven were run in Scotland and two, Carlisle in 1910 and Morpeth in 1913, in England. Though perhaps limited in the scope of its activities the Society was resident in the very birthplace of the most efficient of shepherding dogs, a fact which became apparent as quality exceeded quantity at the trials.

Six collies won those first nine trials, three of them—James Scott's Kep from Ancrum, Thomas Armstrong's black and white Don from Greenchesters, Otterburn, and his half-brother Sweep, with Adam Telfer of Cambo in 1910 and with Thomas Armstrong in 1912—winning the Championship twice. Of the six collies, four of them were close relations of Old Hemp, with Scott's Kep and his son, Sandilands' Don, far enough removed to clear the bloodline.

There must have been a very real danger of the weaknesses of too much in-breeding but there was also the genius of wise and discriminate matings. That the sheepmen of the Borders were indeed discriminate during those pre-war years I think is proved by the fact that those winning collies are remembered today. Scott's Kep, winner at Edinburgh in 1908 and at Perth the following year, is acknowledged as a pillar of the breed. The calm, level-tempered Sweep, a grandson of Old Hemp and winner in 1910 at Carlisle with Adam Telfer, and again in 1912 at Perth with Thomas Armstrong, founded three families which produced four Supreme Champions. William Wallace's Moss from Otterburn, the 1907 winner at Hawick, went to New Zealand and there re-named Border Boss advanced the breeding and prowess of collies in that country. Also responsible for the improvement of New Zealand's collies, Thomas Armstrong's Don, the 1911 and 1914 champion, and T. P. Brown's merled Lad from Oxton in Berwickshire, winner at Morpeth in 1913, were both exported to James Lillico.

When the Society resumed its trials after the war at Lanark in 1919 it was under the secretaryship of James A. Reid, an Airdrie solicitor, who was to become the mainspring of the International Sheep Dog Society. His enthusiasm and energy over 32 years to 1946, his documentation of the history of working dogs, his recognition of their inbred intelligence, and the value of sheepdog trials in promoting their qualities made British collies world famous and in demand wherever sheep were herded, and his organising ability created the Society as we know it today. He started his work of improving the Society in 1919 by creating separate classes of competition, one for farmers' dogs, one for shepherds' dogs, and a final championship of the best of both in a two-day event.

The separation of farmers' and shepherds' dogs came about as a result of complaints from shepherds that they were at a disadvantage in that they had not the same facilities for training their dogs on sheep which did not belong to them, that they had not the means to purchase or breed the best dogs, and that as employees they had not the same opportunities to attend trials as self-employed farmers. This separation continued until 1975 when the Society felt that under modern circumstances shepherds and farmers both had the facilities and scope to compete on equal terms.

Perhaps the most important thing that James Reid did at this time was to create a championship course which fully tested every one of a collie's shepherding duties, those which it would expect to meet in its day-to-day life on the home farm. Good as the trials had been before the war, this immediately raised their prestige and the championship became known as the Blue Riband of the Heather.

Reid's course proved so practical in assessing the qualities of working dogs that with little change it is used by the International Sheep Dog Society today, and all purposeful trials throughout the country are based on its layout. The course is vitally important to the success of a trial—as to some extent are sheep! Unless the course is extensive enough to enable all the sections of the tests to be adequately laid out, the trial is worthless and criticism justly warranted; and adaptable though the collie dog is and capable of mastering any and every type and breed of sheep, give it an honest chance in the usual short space of time—ten to fifteen minutes—it has to work 'magic' with them on a trials test.

There are 47 pure breeds of sheep in Britain and 300 crossbreeds and all have their own particular, and sometimes peculiar, traits. I have seen sheep used in trials—such as Blackface wether lambs which had been folded on turnips in readiness for the butcher—which had never before seen a dog in their lives. When faced with a dog they didn't know whether to trust it or fear it, to trot quietly away as it directed or to stampede away in panic. Often they just stood stock-still, bewildered until the power of the dog's eye made them flee. The result is frustration for the dog and for the handler—and a sheer waste of time for the spectator. When you get the combination of bad sheep on a small course the situation is explosive—sheep scared to death, dog tempers frayed, handlers angry, and spectators wondering what it is all about.

Most sheepmen are sensible enough to remedy the sheep nonsense; some trials organisers are not as ready to make right the course farce. Courses must be good and well laid out to adequately test the work-qualities of the collies taking part, or the whole purpose of sheepdog trials is destroyed and criticism warranted.

We have become victims of our own success and popularity. The breeding of better dogs has created keener and wider competition among farmers and shepherds and television trials have introduced millions of people to a new interest. Greed has often resulted, the greed of organisers to take as many entry fees as possible. Too many entries result in working time being reduced to an impractical level and small courses being set so that tests are inadequate or omitted altogether. Under such circumstances luck becomes too great a factor and in no way can they bring out the qualities of a dog nor show up the faults. I have seen as many trials as anyone in the North Country and judged many of them, and some, including some of the more famous, leave much to be desired. Tradition is good, but it should not impede progress. Sometimes it takes a little moral courage to change something that has been running for years and years but if improvement will be the result the courage must be found.

Walking across the 1,200 feet high rough moor of Deerplay in my Lancashire Pennines with the wind whipping in my face and streaming the long hair of Gael as she trotted at my heel, I remembered how my own Society, the Holme Sheepdog Trials Association, had the initiative to change a good trial on this hill of 250 yards gather and eighty entries to an even better one of 520 yards gather with a reduced entry of sixty. Today the Deerplay Hill trial which asks a dog to cross 520 yards of the toughest hags and peat bog land and climb through 260 feet to gather sheep on the 1,450 feet contour is recognised as one of the best in the North Country. It has proved its worth: at the first event in 1975 many dogs found difficulty in gathering their sheep; today very few miss.

The International Sheep Dog Society is alive to the danger of unsatisfactory trials though in this democratic world it has no power to order trials societies, even those which are affiliated to the Society, to set their courses to an accepted standard. It can only suggest, guide those that are willing, and by example itself set the highest standard as at Sennybridge in 1977, Chatsworth in 1978, and to lesser degree Stranraer in 1979 and Bala in 1980. These were tough testing courses which the collie dog should take in its stride if it is to be efficient on the sheepruns of the world

Fortunately—to counter my lengthy upbraiding of the bad trials and the adverse effects they have on dogs—most of the dogs at these Internationals were capable and reflected their ability and prowess in the shepherding of their home flocks. Winner of Sennybridge, John Thomas' strong 7½-years-old Craig came from work with Speckled-face ewes over high grassland in the Mynydd Epynt near Llandovery; Bob Shennan's mottled Mirk, the 1978 Supreme Champion, shepherded 550 Blackface ewes on 1,000 upland acres in the Carrick district of Ayrshire; the white-headed Zac, taking his second Supreme title at Stranraer, helped Raymond MacPherson in the herding of some 2,000 horned ewes over 3,800 acres of the Tindale Fells in Cumbria; and Tom Watson's little five-years-old Jen, only the fourth bitch in forty years to win the Supreme in 1980, worked with top-quality Blackfaces at Longcroft near Lauder in the Lammermuir Hills.

The BBC too in the filming of 'One Man and His Dog' have run their trials over courses that on occasion have been even more testing than the International courses.

In the Lake District Bob Shennan's Mirk proved his stamina, adaptability and wisdom even more decisively among the rocks and bracken slopes of Rannerdale, as did Glyn Jones' clever Gel and Bracken from Bodfari in winning the Brace contest. Alan Jones' proven Craig and the young Spot from Pontllyfni mastered the slopes and natural obstacles of the fellside course at Austwick in Ribblesdale; and Raymond MacPherson's ten-years-old Tweed, winner of the 1976 World Championship, proved lasting intelligence and strength to conquer the most testing of courses at Cilycwm in mid-Wales. Here also the brace winners, Thomas Longton's Lassie, 5½-years-old daughter of Tot Longton's Jed, and Bess, four-years-old daughter of Tot Longton's Kerry, showed that breeding

Alisdair Mundell's international Cap faces the Blackfaces on his home-ground at Stronyaraig in Argyll.

really counts by emulating their mothers' victory in the same competition.

So with such collies as these firmly 'shooting down' the myth of the weaknesses of so-called 'trials dogs'—let those societies who are in default of the vision of the men of Haddington get back to the real thing and put the dog first, not the entry cash remuneration.

Seventy-five years after that inaugural meeting at Haddington I was one of over 100 directors of the International Sheep Dog Society meeting at Carlisle to discuss methods of limiting the ever-increasing number of entries at National trials. The 27-entry at the first trials at Gullane had risen to 212 at the English National, to 172 at the Welsh National, and to 157 at the Scottish in 1980. These numbers had resulted in England having to extend their event to four days for the second successive year, and the Welshmen having to run dogs until very late in the evening during their three days. Scotland had been able to reasonably contain their entry to the accepted three days. The question of too many entries had to be faced, either by extending the number of days which brought problems of site loan and sheep numbers required, or by the qualifying of dogs in some way for National events.

I course-directed the first-ever four-day National at Penrith in 1979 and again at Tackley in 1980, and whilst organisation went well and dogs were fully tested, extra work and stress is obviously placed on the organisation so that there is a limit to the time extension of these events. That such a problem of too many entries has arisen in recent years does, however, reflect the current interest in the value of trials for the maintenance and improvement of standards of working dogs.

James Reid once said: 'Well may the shepherd feel an interest in his dog; he it is, indeed, that earns the family's bread, of which he is himself content with the smallest morsel; always grateful and always ready to exert his utmost abilities in the master's interests. Neither hunger, fatigue, nor the worst of treatment will drive him from his side; he will follow him through fire and water, as the saying is, and through every hardship without murmuring or repining till he literally falls down dead at his feet.' When he re-started the Society's trials on his Blue Riband course in 1919, James Reid could never have envisaged interest reaching today's heights, though he planned for it.

The first two-day trials at Lanark in July 1919 were still only International— the Nationals as we know them today did not start until three years later. But Lanark showed the way that Reid was planning. The first day comprised preliminary trials in the Farmers' and Shepherds' classes and the best dogs were qualified to take part in the Championship on the second day. Basically this is the plan today, with qualifying trials preceding a championship contest. Only in the allocation of points does the plan differ drastically—and this is a decided and necessary improvement. Compare the tests on Lanark Racecourse in 1919 with those of today. In the qualifying test five Cheviot sheep had to be gathered at 600 yards and fetched straight through one pair of flags set mid-way on the line for fifteen points; driving was triangular as today for 250 yards through two pairs of flags for five points; two marked sheep had to be shed within a twenty yards

Always content. Cyril Bostock's Mick.

diameter ring for five points; the five sheep penned in a triangle-shaped pen without a gate and an entrance of 2′6″ for five points; one of three unmarked sheep to be shed off and worn for five points; and five points were allotted for style and ten for command, to make a total of fifty. The time limit was twenty minutes—time taken being a factor in the judges' discretion.

Comparable points today are 110 without style and command being listed in a test of fifteen minutes.

Ten of the 32 dogs went forward to the championship which was judged out of 45 points with only ten being given for the whole gather which was described as 'running on the blind' a distance of 800 yards to gather five unseen sheep to bring them to the centre of the field before returning for a second five in 'another place' as is today's test for 100 points.

Then the shedding—without a marked ring—asked for the sheep to be run off between the man and his dog with the dog being brought in to turn back every third sheep. Five points were allocated to this test. The sheep were then penned for five points in a square pen with no gate and a four-foot wide entrance. Forcing—driving—'through obstacles as directed' earned ten points, to which work-total of thirty points was added the inevitable five for style and ten for command of the early days. The time limit was, as today, thirty minutes.

The 1919 programme of the 'International' Sheep Dog Trials Society which cost 6d is in today's eyes a fascinating document. Among the 32 entrants, 16 farmers and 16 shepherds, 27 Scotsmen and 5 Englishmen, which ran on Friday and Saturday, 25 and 26 July are such legendary names as Thomas Dickson of Crawfordjohn with Fly, Alex Millar (Burnfoot) with Toss, Tot and Roy, James Scott (Troneyhill) with Sweep and Help, Mark Hayton (Otley) with Meg, William Wallace (Fingland) with Ken, Walter B. Telfer (Fairnley) with Hemp and Midge, Thomas Hunter (Glenburnie) with Sweep, Fly and Nan, Adam Telfer (Fenwick) with Toss, Ben Eyre (Sheffield) with Don and Jed, James McInally (Kirkcowan) with Bessie and Bob, Thomas Gilholm (Prestonkirk) with Somme, George Brown (Longcroft) with Maggie, John Renwick (Alston) with Meg, and David Henderson (Beith) with Nell. Judges were C. B. MacPherson of Kingussie, Captain Butter of Coldingham, and John Maughan of Whitfield in Northumberland, and James Dalgleish of Galashiels and James Scott (Troneyhill) judged the 'type' competition which was in two classes, one for beardies and one for 'other dogs'. Certificates of merit—a good idea—were awarded to all dogs, irrespective of prize-winners, which by their work standard won the judges' approval. Would that we had some such idea today.

There was a special prize of £1 to the competitor 'having the largest family'!

The Lanark plan ran for three years and on each occasion English dogs won the Championship and the Farmers' cup, with Scottish collies taking the Shepherds' trophy.

Almost completed. The collie drives the flock into the home paddock.

The rough-coated Midge, bred at Greenchesters, Otterburn, by Thomas Armstrong in July 1918, and handled by Walter Telfer, son of Adam, the breeder of Old Hemp, was the outstanding collie of this period. At the age of twelve months she won the Championship shield in 1919 and in the following two years, at Hexham in 1920 and at Ayr in 1921, she won the Farmers' cup. Of Old Hemp line, she was sired by the 1911 and 1914 champion Don.

Also of similar blood, S. E. Batty's eight-years-old black and white Hemp from Kiveton Hall, Sheffield, a rough-coated son of the 1910 and 1912 champion Sweep, won the 1920 Championship. A blend of the Old Hemp and Scott's Kep lines, Adam Telfer's three-years-old Haig, a good looking rough-coated tricolour dog from Fenwick, Stamfordham, won the top award at Ayr in 1921. Adam Telfer also won the 1919 Farmers' cup with Toss, a rough-coated brother of Dickson's Hemp who was to become one of the most famous of breeding sires. Nell, a smooth black and white three-years-old bitch with David Henderson of Cockstone, Beith, won the Shepherds' cup in 1919 and 1920; and James McInally's home-bred tricolour Hawker from Kirkcowan completed Scotland's 'hat-trick' of wins in 1921.

One of the judges at the 1921 event at Ayr was E. Jones Jarrett of Corwen, and Wales began to show interest in joining the International competition. The Criccieth Sheep Dog Society sent its secretary, Captain Whittaker, to invite the International Society to Wales, and he was supported by the Hon. E. L. Mostyn —who as Lord Mostyn eventually became the International Sheep Dog Society's president. The following September the International trials were held at Criccieth; Wales had entered the International scene, and the important and lasting step of holding National trials to choose teams for the International was started.

This is the procedure today: each country—and Ireland is now included— holds its National trials in August and the leading dogs form the International team, so that any dog going to the International in September has won its representative 'cap' on merit.

In 1927 the first team contest was added to the International programme, the trophy going to the country with the best overall standard of shepherding; in 1929 came the Brace contest for the best pair of dogs working together; and finally in 1937 the first Driving Championship for the most efficient dog at driving sheep across the course. With the extra spice of international rivalry added, the Society went from strength to strength.

Starting in 1922 as one-day events the English, Scottish and Welsh Nationals grew into two-day trials in 1927, then to three-day events, and the first four-day National was held by England at Penrith in 1979. Each of these three countries is represented at the International by a team of fifteen single dogs, two entries in the brace competition, and one driving dog.

Irish sheepmen, who held their first trials at Dublin in 1888, came into the Society in 1961 when Northern Ireland sent a team of three single dogs to compete at Ayr. Eire joined the entry in 1965, and with collies from the Isle of Man also included in the Irish section, the team, now known as Ireland, has since

1979 sent eight singles, two brace, and one driving entry. Their National event takes place over two days.

At each of the National contests, which are judged by two men from the same country, the awards comprise the National Championship for the top dog of all, the Farmers' Championship for the leading dog handled by a farmer, the Shepherds' Championship for the best dog with a hired shepherd, the Driving title, and the Brace Championship. The aim of every competitor is to get his dog into the team—to win the coveted representative 'cap' in the form of a badge which immediately puts the collie in the top rank, as the results are eagerly sought throughout the shepherding world.

The International, which since 1926 has been a three-day event, is held alternatively in England, Scotland and Wales and has three judges, one from each country. As yet unrepresented on the judges' bench, Ireland is so growing in stature and collie skill that soon it will be able to claim that right, and also to make a case for the International event to be held in Ireland on occasion.

The overall winner of the International trials receives the Supreme Championship, the greatest competitive honour in the sheepdog world, and as at the Nationals, but irrespective of country, the Farmers', Shepherds', Brace, and Driving Championships are awarded.

Today the International Sheep Dog Society is recognised and accepted throughout the world as the leading society dealing with working sheepdogs; its trials are held as the pattern for testing collies and are visited by sheepmen from every sheep rearing part of the globe.

James Reid retired from the Society's secretaryship in 1946 having truly founded the organisation. He was followed into office by T. H. Halsall of Southport, Wilfred Dunn of Nottingham, T. J. W. Evans and Lance Alderson of Darlington, each of whom in his own way added something to the Society's success. The present secretary, Philip H. Hendry, took office in 1977 and has really brought the Society to the fore, his initiative and enterprise bringing acclaim and publicity for the Society's work which has put it in the front rank of agricultural organisations, has attracted valued sponsorship to the trials, and increased the membership to over 6,000.

More than ever is the Society 'international', for though it can only truly minister to the four countries of the United Kingdom—quarantine regulations making the possibilities of true and regular world trials virtually impossible—it has members throughout the world and is consulted by societies of like interest in other countries where it is generally held as the 'parent body', for Britain still leads the world in collie matters.

Chapter 4

Away to me

Sitting on the hill in the rain with Rhaq, Meg, and Gael at my side, I ponder the correctness of trials procedure to best bring out the essential man and dog partnership for efficient competitive shepherding.

The wind screamed cold rain over the top of the field wall and I settled for a moment's rest into the sheltered lee of the stones. My three collies, their coats mud spattered and matted with water, joined me, Rhaq leaning his body against my side, Meg stretching herself on the ground at my feet, and Gael nosing into the gaps between the stones of the wall bottom. She knew that rabbits used the cavities between the stones to hide.

It was a rain blustering morning and though the wind blew with a cold touch, there were signs that spring was returning to the hill. The ewes which the dogs and I had been to check over that morning were heavy in lamb. A flock of some fifty lapwings had flighted from our crossing of the hillside though they had not resented our presence with mobbing display as they would do within days, and a skylark sang its first golden notes of the year. A herd of Bewick's swans flew high over the hill, headed north to their breeding grounds for summer. It was still uncomfortable weather for both man and beast. My waterproofs dripped water from their oiliness and my double-nebbed gillie's hat was saturated. My pipe struggled a little to smoulder.

Weeks and weeks of continuous rainfall had left well drained land soaking, and the sheep, untroubled by cold, did not like the dampness which had penetrated even their woolly waterproof jackets. Their well-being had demanded more and more regular inspections and ministrations as the rains sullenly and relentlessly fell. The dogs were the least perturbed of all. They ran and splashed their way over the soaking ground to gather the sheep with little more than a shrug to clear their coats of water.

I leaned back against the green-lichened stones of the wall. Rhaq laid his head across my knee. Meg settled her head on crossed forepaws. Gael, disappointed that the rabbits were not at home, walked across to the nearest tussock of rushes in the hope that some tiny fur-coated creature might be hiding there.

I looked out across the rain-striped landscape from my sheltered rest by the wall, the lower hill swept from grazing green to warm brown middle ground and further on into the grey mistiness of cloud vapour. Wrapped in the eeriness of that

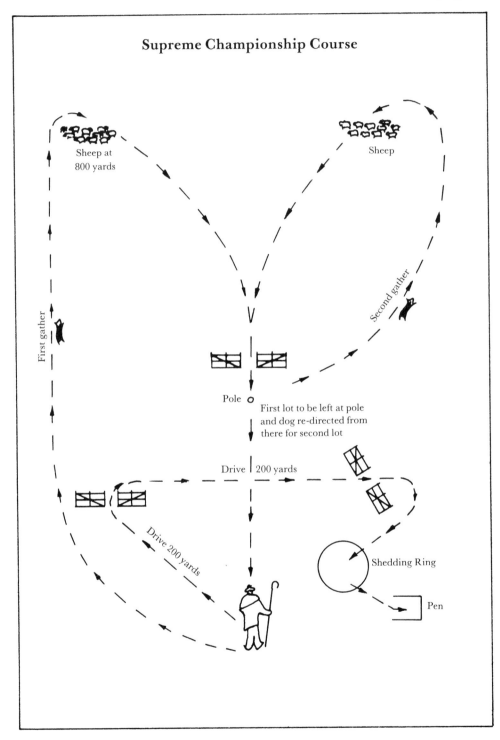

Supreme Championship Course

Sheep at
800 yards

Sheep

First gather

Second gather

Pole ○

First lot to be left at pole
and dog re-directed from
there for second lot

Drive 200 yards

Drive 200 yards

Shedding Ring

Pen

A quiet joke with the workers behind the scenes—the local committee—at the English National at Blackpool in 1966. Local secretary Eric Halsall with Alec Moore, Dick Bradbury and Bill Miller.

cloud was the romance of the Bronte country on the Yorkshire borderland; whilst away to the north the cloud-covered hulk of Pendle Hill brought shivers of the ill-fated Lancashire Witches.

A cold trickle of water down my neck jolted my thoughts to less romantic matters. I wiped away the water with my neck cloth and Rhaq lifted his head to my movements. Always he must be involved. It was good to have his friendship and respect. Rhaq, Meg, and Gael were my constant companions and we shared the changing patterns of life on the hill in a comradeship that was total. Devoted to my ways, their one desire was to please and they were utterly faithful. Aware of their varying temperament and character, I respected the expertise of their craft, a blend of inherent intelligence and experience in the ways of sheep.

In Rhaq, who was senior partner at six years old, this blend of wisdom and knowledge had brought a method akin to genius. With courage and stamina to match, he was the ideal shepherding dog. Proud and capable, he was a handsome prick-eared dog, black in colour and rough coated. Meg at three years old was equally wise and reliable and she had a gentle nature which persuaded sheep to her way. The baby of the trio at eighteen months old, Gael had a mischievous and independent streak, but was totally committed to my wishes.

Never did Rhaq, Meg, or Gael ever fail me or let me down and I never ceased to wonder at their intelligence and devotion to their craft. I was privileged to see such character every day; visitors to sheepdog trials and viewers of 'One Man and His Dog' have come to know the uncanny skill and appeal which sets the working collie apart from other dogs.

I did not linger unnecessarily on the hill that stormy morning. It was Saturday and there was to be a sheepdog trial over in the next valley. It was the beginning of March and towards the end of the winter nursery trials season, the period when sheepmen tested their young dogs on the competitive field. I had not competed at sheepdog trials, nor have I since, believing that as an agricultural journalist it is more honest to be able to report and criticise without being prejudiced by competitive involvement. Trials have fascinated me ever since as a youngster in the Yorkshire Dales I came to respect sheepdogs, and I have organised, directed, and judged very many trials at all levels, finding a broader interest by not being concerned in the outcome of the contest.

Sheepdog trials societies are friendly organisations usually comprised in the main of farmers from the locality, with a sprinkling of other interested persons from the village. We of the Holme Sheepdog Trials Association invite the local Scouts to provide the refreshments, and the Women's Institute have held a stall on occasion. The fell-race to the top of Thieveley Pike above the Cliviger Gorge is handed over to a nearby club of harriers, so that each section is the best of its kind.

Every society needs a good secretary. Secretaries are a much maligned race, blamed for everything that goes wrong, and credited with little that goes right. They are the backbone of every trials society, the men—and women—who have all the graft and unglamorous work of arranging and letter-writing to do. It is always difficult in a voluntary organisation to give members their duties. If you insist that something be done your way, you are a 'bighead'; if you sit back and

Richard Fawcett and Glen come through the 'maltese-cross' at Husthwaite in North Yorkshire. Glen subsequently went to Hubert Bailey in Georgia, U.S.A.

A good shed taken by Ron Railey's Ed at the English National.

do nothing, you are 'useless'. So you can't really win! Tact and diplomacy are possibly more essential qualities than sheepdog knowledge—which can always be gained or supplied by other committee members—in the character of a good secretary.

I have been fortunate in the quality of my colleagues during the many years I have been either secretary, chairman or president of my own society. Secretary Danny Wild, of Rakewood, combines organising ability with a life-time's experience of dogs and sheep, and Brian Crawshaw, of Healey above Rochdale, the chairman, also has years of experience of shepherding, so that their expertise reflects in the quality of our trials.

The society meets in the village pub and apart from organising a list of winter nursery trials our two main events are held in June and September. The June trial is the moor trial on Deerplay Hill which has become quite famous for its exacting test, and the autumn event is held in the valley on a tree-dotted field split by the infant River Calder over which Gritstone sheep are worked by the dogs. This event is part of the ancient Sheep Fair of Holme, believed to be one of the oldest in England, dating back to Elizabeth I, and held at the entrance to the Cliviger Gorge lined by high gritstone crags which Harrison Ainsworth in his book *The Lancashire Witches* records as being the haunt of eagle and wolf.

When we sit down for committee meetings, the main items to be arranged are availability of field, for hay-time can get very late in a wet East Lancashire, availability of sufficient sheep and the gathering of them from the adjoining hills which takes a full day, and the programming of a willing and capable staff comprising shepherds at the holding pen, course-director, and timekeeper. These three items must be the chief concern of any society preparing to hold a trial. They are really of equal importance, for without any one of the three the trial is doomed to failure.

I have written elsewhere of the absolute necessity of a suitable field in which to lay out a course which will test the dogs adequately. Sheep, in sufficient numbers so as not to be worked more than twice and preferably only once as in National contests, should be used to dogs—which is to say sheep that are normally well-shepherded in their home environment so that the competing dogs have a fair chance of mastering them to trials tests in ten to fifteen minutes. Staff, particularly the lads who will be setting the sheep at the gathering post for the dogs to collect, are equally important, and sheep-sense is an essential requirement. A trial can be spoiled by the way the sheep are brought from the holding-pen; they must be handled quietly and not upset, to make the competition fair for all.

The setting-up of a trials course to use the land available to the best advantage is also a job for the knowledgeable. Based on the layout recommended by the International Sheep Dog Society for their National trials, which is ideally the scope for local trials, the distance between the handler—marked by a single upright post on the field—from where the dog is sent out to gather, and the spot— also marked by a single upright post—from which the sheep are to be gathered should be around 400 yards. The post which marks the 'site' of the sheep should be set to allow plenty of room for the dog to run well behind the sheep, and the handler's post set well in front of the spectators and judge's position to enable sufficient scope for the small flock of sheep to be turned round the back of the handler at the start of the driving test. These positions are crucial. In the line of the 'fetch'—the direct route of sheep and dog back to the handler—is set the first obstacle to be negotiated, a pair of gates seven yards apart and about one-third of the fetch distance from the sheep gather. The driving test is over a triangular course, and the first 'leg'—the 'drive away'—starting from the handler's feet for 150 yards to another pair of gates; the second 'leg'—the 'cross drive'—for 150 yards across the front of the handler to another pair of gates; and the third 'leg' to complete the triangle of 450 yards back to the handler and into a shedding-ring forty yards in diameter, physically marked on the ground with sawdust. The pen should be set nearby the shedding-ring and is built of hurdles to the dimensions nine foot by six foot with a hinged gate of six foot. To the gate is attached a six foot long rope which the handler uses to negotiate the gate at the penning test.

The placing of the holding pens, one which holds the flock of sheep for use in the trials and the other—the exhaust pen—into which the sheep are taken after being used in the trial, is very important. They should be sited so that the sheep held within will not be visible to attract the attention of the sheep being worked over the trial course or to divert the dog from its purpose of herding the trial sheep. Our holding pen is tucked into the corner of the field against the stone

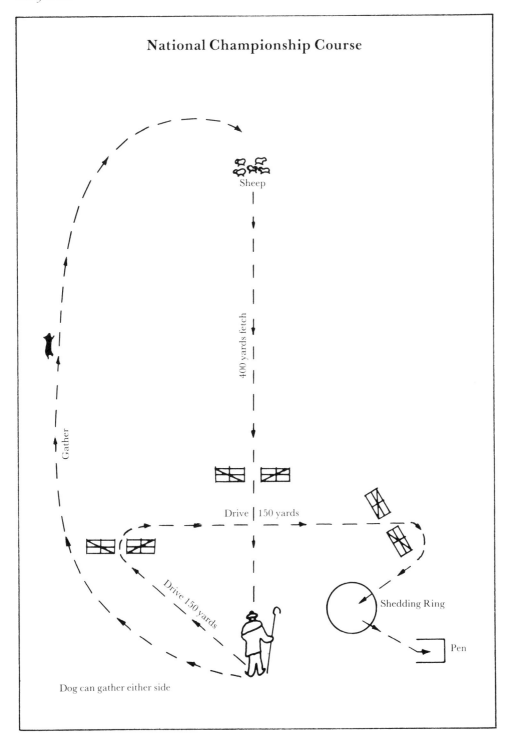

National Championship Course

Sheep

400 yards fetch

Gather

Drive | 150 yards

Drive 150 yards

Shedding Ring

Pen

Dog can gather either side

boundary wall and the exhaust pen is hidden away from sight among a fringe of rhododendron bushes. Wherever sited the pens should be screened with sacking so that the sheep inside are unseen.

This is the general type of layout for most trials, but it varies of course dependent on the size and contour of the land available. Some trials do not include the shedding-ring, some incorporate a 'Maltese-cross' which is a narrow passage formed of hurdles through which the sheep have to be put, and the South Wales layout is entirely different. But all trials courses are set out to test gathering sheep, fetching and driving sheep through obstacles, and penning sheep.

The provision of such ancillary items of equipment as a score-board, loud-speaker, marquee shelter and seating, are also arranged at our committee meeting. The lack of information and explanation such as which competitor is running, what points a dog has scored, is one of the big criticisms levelled by visitors to sheepdog trials.

We are fortunate in having a stream on site so do not need to provide drinking water for dogs—and sheep—but, though most handlers carry a can of clean water in their cars for this purpose, trials societies should not overlook this very vital service.

Completing the staffing of the event is the judge, who is positioned immediately behind the handler on the field, the timekeeper, who invariably sits with the judge, and the course-director, who has a roving commission but who is usually identified when signalling by flag for sheep to be released for the trial.

Course-directing properly is an important job and is vital to the success of a trial. In effect it is stage-managing the whole event, seeing that everything flows smoothly, that every competitor gets equal chance of a good trial, and that everyone goes home happy after a good day out. Efficiently managed, there

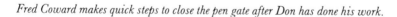

Fred Coward makes quick steps to close the pen gate after Don has done his work.

should be no hustle and bustle at a trial, the atmosphere should be relaxed and no competitor should be rushed. I have course-directed from nursery to international level and I learned the importance of the job from the most experienced of colleagues, from Jim Wilson, who won nine Supreme Championships before he took the job of Scotland's course-director, from his successor, Willie Hislop, and from Welsh course-director, Bill Jones. The years I spent as England's representative in partnership with Willie and Bill at the International trials were the happiest and most revealing of my international involvement. I also well remember course-directing the first-ever four-day National, held by England at Lowther Park, Penrith, in 1979, which was a pioneering step in the history of the Society.

Ernest Dawson, of Littleborough, course-director of the Holme Association's early trials showed me how to get through the biggest of entries without upset; Frank Tarn, former chairman of the International Sheep Dog Society, demonstrated that the little things were important for success; Will Fife, my predecessor with England, taught me never to get frustrated whatever went wrong. Some of my happiest stints of course-directing were with Jim Heap at the Nelson Agricultural Society's trials where for some reason it was always felt necessary to provide a case of beer for the officials and where the shepherding tests were over a course too small for wild sheep but on which the legendary Learie Constantine made cricketing history in his days in the Lancashire League. Perhaps the refreshment was to ensure that we worked hard in good weather. Looking back, it always worked, for Nelson is remembered for its scorching hot days—I think!

The judge at a sheepdog trial is of course the VIP. The International Sheep Dog Society holds a list of 'approved' judges from which the National and Inter-

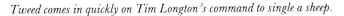

Tweed comes in quickly on Tim Longton's command to single a sheep.

national judges are chosen, and this is a list of people prepared to judge who have been elected by the Directorate and regular competitors of the Society. There are equally competent—some even more so!—people who are capable and willing to judge, and my society works on the principle of having different judges from various parts of the country each year. My point to trials societies is, do not forget the judge on the day. The judge should be offered every hospitality—such as a cup of coffee—to make his onerous task as pleasant as possible. This may sound like stating the obvious but I have sat alone judging a trial from eight o'clock in the morning until eight o'clock in the evening without being offered a cup of coffee or a bite to eat.

Judges—being human—vary in their interpretation of the degree of fault in a collie's work as the judging seminars of the ISDS have vividly illustrated, but all agree on the basic principle of what is good and what is bad in a collie's work.

Apart from the extent of concentration over a longer period of time, I find little difference between judging at nursery, novice, open or national level. Though not as vital by any means, it is often more difficult to place awards at nursery trials than in Open Championships—poor running is more difficult to judge than good running. Most open trials are judged by one person though in some parts of the country societies prefer two; the Nationals are judged by two people; and at the International three judges officiate each marking his score-sheet individually to his own decisions, the final pointing being the aggregate score.

And so we have set the scene, the course-director waves the flag to signal the shepherds to release five sheep at the far end of the field, the competitor, collie quietly trotting at his feet, walks to his place at the post. We have a National trial before us and the stillness settles over the watchers. Atmosphere at a trial becomes vibrant and intense, for though perhaps 100 men and dogs will be through the same procedure during the day the routine is never repetitive. Each pair is a new experience and refreshing in their method of meeting the challenge.

When such men as Alan Jones and Glyn Jones for Wales, Raymond MacPherson and Tot or Tim Longton for England, Bob Shennan and Tom Watson for Scotland, or Jim Brady and Tim Flood for Ireland go to the post there is always a hush over the crowd of watchers.

At the post, before the collie is sent out to gather the sheep, the man and his dog hold the maximum points, for the method of scoring or marking is to deduct points for faults in the work. Each section of the work is judged out of a set number of points, together totalling 110.

Standing with his back to the audience, his nerves perhaps just a little jumpy, the handler is entirely dependent on the cooperation of his dog. The extent of their partnership, friendship, and trust in each other is about to be tested to the full. They are alone on the field, detached in a remote arena for a fifteen minutes test which will demand all the perseverance, patience, and talent of both. A whispered word and the dog is away, moving across the ground with a noiseless and machine-like power towards the sheep at the opposite end of the field.

The dog may be sent away on either the right- or left-hand side of the course on the gather, whichever the handler decides. He should sweep out quickly and quietly, and without further instructions from his master, on a route which will bring him to the point where he can 'cover' the sheep so as to block any thoughts they may have of escaping him. Should he cross the course before reaching the sheep and gather them from the opposite side to that which he was directed, he will be heavily faulted, at least half the twenty points allotted to this section of the work. He will also lose points for requiring extra commands to find his sheep, for stopping on his way out, for going out far too wide in the line of gather, for coming in too tight and scattering his sheep, and for failing to cover his sheep at the end of the outrun.

The next move which the collie makes is to me the most decisive of the whole trial. When he moves up to take control of the sheep at the 'lift' to set them on their way down the field towards his master he must immediately assert his authority over them. It is his first contact with the sheep and he must show that he is the boss to be obeyed. A show of weakness here and the sheep will contest him all the way round the course. Quietly moving up, the dog must dominate the sheep and send them trotting on the way he dictates for the maximum ten points. At no point is the handler more pleased than to see his dog walk up with purpose and ease the sheep away.

There are two extreme faults to be down-pointed at the lift, one for weakness in controlling the sheep, usually requiring whistled and shouted commands of encouragement from the handler, and the fault of over-reaction, the brash tearaway dashing approach which scares the sheep into panic flight.

To bring sheep directly to his master is the most natural action of the collie so that the test of 'fetching' the sheep down the field is possibly the easiest section of

Every collie which competes at the National and International trials receives a veterinary inspection for fitness. Alan Leak's Roy passes this test at Stranraer 1979.

Left *Richard Fawcett's Tess herds Swaledale ewes on the snowbound fells above Wensleydale in Yorkshire.*

Right *Sheep that will test any dog. Strong crossbred ewes leave the holding pen at Tackley, 1980.*

the trial and is judged on the dog's ability to keep his sheep in a straight line—bringing them through a pair of gates set seven yards apart—and to keep them moving at an easy steady pace for twenty points. Faults here are for loss of control resulting in the sheep straying off line, weaving about on their course, stopping to graze, and the other extreme of rushing and chasing the sheep. Failure to guide the sheep through the gates is, of course, faulted.

With the action on, the handler is usually more relaxed than at the anticipation, and his whistled commands, confident and calm, or urgent and demanding, bring quick reflex action response from the dog. In the full flight of speed the collie drops motionless as though poleaxed; on a second's acceleration he is up and away to check a straying sheep; tested, he gentles his charges with the supreme stealth of a half-crawl, his deliberate steps compelling and hypnotising. The 'fetch' is completed when the sheep are brought to the handler and the five sheep, nicely bunched and comfortably moving without panic or fear, are turned round the back of the handler in as tight a line as possible for good marking, to start driving away for 150 yards. The direction of the 'drive away', either to right or left, is determined when the course is erected.

At no point in a trial can either handler or dog slacken their concentration, and the driving swings the control from in front to behind and calls for lessons well-learned from the dog. Driving is against the natural instinct to be bringing sheep to 'the boss', so control, a firm steady mastery of the sheep at the right pace on a straight line, will be tested. There is no more satisfying sight than a flock of sheep moving quietly and contentedly away with a black and white collie slinking a few yards behind and driving them on the correct line. At the end of the 'drive away' of 150 yards is the first set of drive gates through which the sheep must pass.

Commanded to flank his sheep—move round to turn them—he will next 'cross

'drive' for 150 yards, moving the sheep across the field in front of the handler, some 130 yards from where the man stands, and through the second set of gates. 'He's left it too late . . . they're going too fast . . . he's not going to make it . . . blimey, he's done it . . . they're through!' are the sort of hushed comments in the crowd when gated obstacles are approached.

It is a relaxed feeling to see the dog come sweeping round with a masterful flanking move to turn the sheep tightly after the gates. The final 'third leg' of the triangular course of driving is the simplest, really back to the art of bringing sheep as the dog drives them back to his master.

Driving points are marked out of thirty and faults are lack of push or power to keep the sheep going in the desired straight lines, too much power or lack of restraint resulting in a galloping race, going too wide on the turns and, of course, missing the hurdles.

The dog completes his drive by bringing the sheep into the shedding-ring. If there can be a moment's lapse of concentration out on the field without dire results there can be no such luxury in the shedding-ring. Two of the five sheep are marked with red collars (which in no way upset their normal behaviour) and the shedding test to separate two of the three unmarked sheep from the remainder within the ring for ten points. This test, often spectacular in outcome is based on the necessity to separate sheep into different groups for inspecting, dosing, culling on the home farm, and is one requiring absolute and instant cohesion between man and dog.

It is a test of temperament, for after the complete flow of movement of the trial to this point, the collie is asked to become almost immobile as he holds the sheep steady with the strength of his eye for his master to manipulate. Then the dog must spring into action to come between the two and the three sheep. There must be no hesitation in the collie to come through the gap and he must not waver a second. This stage tests quickness of decision in the handler and immediate reaction from the dog for, as throughout a really successful trial, both must work as one.

Faults in the shedding-ring are fear and cowardice in facing the sheep, ragged and rash work, failure to act on instruction, too much work left to the handler, and opportunity lost.

Next test is the penning of the sheep for a maximum ten points. After shedding, the five sheep are united and herded into the pen. Again close teamwork is required for full points, the collie taking one side, the handler the other. The handler controls the gate by holding the end of a six foot long rope fixed to the gate. The collie should again be quietly in control, watching to prevent any breaks—any escapes—by the sheep, holding them steady by the strength of his eye, applying or easing off pressure to settle the sheep so that they have no alternative but to enter the pen. Awkward sheep that will not enter the pen, though held and unable to escape the authority of man and dog, call for absolute control of temper—the repression of mounting irritation in the man and tireless tenacity in the dog.

The cardinal sin in sheepdog trials of loss of temper resulting in 'gripping' or biting the sheep could lead to disqualification, and points will be lost for harrying the sheep, for any unsteadiness or slackness in holding them, for rash moves, and for loss of concentration or interest.

The final test for ten points is the 'singling' of one of the two red-collared sheep,

Llyr Evans and Chip, England's 1976 National Champions, in the final stages of the Supreme test at the Lockerbie International.

when the dog is asked to take one of the marked sheep away from the small flock. Sheep bunch together in small flocks and to 'cut one off' is a test of patience, concentration and courage. The man must bide his time and manoeuvre one of the collared sheep to the edge of the flock so that the dog can on command move in quickly to cause the separation.

Then follows the test of courage and strength of will in the dog which must 'wear' or hold off the sheep from rejoining the other four. This is often a very testing and tense situation and the collie must show his absolute dominance over the sheep until the judges are satisfied with a shout of 'That'll do' to end the trial. Failure to respond to his master's call to 'come through' and cut off the sheep, cowardice in facing up and lack of power to dominate the sheep are all down-pointed.

Success in sheepdog trials, indeed the hallmark of success in practical shepherding comes through the complete partnership of man and dog with total understanding and confidence in each other. Each has a role to play, the handler seeing the purpose and guiding, the dog answering whilst using his own intelligence in the method of his contact with the sheep. Quiet control without undue commands, absolute mastery of the sheep without pressing dominance, and all the work completed within the allotted time of fifteen minutes will bring good pointings. Only in exceptional circumstances—a particularly stubborn ewe facing up to a dog may need a sharp lesson by a nip on the nose—is gripping tolerated. The handler is not allowed to touch the sheep. Pure practical, sensible shepherding, where the sheep are treated with respect, will win sheepdog trials.

This trial as judged is the one used by the International Sheep Dog Society at their four National events, and this is the test also used on the first two days of the International as qualifying trials when the 53 dogs from England, Scotland, Wales and Ireland are further graded to the top fifteen for the big test, the Supreme Championship on the third day. It is the trial with all the basic sections of outrunning, gathering, fetching, driving, shedding, and penning sheep on which all open trials are patterned, though they may vary in exact layout and in the number of sheep used for the trial. The Supreme Championship is the most exacting sheepdog trial in the world. Judging criticisms are exactly as we have discussed with the work extended, total points increased to 160 and the time allowed for completion to thirty minutes.

There are two separate gathers to be made by the dog, the first for ten sheep at half a mile distance, and the second—after the dog has brought this first flock half-way down the field and through the fetch-gate—away a quarter-mile to the opposite corner of the course for another ten sheep. This second flock is also brought on the fetch through the gate to join the first ten sheep, and then the whole twenty are taken on a driving test of 600 yards similar to the triangular National layout. Five of the twenty sheep are marked with a red collar and in the shedding-ring the dog has to separate these five, and the final test is to put these five into the pen. It goes without saying, though some people have raised the point to me, that each contestant in trials has fresh sheep.

Possibly the most popular contest with spectators at many open trials and at the

Steady on the fetch. Michael Csernovits' Mick from Berkshire.

Nationals and the International is the brace competition. The skills of two dogs working together under one handler never fails to enthral the audience.

Ten sheep are herded and the judging of the work is on similar lines to single-dog work with the big difference being the assessing of the partnership of the dogs. Each dog must do its share of the work. Sometimes one dog is jealous of its partner and tries to take all the limelight; in reverse, one dog may be a little lazy and let its partner do all the work. More than ever is a brace contest a test of shepherding partnerhsip with the handler on his toes to give the right command to the right dog at the right time.

The routine of gathering, fetching, and driving the sheep is similar to single-dog work. Each collie takes its own side on the out-run and whilst they are permitted to cross over at the back of the sheep they must then work on the side they have taken. To change sides during the actual herding of the sheep is a fault to be heavily down-pointed by the judge. In the shedding-ring one dog divides the flock into two packets of five, then proceeds to pen one group. The pen has no gate to close on the sheep, and having penned, the dog is left at the opening to prevent them from coming out again. This is often a test in itself, for a keen dog will be tempted to leave its post to help its partner pen the second group of sheep into the second pen.

Though they will work two, and often more dogs at one time in gathering their sheep from the hillside at home, some handlers decry brace running in competition. They say that with a partner to rely upon, a dog's concentration can be spoiled for singles competition.

My old friend Len Greenwood from the Pennine Hills who won more brace contests than most always used to say that 'a good dog can do anything—moor work, singles competition, brace competition'. He believed brace running taught a dog extra discipline and made it respect its working partner.

The other shepherding contest which can be seen at the International is for the Driving Championship when the dog is required to muster fifty sheep and drive them some 800 yards up the field. He must show that he has the power and authority to drive the flock without faltering, keeping them going away from him at a steady trot, nicely bunched and on the line required. The sheep must not be allowed to stop, graze, break away, or straggle out of control.

Each country is represented by one dog which is chosen by the judges at the Nationals on its prowess in the driving section of its ordinary trial. Spectators at trials also have a role in the proceedings—a passive one! Whilst a dog is working, silence is the rule and appreciation should only be shown at the completion of the trial. Actually most dogs take not the slightest notice of crowd noises, intent on their job and ears open only to the commands of their handler, but an inadvertent whistle or shout could be misinterpreted and some dogs are indeed a little nervous. Crowd noise is more likely to break the handler's concentration. Unless you have stood in front of the crowded grandstand as at the International, it is impossible to realise the amount of noise which comes from a massed murmur of voices and it can be very distracting.

The route to the Supreme Championship for a collie is an exacting one. After his basic schooling on the home farm he will receive his blooding into competitive shepherding in nursery trials. These are held during the winter months, October to March, on host farms—the dogs go to the sheep wherever available, usually wintering hoggs, and wherever a suitable course can be set up.

Matching the standard of the collies, the courses are minor versions of open courses with reduced distances of gathering and driving. Held on Saturday afternoons, nursery trials are friendly affairs. We gather without fuss, working clothes are the order of the day, and that is usually waterproofs, for windswept rainstorm and snowfall are often the conditions met with. The high sides of a

The red-coated Tweed eases heavy ewes into the pen for Tim Longton at the 1980 English National.

Land Rover or the field boundary wall are the only shelter and there are few spectators other than the competing shepherds and farmers.

Friendly yet highly competitive, the main interest of the watchers is to see the fresh crop of young collies which come out each season. Entry qualification is simple—nursery trials are open to a collie that has not won anything at all in competition. It is revealing to recall the collies which from this level have gone to the top: Jim Cropper's Fleet and Clyde, sons of John Bathgate's Rock and John Bonella's Trim, ran the Pennine nursery fields in 1966 and 1968 and went to Bala in 1973 to win the International Brace Championship; Tot Longton's wise old Rob from the Conder Valley in North Lancashire left the nursery courses to win forty Open Championships, five caps, and three National and International Championships for England; Alan Foster's rough-coated Dart from a Dalesbred herding above Lake Windermere in Cumbria won the 1977 Windermere-Northern Inter-club Championship and graded up to win the 1980 International Shepherds' and English National titles.

The step from nursery status is to novice competition which, with slight variations dependent on the promoting society, is for collies which have not won a first, second, or third prize in open competition. Jean Hardisty's little black and white Flash won her first novice victory over the tricky course of Rydal in the Lake District in August 1976 and progressed to win the 1977 English National Championship at Swinhoe on the North-East coast to make history for her mistress, the first-ever lady to win a National title.

Having cleared the novice hurdle a collie enters the open contest and finds that with entries approaching the 100 mark at so many events he has to be good to win even one.

The successes of Tot Longton's clever Rob, Llyr Evans' Supreme Champion Bosworth Coon from Whittlebury in Northamptonshire, and the two Ayrshire bitches David Shennan's tricolour Maid and Peter Hetherington's adaptable Nell, all of whom won over forty Open Championships, are close to the realms of fiction and fairy-tale romance.

The next step to stardom from the open field is to win an International cap at the National trials where the best collies in each country receive the major accolades of National Champions in the separate classifications. A National Championship is a great honour, the highest any country can grant. All success up the sheepdog ladder is on merit of working ability. The honour of a dog representing its country is purely on its own merit, the officials of a country do not sit round a table and choose an International team as with most sports.

Chapter 5

Of the same mind

I discover the true friendship which leads to mutual understanding between man and dog and see the results in such Supreme Champions as William Wallace's Meg, Mark Hayton's Glen, and the one-eyed Roy, the most famous of all Jim Wilson's champions. The years 1922 to 1938.

Success in trials—and more important of course in the daily routine of shepherding—depends on a true partnership and understanding between man and dog. The ultimate partnership is when man and dog are of the same mind rather than of two separate minds, however well blended.

Let us not forget in our enthusiasm for trials, and I make no excuses for repeating this often for the trials 'bug' can be all-consuming, that the collie dog is basically a tool of the sheepman's trade—as much as the plough is to the arable farmer. The dog is indeed the shepherd's most vital tool in the work of flock management. So, how much better and how much more efficient be that tool if it is a living, willing, self-acting servant—never slave—who has the same purpose in mind. The tractor man in his heart of hearts deplores the passing of the heavy horse. You can talk to and make friends with a horse: a tractor is a little non-commital.

For true efficiency man and dog must blend in temperament and each must have regard for the other. With the right man and the right dog it goes much deeper and develops into true friendship. The most successful shepherds treat their dogs as friends and the dogs respond. Mark Hayton, farmer of the Dales country, teacher of trials champions, and wise in the ways of his dogs, said 'A friend is one who knows all about you and loves you just the same. Your dog usually knows quite a lot about you.'

A shepherd spends so much time with his dog that friendship is essential. Tim Longton, who farms Dalesbred ewes on the high remoteness of Clougha Fell in North Lancashire, says 'They're tremendous pals, they never seem to let you down.' Raymond MacPherson, dependent on collie help to farm 3,800 bleak acres of the Tindale Fells in Cumbria, says 'I am constantly amazed at their ability.' Glyn Jones, whose Welsh Mountain ewes graze the Clwdian Range in North Wales, says 'Each is an individual and must be respected as such.' Tim Longton, Raymond MacPherson, and Glyn Jones have all won the Supreme Championship on the trials field.

It is just impossible to live with a dog of the nature of a collie for any length of time and not make friends. My black-coated Rhaq who spent the whole of his life in my company was the best pal I ever had; Meg was the most devoted companion a person could have; Gael was the most loveable of collies. All their faults disappear in memory. True friendship with a dog is usually founded during the teaching period when emotions are invariably stretched to the extremes of patience and understanding. Then temperament—and temper—will be sorely tested.

Basically, teaching and training fall into two distinct categories. The first is what I call the 'yo-yo' method when the man inflicts his dominant personality wholly upon the dog and divests it of its own intelligence so that it dare not make a move unless the string is pulled. As an obedient slave it is totally lost when called to use its own initiative. The second method is to teach the dog to use its inbred intelligence, to understand what it has to do and the reason for doing it, to act as a partner, even though in most cases as a servant—but always with respect.

The first method of training brings earlier results, for 'brain-washing' can start young; the second method of teaching brings lasting results. Friendship and understanding come initially from choosing a dog with the right temperament, it matures to efficiency if that dog has the inbred intelligence and the man has the 'know-how' to develop it. Choosing the right dog for both temperament and intelligence is consequently of paramount importance, but that decision which was something of a gamble in earlier years is today much easier. The odds in choosing the right partner have been reduced by the shop-window of sheepdog trials. Now one can see the qualities and the faults of the leading bloodlines, families of dogs, and choose accordingly.

The blood of champions runs through the veins of most of the International and National winners, going back to Old Hemp and the off-shoots of the main family-tree which he created, and whose importance and influence is discussed more fully in *Sheepdogs, My faithful friends*. Today by watching trials competitions we are able to choose the sires and dams which will give the basic personal requirements. It is then up to the man to encourage and develop that partnership for successful shepherding.

In choice of bloodline we are in effect talking about progeny-testing as the agricultural world knows it, the method of assessing the quality of a dog or bitch by examining the success of its offspring. A proven sire is one having an adequate number of competent progeny. But remember, comparisons are only really valid under like conditions. The best hill dog in the world will find the lowland sheep mentality more placid and their grazing pastures less exacting but frustrating until he adapts to the new life-style. In the progeny-testing context I purposely decline to list some of the more obviously accepted collie sires in recent years for only their successful progeny have been measured—their failures are unaccountable!

Would that the International Sheep Dog Society could be persuaded to produce a Stud Book which included only collie dogs which had a working and breeding record. How much more valuable would it be than the mass of dogs registered today because they have been born on the 'right side of the tracks' and with no proof that they will ever see a sheep or will be worth even the paper they are registered on. It is a system which only proves parentage and does not guarantee the working quality of a registered dog! However, the ISDS Stud Book is a work of classical proportions and its knowledgeable perusal will provide many answers to the genetic standard of the individual.

As with all 'herd books' genuine mistakes of pedigree will have been made, particularly in the foundation days, and I suppose it is easy to exaggerate the importance of remote ancestors. But before I appear to contradict all my previous emphasis on the 'right' families it is a fact that the blood of Old Hemp runs in today's champions. That most reliable sheepdog historian, John Herries McCulloch recorded the early years of Old Hemp's influence and, boosted by the skills of such collies as Wilson's Cap, McKnight's Gael, Gilchrist's Spot, Whitehope Nap and Wiston Cap, two of them Supreme Champions, the line has been invigorated and enhanced. So much is dependent on the individual to use the 'facts and figures' of records wisely and to take the trouble to seek what for him will be the ideal shepherding partner.

Take heart, whilst searching for the right temperament, in that many subsequent champions did not find their true partner until late in life. The greatest of driving dogs, the big tricolour Welsh Jaff did not come to partner Dick Hughes until he was four years old. Together they won three Welsh Driving and three International Driving Championships and two Welsh National titles.

Of the right temperament to blend with the ways of her master—and of the right breeding—was the 2½-years-old black and white Meg who with William Wallace of Otterburn in Redesdale won the first Supreme Championship after Wales had joined the reorganised International Sheep Dog Society in 1922.

Jim Wilson's Cap, the great hill-dog whose family made trials history.

It was an eventful year for Meg. In August she left her home duties at East Farm by the Rede to go to York to qualify for the English International team; a week later she was stolen but found in time to go to the International at Criccieth in Wales in September, and there, unperturbed by all the fuss, she put a fairy-tale ending on her adventures. With all the composure and resilience of her breed and in a most matter of fact manner she ran possibly the finest sheepdog trial ever seen. She was faulted only a single point by one of the three judges, the other two giving her full marks for an aggregate score of 179 of 180. Her victory was a superb triumph for good breeding and sound schooling. She had perfect understanding with her master, accepting his every soft-spoken word of guidance whilst drawing on her own intelligence and initiative when necessary.

Trim and supple, with the intuition of the female, the light of wisdom shining in her almond eyes, Meg was of direct line from both Old Hemp and Scott's old Kep. Her sire was Walter Amos' Tip, brother of Haig the 1921 International Champion, and her grandsire was her master's clever Glen, a descendent of Kep. John Hedley's Nell was Meg's mother, taking her heritage back to her master's Moss—Border Boss of New Zealand—to Dickson's Hemp and Thomas Armstrong's champion Sweep, the grandson of Old Hemp. Meg was well tempered and happy to be handled by her master's son, W. J. Wallace, who became as famous as his father in later years.

Whilst still in his teens, W.J. worked Meg over the Kelso trials course by the River Tweed when she unaccountably got her sheep into the water. Again showing that implacable nature, and swimming out to gather the sheep as though it was a regular occurrence, she completed the trials test in such grand style that in spite of the river incident she won third prize.

In 1938 W. J. won the Supreme Championship with Meg's granddaughter Jed at Southport.

The quality of Meg's temperament and inbred intelligence coupled with a daily experience in the ways of sheep was proved again in 1926 when she came close to making sheepdog history. In the International trials at York she ran second in the Supreme contest, beaten in the outfield by Mark Hayton's young Glen and thwarted of the honour of being the first bitch to win the Supreme honour twice.

Few but the romantics, could begrudge Mark Hayton that victory, the first and only Supreme won by one of the most respected and legendary personalities in the sheepdog story of the 1920s. A true gentleman of the country, Mark Hayton studied canine behaviour, treated his dogs with respect, and earned their loyalty in his farming of the Yorkshire fells above Wharfedale.

Glen was a 2½-years-old rough-coated tricolour dog when he won the 1926 Supreme title, setting the winning standard in a 21 minutes work stint in the first run of the contest. Sound in every section of his work, he also was of proven line, the grandson of George Brown's famous Spot the 1923 champion and, when exported to America after his 1923 victory, the foundation sire of the North American Sheepdog Society's Stud Book.

Classed as a canine genius because of his exceptional knowledge and ability to learn, Spot ran almost as good a British Supreme as Wallace's Meg the previous year, losing only 1 ½ of 180 aggregate points. In America with Sam Stoddart of New Hampshire the Scottish dog had a great influence in raising the shepherding standards.

George Brown was the first Scottish shepherd to win the Supreme, adding this top accolade to his 1922 International Shepherds' Championship and the 1923 Scottish National Championship which he also won with Spot. Five years later he again won the International Shepherds' title with Spot's son, Spot II.

Wales, in international competition for three years, scored their first major success in 1924 when Thomas Roberts from Corwen in Merionethshire won the Supreme title at Ayr with his 3-years-old rough-coated Jaff. A calm and clever black and white dog, Jaff was nicely marked with white chest, face blaze, and forelegs, and was in line to former champions Telfer's Haig, Wallace's Moss, and Scott's old Kep. He in turn passed his skills to his son Jaff II to win the 1938 International Farmers' Championship. The blood-links of the top dogs at this period of Border Collie history was close, all of them being descendents of Isaac Herdman's Tommy, who was bred by William Wallace at Otterburn, a grandson of Old Hemp. Himself only moderately successful in trials, he nevertheless had the qualities of strength and an intelligence close to genius which were to give great strength and character to the Border Collie breed.

Two of Tommy's kin, the sturdy rough-coated Hemp, and the gentle, stocky little Loos, were perhaps the most consistent breeding pair of all time, their matings producing good and intelligent collies with the stamina for hill work.

Hemp, a great-grandson of Tommy, was bred in November 1916 by Adam Telfer in Northumberland and went to Thomas Dickson at Crawfordjohn. With the Scottish farmer he won the International Farmers' Championship in 1924 and came close to the Supreme the following year, only one point down on the winner, Sandy Millar's Spot, the reigning Scottish Champion. Loos, a great-great-grand-daughter of Tommy, was bred by the International Sheep Dog Society secretary James Reid in May 1921 and went to Scotland's William Wallace of Fingland, Dalry, in Galloway when only a puppy. She had her moment of trials' glory when she was just over four years old, winning the Farmers' Championship and the qualifying trials at the 1925 International event at Criccieth, down-pointed 1 ½ of 55 points by the English judge, one on her singling test by the Scottish judge, and only half a mark on her lift by the Welsh judge.

Successful though they proved at International level, Hemp and Loos are best remembered for their breeding potential. Hemp was the ideal stud-dog and Loos mothered collies which won eleven International and sixteen National Championships.

One man who quickly realised the quality of the Tommy, Hemp, Loos bloodline was James McMorran Wilson, the most successful of all sheepdog handlers. Farmer of quality Blackface sheep in the Southern Uplands of Scotland, first at Holmshaw near Moffat in Dumfriesshire and then at Whitehope Farm at the head of Leithen Water above Innerleithen, Jim Wilson won 55 National and International trophies, including nine Supreme Championships, in nineteen years of international competition.

Left *William Wallace at Southport in 1938 with Jed and Foch, Supreme Champion and Reserve Supreme.*

Right *Twin lambs with weather protective jackets are gentled to their mother by Glen, a collie who overcame plastic hip surgery to continue serving his master Evan Evans at the Trawscoed experimental farm in South Wales.*

Below *John Jones' Jaff from Corwen, 1935 Supreme Champion.*

J. M. as he was known to the sheepdog world had an exceptional way with collie dogs and they served him faithfully on the high windswept sheep-runs of the Borders and on the trials fields of Britain. A modest man, he was an efficient farmer who got the best out of his animals by understanding their ways. Gifted with the patience so necessary when dealing with livestock, he trusted his dogs in the management of his sheep and had faith in their inbred ability. They were vital to his livelihood and such was his rapport with them that, with little other schooling than their work on the hill where he taught them the joy of their natural skills, they won 12 Supreme trials Championships, nine in his company.

The first of these nine successes came in 1928 when he was 27 years old and in partnership with a bonnie bitch which cost him a mere £4. Fly was a daughter of Dickson's Hemp and Wallace's Loos and at 2½ years old at Llandudno, working Welsh Mountain ewes with the watchful and alert concentration which marked her style, she won the Supreme title for Scotland. Black and white and healthy and wise, Fly returned to Llandudno in 1931 to win the International Farmers' Championship. Easily blended, Fly partnered three of her work-mates, Craig, Nell, and Roy to win the 1931, 1933, and 1934 Scottish Brace Championships. The year after Fly's Supreme victory her half-brother Craig, also sired by Dickson's Hemp, won the International Farmers' Championship for J. M. at Morecambe, and the following year went right to the top to win the Supreme at Ayr. A strong, handsome dog, though he had a streak of sulkiness in his nature, Craig also won the Scottish National Championships of 1931 and 1932.

Invaluable for his work capacity with the Blackfaces at Holmshaw and supreme on the trials field, Craig is also famous as the sire of Roy. One trials record which seems unlikely to ever be beaten—or even equalled—is that of Jim Wilson's Roy, a dog who virtually lost the sight of one eye in a fight with his half-brother Jix before he really started his working life.

As though to offset his physical defect—though it never really seemed to bother him—he developed an extraordinary intellect and his method of sheep control grew akin to genius. It earned him his three Supreme Championships. Three collies before him, Scott's Kep and Armstrong's Sweep and Don had won two International Championships, and three collies since, Jim Wilson's Glen, David Daniel's Chip, and Raymond MacPherson's Zac have won two Supremes, but no other collie has won the highest accolade of the sheepdog world three times.

Quickly adaptable to the whims of the sheep he met at the end of a trials outrun, Roy spotted possible troublemakers immediately and asserted his authority with a manner that was purposeful and decisive. Starting to herd, he geared pace to suit the nature of the sheep yet kept enough pressure to counter any hint of rebellion. His calm and methodical action, so confident and sure, eased sheep of their fears to give him complete control. Such initiative and wisdom in handling sheep, coupled with immediate response to the guiding instructions of his master, gave him two victories at the Cardiff Internationals of 1934 and 1937 and one at Ayr in 1936.

Sired by Craig, Roy was born on 7th April 1931, a good-looking black and white son of Wallace's Loos. Handsome is as handsome does and in addition to his trio of Supremes he won the International Farmers' title in 1935 and, so forming a sisterly partnership with Nell who knew so well how to deal with his occasional touch of 'lordliness', won the 1937 and 1938 International and the 1936, 1937 and 1938 Scottish Brace Championships. In a most un-brotherly way the champion prevented the clever little Nell from winning a true 'hat-trick' of Scottish National Championships, beating her by half a point in the 1937 event at Peebles after she had won the 1935 and 1936 titles. She compensated by winning the 1939 National before World War II brought an end to her trials career.

Nell was a delightful collie, a half-sister of Roy, both being from Wallace's Loos, and she was one year older which enabled her to treat him as the junior of their remarkable partnership. Sired by Dickson's Hemp, Roy's paternal grandsire, Nell had a commanding manner which stood no nonsense from sheep and she was ever willing to do more than her share of work on the hill.

Further emphasising the quality of the bloodline which Jim Wilson held in such regard, Roy's litter-sister, the black and white rough-coated Nickey won the 1933 International Farmers' and Scottish National Championships before going to Edgar Ferrier in Australia.

World War II interfered with sheepdog trials but not with shepherding; indeed the skills of collie dogs became more important than ever in managing Britain's sheep flocks to provide food for the nation. With the flock at Whitehope during those years of war the tradition of sound, efficient shepherding was kept with the big white-headed Cap, of the Tommy, Hemp and Loos lines as his predecessors.

Strong and wise, enjoying his true vocation on the high sheepruns where his energy never flagged and where his intelligence in the ways of sheep was fully tested, Cap was content to share his skills with the master he loved in the

The most willing work-force in the world. George Mitchell's Glen, Jaff, Moss and Roy from the Yorkshire moors.

loneliness of the Border Hills. It was in later years that those skills were fully and more widely recognised, and then, by the quality of the family he created. Cap became the perfect example of a progeny-tested sire when his breeding successes established his fame. He was a great hill-dog with the stamina, health, and wisdom of his calling, and he was able to pass those qualities to his sons and daughters.

His daughter, John Kirk's Nell, a big black-coated bitch of kindly temperament mothered by McCaskie's Moss, had three of her sons in the top three placings at the International trials at Worcester in 1948. The winner, Jim Wilson's Glen, a five-years old black and white son of Willie Hislop's Glen, was earning his second Supreme Championship, his first at Edinburgh two years previously. Glen also won the Farmers' title at Worcester, and had won the Scottish National in 1946.

Placed second at Worcester was Wilson's Moss, a 2½-years-old son of his master's Mirk. Marked as third was Glen's older brother, Willie Hislop's Sweep who also won the Driving Championship at the same event.

Cap's grandson Mirk won Jim Wilson his eighth Supreme Championship at Ruthin after having won the Scottish National at Dunoon in 1950; his great-granddaughter Tib won the 1951 Scottish National for J.M.; and his great-grandsons Bill and Whitehope Nap ran first and second for Wilson's final triumph at the 1955 International—such is progeny tested.

Left *Fit and active and overlooking 700 South Country Cheviot ewes at 10-years-old—Geoffrey Billingham's Trim from the Bowmont Valley.*

Right *Mary Heaton from North Yorkshire, one of the most competent of lady handlers, works Moss over the Penrith National course in 1979.*

In spite of Jim Wilson's astounding success on the trials field he did not have all his own way between the war years, from 1919 to 1939. Perhaps his greatest rival was another legendary Scot, Alex Millar from Highbowhill at Newmilns in Ayrshire who also believed that 'like breeds like' and proved his point with one main bloodline which produced collies to win one Supreme, three International Farmers', three International Brace, and nine Scottish Nationals—seven of them in succession. Of the 18 Scottish Nationals held between 1922 and 1939 Jim Wilson won seven and Alex Millar won nine.

The sort of rivalry these two used to have is reflected in the International Farmers' contests of two consecutive years. At Llandudno in 1928 Millar's Ben won with Wilson's Fly second, three points dividing them, and at Morecambe in 1929 Wilson's Craig won with Ben second, two points between them.

Between the war years twenty Internationals were held and England won ten and Scotland seven, five of them going to Jim Wilson. Wales in their seventeen years of competition won three. Scotland won ten Farmers' Championships, England eight, and Wales two; and Scotland dominated the Shepherds' scene, winning sixteen of the twenty contests, England and Wales taking two each.

Alex Millar, better known as 'Sandy' Millar because of his colouring, had a trials prowess to match his 6' 6" stature and a practical experience of dogs which took him back to driving sheep from Ayrshire to the markets by the Clyde. One of his best road dogs was a half-bearded collie Frisk who also followed his sire, the black and tan Bruce, winner of three New Cumnock championships, as a trials winner.

The rough-coated black and white Spot, a strong forceful dog who blended perfectly and with unusual ease with the big man, was Sandy's first champion collie, winner of the 1925 Supreme and four Scottish Nationals. Dominant in manner, Spot was of breeding from former champions Armstrong's Don and Scott's Kep.

Also of Don's bloodline were Tot, Millar's 1924 Scottish National winner, and Mirk, his victor in 1928 and 1929, and the smooth-coated Ben, partner with Mirk in three International Brace wins and twice the International Farmers' Champion and 1930 Scottish Champion, was mothered by Tot. Ben, winner of the Welsh Cambrian Stakes in 1929, was sent to the New Zealand sheepruns but his son Ken carried on the home successes with the 1934 Scottish and International Farmers' Championships. When Spot won the Supreme in 1925 he lost six of an aggregate 165 points from the three judges. Each of the judges marked out of a mere 55 points and fifteen of these were given for the very personal and flexible opinions of style and command—interesting when today for the same work each judge has 160 points to allot, style has gone, and command is assessed in each section of the work and not as a separate item. At most open trials of any standing the shepherding is judged out of either 90 or 100 points today. Though the International trials courses and tests have not changed to any marked degree over the years, the system of pointing has rightly changed.

Welsh sheepmen had to wait with growing impatience for a repeat of Thomas Roberts' success with Jaff in the 1924 Supreme Championship and it was not until 1933, and again at Ayr where Roberts had been successful, that they acclaimed their second Supreme to an equally patient rough-coated dog, the eight-years-old Chip with George Whiting of Aberdare in South Wales.

Between 1924 and 1933 the Welsh trophy cupboard had been rather bare, a remnant of prestige having only been salvaged by two victories in the Shepherd's class by Evan Pritchard's Welsh Champion, the black and tan Juno from Llanor, Pwllheli in 1926, and John Evans' black and white Hemp from Llandudno in 1931. Wales did however complete the pre-war period with another Supreme Champion, John Jones of Tan-y-gaer, Corwen taking the 1935 honour at Blackpool with his two-years-old Jaff, a great-grandson of Roberts' Jaff, the 1924 champion.

One of the best known and most respected handlers of the present time, Meirion Jones of Pwllglas near Ruthin is the son of John and equalled his father's success in 1959 with Ben, a 3½-years-old grandson of Hughes' Jaff.

The two Welsh Supremes, George Whiting's Chip and Jones' Jaff were both related to the 1923 champion, George Brown's Spot. Wales had to wait until 1953 for their first victory on their home soil when at Cardiff John Evans of Magor in Monmouthshire won the title with the four-years-old Roy, another grandson of Hughes' Jaff.

England, who led the trophy race up to the war, were very dependent on the skills of Northumbrian farmers and the clever collie families they had slowly and methodically established. From the sheep lands of the Derbyshire–Yorkshire border John Bagshaw, one of the stalwarts of the famous Longshaw trials, won the 1927 Supreme with his experienced seven-years-old Lad, a son of the 1920 champion Batty's Hemp; S. E. Batty himself added the 1929 title with Corby; and another Derbyshire handler, John Thorp of Derwent and his tricolour Jess, a four-years-old daughter of Mark Hayton's 1926 winner Glen, won at Llandudno in 1931.

These collies, together with Walter Telfer's Queen, line-bred to Armstrong's Don and winner of three National Championships and the 1932 Supreme, were of the Border heritage. Appropriately in what could well have been the last International sheepdog trials it was a true Border Collie which won the last Supreme Championship before the war, at Southport in 1938.

Jed, a wise and experienced eight-years-old granddaughter of William Wallace's 1922 Supreme Champion Meg, won the title for Wallace's son W. J., the young farmer who had worked his father's old champion through the waters of the Tweed in earlier days. Jed beat her kennel-mate Foch into second place by 7½ aggregate points in the final in a great personal triumph, tinged with sadness for W. J. The triumph of the two dogs was not able to be greeted by their great playmate for whom they were still pining, W. J.s four-years-old son Willie who had died earlier in the year.

Nor did the tragedy cease, for within two years both Jed and Foch died. Jed died the following year after having won 146 trials prizes and Foch was accidentally poisoned a year later. Jed, a keen bitch with a broad white neck ruff had won England's Championship in 1933 and was by Wallace's Moss, son of Meg, and out of Heslop's Maddie. Foch, a tall leggy dog, was out of Jed's sister Fly and consequently also related to Meg.

W. J. Wallace left the North Country to live in Sussex and his prowess in breeding and working sheepdogs had been remembered, since his death in 1976, by the holding of a memorial trial in aid of Cancer Research each year in May by the Standean Sheepdog Society at Brighton.

Chapter 6

On national service

Describing the important role of the collie dog in providing food for a nation at war, and in peace how its skills held the people of London 'goggle-eyed' in wonder when it took the bustle of city life in its stride. The years 1939 to 1960.

On the cold Border hills, the bleak grazings of Snowdonia, the windswept slopes of the Pennines, or amid the green pastures and relative calm of the lowland plains, the working collies of Britain were totally committed during six years of war to assisting in the production of food and clothing. For those years they were wholly engaged in their basic duties of helping man care for his sheep and cows to provide meat, wool and milk. Trials had to be forgotten from 1939 to 1945, whilst collies played a vital role in the all-out farming operation of Britain to produce essential home-grown food for a nation at war.

The cancellation of trials for those six years was not a bad thing for the Border Collie breed. With every sheep and lamb, cow and calf really counting, farmers became even more fussy in the welfare of their stock, in eliminating or at least reducing to a minimum the stress and strain of their handling. Consequently farmers became more aware than ever of the qualities of a good herding dog. They needed a collie which was in sympathy with stock, a collie clever enough to anticipate the actions of stock and with the initiative to prevent trouble before it arose, a collie with controlled power and amenable temperament which would order stock without undue hassle. The careful handling of sheep can save tons of mutton in one flock alone. It was a time for reflection and whilst going about their job in the tranquillity of the high hills farmers and shepherds began to appraise the standards of their dogs more critically than ever before.

Without trials to attend every weekend there was a little more time to consider and study the selective breeding plans of the earlier shepherds. All breeding is a risk but it can be turned into an art and the Telfers, the Armstrongs, the Browns, the Wallaces and their kin of the Borders had done just that in bringing the wartime collie to an efficient farming assistant. Bred into the dog was the ability to round up sheep and cattle, it was temperamentally suited for work with other animals, it was healthy and fit for a long life in arduous surroundings, and above all and by far the greatest achievement, its canine mind had been developed to reason and think, to temper instinctive reaction.

As Mark Hayton said, the ability to handle sheep efficiently was already bred into the dog, it was the shepherd's job to teach it how best to make use of such skills.

Earlier I have written that the start and growth of trials by the gathering together and testing of potential breeding stock played an important part in the sheepdog's growth of stature. I am convinced that this was certainly true in the early 1900s, but I am prepared to listen to those who say that the number of trials held up and down the country just prior to the war—and even more so today—also had some adverse effects. Who would challenge the wisdom of W. S. Hetherington of the famous Wiston brand of dogs who believed that dogs got too much trialling—and the successful ones too many bitches—when the mobility of the motor-car made it possible for dogs to be run at two or three trials in the same day?

That the best dogs were able to attend and win more trials and thus highlight their ability and increase their breeding use can be argued two ways—it leads to either the narrowing of bloodlines or the full use of dominant lines. In effect we are back to the breeding skill of the individual person, his assessment of the dogs—and bitches which are equally important in any breeding programme—and his ability to make full use of whatever potential is available.

The loss of mobility when the brake went on the holding of trials did not harm the breed. Successful breeding continued, but the difference between the early 1900s and the war years was that by 1939 the blood was available and its source known. The break from trials competition gave a breathing space during which more thought, more investigative time, and more relaxed interpretation of quality could be put into a breeding programme.

And it worked. To the National and International trials between 1946 and 1950—the 'harvest' period of the war years—came some of the best collies ever seen. From the sheepruns of the Borders came Jim Wilson's Glen of the brisk manner and his six-years-old Mirk, both grandsons of the white-headed Cap, to win the 1946, 1948 and 1950 Supreme Championships. The easy, disciplined rhythm of Glen's shepherding and the perfect understanding he had with his master in the 1946 final had that hallmark of quality which had been cleverly planned and bred for. John Gilchrist's first Spot from Haddington, descended from former champions Wallace's Moss, Scotts Kep, Millars Spot and Wilson's Craig, was four years old when he won the 1947 title at Cardiff; Tom Watson's clever prick-eared Nell, daughter of Wilson's Cap, from Eccles near Coldstream in Berwickshire took the 1949 and 1950 International Shepherds' Championships; and Willie Hislop's Sweep, a most skilful black and white collie won the 1946 International Farmers' Championship. All these four handlers served Scotland well, Jim Wilson to the very peak of trials honour, John Gilchrist to International points with Spot II, Tom Watson to further Shepherds' successes and eventually in 1980 the Supreme with Jen, and Willie Hislop, who after many representative honours, continued to serve his country—and to teach me the efficiency of course directing—at International level.

With Welsh ewes in the Black Mountains of South Brecon, David Daniel's coolly efficient and strongly determined Chip won Wales her fourth Supreme

Jim Wilson, nine times the winner of the Supreme International Championship, with Whitehope Nap and Bill at Edinburgh in 1955.

honour at Ayr in 1949 and, a dog for the big occasion, repeated the success in 1952; John Evans, farming at Magor in his native Monmouthshire in 1947, won the International Farmers' title with Juff; the great Hughes' Jaff of the balanced concentration and power from Anglesey won the Welsh Nationals in 1946 and 1948; Bill Miles of Berthlwyd Farm, Treharris in the Welsh valley of Glamorgan, won the 1949 International Farmers' Championship during a successful eleven-years-old partnership with the smooth-coated Wally; and Herbert Worthington of Abergavenny took the Welsh Shepherds' honours in 1946, 1949 and 1950 with two North-country bred collies, Kep and Moss, and the rough-coated Maid from Scotland.

From the Peak of Derbyshire where he worked with 1,400 Swaledales over 5,000 acres, Ashton Priestley's smooth-coated Pat, son of Joseph Relph's Fleet of *Loyal Heart* film fame, won England's first post-war Supreme at Blackpool in 1951 after taking the International Farmers' title at Ruthin the previous year; from the Cheviots on the Scottish Border at Mindrum, Bob Fraser's mottled black and white Nickey, a responsible and hard-working collie of a world famous line, won the 1948 International Shepherds' Championship, and Bob took three England titles in four years with Sam, Nickey, and Lass, two grandsons and one granddaughter of Wilson's Cap.

Tot Longton's prick-eared Mossie from North Lancashire led 72 entrants on Swaledale ewes over Bakewell's showground to win England's National title in 1950, the first of the many International honours to her master whose father had won the English Championship the year before at Morecambe with Dot.

Remember the successes of the Hyde Park trials organised by the *Daily Express* immediately after the war when, as much at home as on their native fells, collies worked Swaledale ewes with Park Lane on the skyline and against the background hum of London traffic in a steady relaxed manner which 'held the crowds spellbound.' Here, really for the first time we got the 'layman's' reaction to the skills of working collies, and again with a rather 'surprised discovery' of the appeal of clever dogs, the *Daily Express* reporter of 1949 wrote of the Hyde Park event: '200,000 people standing in the sunshine 30 and 40 deep round the arena and held silent in the middle of London on Derby Day by an event which has neither balls, bats, bookies, nor blows'. They were watching an enthralling display of canine intelligence, and the few farmers and shepherds who had joined them recognised work well up to pre-war standards, with youth in the shape of the two-years-old Ben slipping gracefully and naturally into the pad-prints of his ageing kennel-mate, the twelve-years-old black and white Lad, former winner of the 1947 Welsh National title under R. O. Williams from Trescawan, Llangefni, on Anglesey.

They saw that the rough-coated black and white Ben with Sandy Millar had a style of authority akin to his mother the former Scottish champion Tot; and that another Scottish dog, Tom Bonella's black and white Glen from Kinross, was similarly showing traits of his great ancestor Wilson's Cap.

They noted how Willie Bagshaw's soft Yorkshire commands brought out the

A good collie is adaptable—Glyn Jones' Bwlch Bracken is equally capable on cows or sheep.

skills of his Mac to reflect the ability of his sire, Mark Hayton's Pat, Farmers' Champion of 1936. From Blyth near Worksop, Mac won the English Championship in 1946 and took honours at Longshaw and Dovedale in Derbyshire.

From the hills of the Lake District where two winters previously they had saved the lives of numerous sheep by locating them under the worst snow blizzards for years, Joseph Relph brought Fleet, the film-star dog, and Spy, son of Wilson's Cap, his partner in the winning of the 1948 English Brace Championship.

From the 'hills of gold', the gold-mining district in Merioneth, Welshman John Jones, whose pre-war record of training dogs to herd his Mountain ewes at Trawsfynydd was second to none, showed he had lost none of his skills with Jim and Jaff. Winners of the 1947 Welsh Brace title, both were blue-blooded, Jim by Wilson's triple Supreme Roy, and Jaff, by the great Welsh driving dog Hughes' Jaff. Jim won the first Longshaw Championship after the war and again in 1948. Jaff won the Cambrian Stakes in 1948 and joined his sister Dovey to win the 1949 Welsh Brace title.

From the herding of a Black Welsh Mountain flock of ewes on the slopes of Caerphilly Mountain above Cardiff, David Stone brought his 1948 Welsh winners Jaff and Jake to the city.

One of the best 'non-working' compliments paid to the temperament of the post-war Border Collie was that of a hotel proprietor when the 1949 International went to Ayr: 'I wish all my guests were as well behaved as the dogs.'

It was obvious that the working collie had 'wintered well' during the war. Trials societies too were more than ready for the re-start of their competitions and

Content in her trust of David Carlton's international Tony, this mother ewe allows David to minister to her lamb.

the Lake District Sheepdog Trials Association ran a small trial in conjunction with a hound-trail at Ibbotsholme, Windermere in 1944, which was won by Jack Mason's Jed from Barbon. The Association returned to their true venue, the famous Applethwaite Common course, the following year when Bill Huddleston's Mossie from Caton in North Lancashire was the winner.

Longshaw in North Derbyshire also ran their first post-war event in September 1945 with 67 collies watched by 5,000 spectators. Featured on BBC Radio Newsreel, the Open Championship went to John Jones and the 6½-years-old Jim from Trawsfynydd. It was a champions' 'meet' with Willie Bagshaw's six-years-old Mac, Willie Hislop's Scottish brothers Tam and Sweep out of Kirk's Nell, Francis Goldthorpe's Shepherds' Champion Roddy, Dick Hughes' famous Jaff, and Len Greenwood's three-years-old International Dot in the prize-lists.

The following year, 1946, the Cambrian Stakes re-started at Llangollen with one of the best known of Welsh handlers, Griff Pugh of Sealand taking the championship with Moss. Griff repeated his victory the following year with Sweep. In 1946 also, the International Sheep Dog Society got going again, though after having kept interest alive during the war years, James Reid announced his retirement as secretary, but not before he had arranged the English National with 62 entries at Ilkley in Yorkshire's Wharfedale, the Scottish National with 76 dogs at Stirling, and an entry of 53 Welsh collies at Llanfairfechan in Conway Bay.

The International was held at Carrick Knowe golf-links at Edinburgh on three September days under the judgement of William Wallace of Dalry, J. V. Allen of Patterdale, and Capt. T. M. Whittaker from Portmadoc. They judged the qualifying trials out of fifty points each, including five points for style. The outrun and lift at ten points total were only as valuable as the fetch. Fifteen minutes were allowed for the work. The double-gather Championship was marked with sixty points by each judge, thirty being allocated to the total gathering and fetch, with ten points for shedding and five for style. Thirty minutes were allowed for the full test. This was also the test for the Shepherd's title. The Brace test was judged from fifty points by each judge, with only a total of five for the joint outrun—half the number allotted to penning—and again five for style.

Today we would all consider these pointings and their allocation to be totally impracticable—and those 'style' points are frightening! Jim Wilson's Glen scored 172½ of 180 aggregate points, unfaulted in shedding, penning, and style, for the championship; Donald MacLeod's Garry from Comrie in Glen Earn won the Shepherds' title on 153½ of 180; Willie Hislop's Sweep was top of the qualifying list on 144 of 150; and Arthur Hayton, Mark's son from Otley in Yorkshire with Paddy and Barney gave England their only success by winning the Brace honour on 136½ of 150 aggregate points. The Driving Championship went to Dick Hughes and Jaff for Wales.

Contested by these champions and by such as Joe Relph's Fleet, John Thorpe's Jess, Willie Bagshaw's Mac, Mark Illingworth's Meg and Monty; Francis Goldthorpe's Roddy and Dan, John Evans' Juff, David Stone's Jake, John Jones' Jaff and Jim, Bill Miles' Wally, Herbert Worthington's Kep, John Gilchrist's Spot, Jimmy Millar's Drift, Sandy Millar's Jock and Ben, and David Murray's

Toss, all of which won a National or an International Championship in their careers, the quality of the dogs in the first post-war International augured well for the breed; and the programme was, through subsequent success and breeding potential, to become a sheepdog *Debrett*.

The whole theme of living at the end of the war was one of re-building. In sheepdog circles this was not necessary. The breed had not suffered, indeed could be said to have benefitted from the trials rest. What had become obvious to those who seriously considered the collie's future as the perfect working dog was the responsibility of correctly interpreting the results of the trials field. To interpret them wrongly, to glibly accept that every winning dog is naturally and automatically the ideal partner for every bitch puts an awful responsibility on, for instance, the Supreme Champions of the International trials on whom the full glare of the publicity spotlight falls each year.

Any collie which wins a Supreme Championship—be it a dog—gets more than its fair share of bitches and thus has some influence on the breed as a whole. The exact degree of impact is obviously dependent on the usage of the winning sire.

Fortunately—and by studied design—the tests of the International Sheep Dog Society to acclaim a Supreme Champion are tough and demanding and so it is in fact a good, hard-working and clever collie which wins this top accolade. 'The Supreme test is absolutely unique,' said Lord Mostyn in 1955 when he was president of the International Society, 'and the dog that wins it is a very great sheepdog indeed.'

It is a practical, strong-working collie for the tests are so exhaustive and revealing that had it not the stamina for the physical work and the intelligence for the skilful work, it would be hopelessly outwitted by twenty virile sheep. It is not a 'lucky' collie, for it would be stretching fact just a little too far to consider that good fortune could stay with one dog long enough to take it through two qualifying and one final series of tests of a total hour's duration. It has to be an adaptable, reliable, and wholly responsible dog to maintain the highest of standards through such tests.

And where this dog—this Supreme Champion—has been bred from with thought and discretion, the Border Collie breed has benefitted. Consider the influence of the Wilson line, and of John Gilchrist's 1947 Supreme Champion Spot to Glyn Jones' Gel, Elwyn Griffith's Craig, Tot Longton's Rob, Martin O'Neill's Risp, and to his master's younger Spot, Scottish Champion of 1965 and 1966; of David Daniel's clever Chip, 1949 and 1952 Supreme, to his son Ken, 1960 champion; of Llyr Evans' Bosworth Coon, the 1968 champion, to such successors as Raymond MacPherson's dual Supreme Zac; of John Evans' very adaptable Roy, 1953 Supreme, to his Welsh son Alan Jones' 1961 Supreme Roy, and to Mrs Barbara Carpenter's Brocken Robbie and Michael Perrings' Kyle, and to Wiston Cap whose three sons, John Murray's blue-fronted Glen, John Templeton's 4½-years-old Cap, and Gwyn Jones' strong-working Bill, and three grandsons, Gwyn Jones' white-headed Shep and Bob Shennan's mottled Mirk, and Wyn Edwards' handsome Bill, emulated his 1965 Supreme success.

Of the very few bitches—only the second in 29 years—to take the Supreme honour, Thomson McKnight's clever Gael, daughter of Whitehope Nap, was outstanding. Always well-mated, she mothered sound, efficient work dogs and International and National Champions. Trials showed the qualities of these dogs to the world at large—thus playing their true role in the shepherding pattern. Trials also showed that there were lean years in collie efficiency, though there have always been individuals to offset the general depression.

Have trials perhaps an even more important role in flashing the warning lights to show us when and where things are going wrong? They certainly leave us in no doubt when such is the case by their grim boredom, though to the uninitiated in the finer details, they then often present a greater spectacle. A somewhat ambiguous statement—but sheep dashing suddenly out of control does awaken the sense of humour in most folk.

The danger with general decline is that too much importance and quality can be put on the individuals which do rise above the rank and file to catch the eye. Fortunately the likes of Jim Wilson's 4½-years-old Whitehope Nap, Scottish Champion and Supreme reserve in 1955; George Redpath's adaptable Moss from Jedburgh, third in 1955 and the winner the following year; William Work's six-years-old Ken, with 700 South Country Cheviots at Hermitage near Hawick, 1955 International and Scottish Shepherds' Champion; and David Murray's Vic and Number, father and son team from a Blackface herding near Peebles, and Brace Champions in 1955 for the third successive year, were really good and showed their skills in their trials work.

Beaten over the Craigentinny course between Leith and Portobello by his kennel-mate, the four-years-old Bill who was later sold to Ray Parker in America, Whitehope Nap was to become one of the most important sires in the history of the breed. He was a sire who had a great influence in improving the day to day shepherding of the Borders and the North of England, for farmers and shepherds liked his style and action which stood no nonsense and got on with the job of handling stock under all conditions. Nap was a well-coupled dog with plenty of power and authority and he could pass this on to his progeny, so that he became renowned as a sire of solid, reliable, and clever stock-dogs. Medium sized, bare skinned, and endowed with more than his share of brain-power, he sired strong, healthy, fast moving and quick thinking dogs which, in the right hands, also won trials championships. Most of the Supreme Champions of the past fifteen years carry some of his blood.

One of the collies which Nap beat on the Supreme trials field in 1955 was Glen, the five-years-old black and white Welsh National Champion handled by Harry Greenslade who was a coal-miner from Cwmcarn in Monmouthshire's Ebbw Vale. One of the few men who trained and worked collies as a hobby though his interests were among the small hill farms above the Welsh valleys, Harry was also one of the most competent after nine years, and he again handled Glen, line-bred to Wilson's Cap, to the Welsh championship in 1956 and to the International Farmers' title a month later with work over the Llandudno course marked at 147 of 150 aggregate points.

A great believer in testing by properly laid-out trials, Harry taught his dogs

Collies control the Blackfaces in a tight flock across the foot of the hill.

their craft on Mynyddislwyn, the mountain which towers above his native valley and over which is held one of the best sheepdog trials in the country in mid-July. A stronghold of the South Wales style of testing, Harry remembers how Jim Wilson came from Innerleithen to adapt his collies Glen and Mirk to take the leading prizes at the contest.

The 1956 Supreme, George Redpath's rough black and white Moss from Harden Mains by Jedburgh in the Borders gave a very practical stint of shepherding in windy, command-destroying conditions and used all the experience of his eight years to master Mountain ewes over an undulating course, baulked by hedge and banking on the second outrun. He was a good sound dog who had already won the 1952 International Shepherd's title over the big course and, his work-mate Coon, a grandson of Hughes' Jaff, having won the Shepherds' title earlier in the 1956 event, gave his master a unique honour—the first man to win the Supreme and the International Shepherds' honours in the same year.

John Thomas from Llandovery equalled his record in 1977 when his rough-coated Craig won both awards, though the Shepherds' award was won over the shortened qualifying course.

The famous Longshaw Trials in North Derbyshire with Mark Illingworth handling Spot.

The year 1956 had some very practical collies standing at the top of the Supreme list. Lancashire farmer Tot Longton had his nine-years-old Bute on the reserve championship mark and his prick-eared Mossie, English Champion earlier that year, on the fourth marking. Bute and Mossie were as good a pair of working dogs who ever came together to work Tot's milk-cows and fat-lamb producing ewes in the Conder Valley near Lancaster. They showed their partnership understanding in taking the 1954 English Doubles Trophy.

Splitting Tot Longton's Lancashire pair at the Llandudno International was the rough-coated Tibbie whose handler, then at his first International, was to become famous in the top flight of competition. Meirion Jones, son of John Jones who won the Supreme in 1935 with the smooth-coated Jaff, was 23 years old and he had been working collies at trials since he was twelve years old. From Llandrillo in the Berwyns, his hard work and dedication paid off, the three-years-old Tibbie, a black and white granddaughter of Wilson's Moss, taking third placing at Llandudno, and three years later at Cardiff he won Supreme honours with the 3½-years-old Ben, a grandson of Hughes' Jaff.

Confident and easy in his way with collie dogs, Meirion, who now farms Welsh ewes and beef cows at Pencoed, Pwllglas, above the Vale of Clwyd, has that gift of cool and assured understanding which brings out the full qualities of his dogs on the trials field and which has brought four International and five National Championships. In 1979 his black and white Craig won the Welsh National, Farmers', and Driving Championships at Llyswen, and partnered by the younger 2 ½-years-old Ben at Stranraer won the International Brace title.

Blustery wind conditions impaired contact with the handlers and made collies use their own initiative at the distance of the 1956 Supreme, and the 1957 International at Loughborough in Leicestershire was even worse—with unnatural noise interference. Traffic bustle from the busy A6 road alongside the course upset communication to the extent that the Shepherds' Champion, Mark Illingworth's clever little Fly from Wensleydale in Yorkshire won the title with a score 27 ½ points less than her third-place marking the previous year.

Again collie initiative was well tested and Fly, a trim little bitch of Wilson's Cap line in work with hill ewes above Semer Water, was masterful in her herding of heavier Halfbreds. 4 ½ years old, Fly complemented the success of her half-brother, John Holliday's rough-coated Moss, equally controlled and determined in his winning of the Supreme Championship under the same distracting conditions. Both collies were sired by John Holliday's Roy, the 1951 English champion.

Never better was the temperament and adaptability of the Border Collie seen than at Loughborough. Both Moss and Fly came from the isolation of Dales shepherding where a quiet, relaxed environment was their daily lot, and yet they settled to work of the highest calibre on stronger heavy sheep amid the noise and bustle of city life. Adaptability had been a topic five years earlier when the English National was at Loughborough and John Nelson took the seven-years-old Tweed, a grandson of Mark Hayton's champion Pat, from the loneliness of Woodside Farm, North Stainmoor above the Eden Valley to win the Shepherds' Championship. John said of the big occasion 'I'm sometimes so scared I can't whistle, yet Tweed takes the crowd in his stride and knows what to do even when I can't tell him.'

The course for the International in 1958 at Camperdown, Dundee in Tayside was much more of a practical test with Blackface ewes to be gathered from a rough hillside intersected with gullies and covered with bracken. It found the weaknesses and not one of the shepherds' collies completed the work, shedding being the major problem, but it also added to the quality of the Supreme Champion, a six-years-old rough-coated Scottish dog Tweed handled by a Welshman, John Evans of Tidenham in Gloucester, representing England under the residential rule.

Tweed, a tricolour son of Jim Wilson's Moss and Robert Anderson's Trim, won the English National at Chatsworth the following year. Technically an English win, this Supreme Championship was the only individual championship missed by the Welsh team. Robert Thomas of Aberdesach and his handsome Roy won the Shepherds' title: Ivor Hadfield from Prestatyn won the Brace honour with Jean and Roy; and two farmers from the Valleys, David Daniel from Ystradgynlais and Allan, winner of 21 first-prizes in a single season and son of his master's double Supreme Chip, took the Farmers' Championship, and Bill Miles of Berthlwyd, Treharris, won the Driving title with the prick-eared Kay.

Meirion Jones and Ben, winners of the 1959 International, were hard pressed to a single point by John Templeton of Mauchline in Scotland whose lapse in the shedding ring with Roy cost him the title.

Wales benefited from a national intensity in breeding good collies and testing well with meaningful and practical trials which sorted the dogs and gave handlers hard experience in the late 1950s. Meirion's victory at Cardiff—when all but the Driving Championship went to Welsh collies—was the start of a remarkable run of international success for Wales, the first of six successive Supreme Championships. In those six years Wales won half of the championships available—two Farmers', two Shepherds', five Brace, and four Team. In fifteen years from 1956 to 1970 Wales won the Brace award twelve times. Only in the field of driving were they barren—after Bill Miles' win with Kay in 1958 they waited until Wyn Edwards' Jaff earned the honour at Stirling in 1967. Typical of the sound, reliable Welsh dog which was capable of taking the hard work out of shepherding and was also capable of winning sheepdog trials was Eurwyn Daniel's home-bred Ken, the winner of the rain-lashed 1960 International at Blackpool.

Ken, a descendent of Jim Wilson's famous one-eyed Roy on his dam's side, was the son of Chip, twice Supreme Champion with Eurwyn's father, David, and Chip, bred in Scotland by David Dickson of Hawick, was one of those sires which the shrewd Welsh farmers used to advantage. Chip and his like left some good progeny on the Welsh sheepruns, dogs which were sound, reliable, accurate and straightforward, and it was these qualities of good sensible shepherding which won Eurwyn's four-years-old Ken the 1960 Supreme.

My memory of Blackpool is of mud, rain, rain turning to downpour, and more mud, much of it plastered on the black and white coat of Lancashire's Spot, striving valiently under Tot Longton to become the home county's first Supreme. He ran hard and well and failed by only 8½ points—also beaten by one point by John Rutherford's big black and white Sam from Boundary Farm, Kineton in Warwickshire.

Sam, of Hughes' Jaff and Gilchrist's Supreme Spot lines, was one of the dogs who sensibly solved the problem of the obstacle that wasn't! This was the strangest memory of Blackpool's Stanley Park course—the tarmacadam footpath which became a stream, at least so thought the sheep. Initially dry and presenting no problem for the sheep to cross, the path soon became wet and shiny in the downpour and though it never held water it presented a great psychological barrier to the sheep. Trotting happily on the fetch to the dog's command, they stopped in sudden panic at the edge of the path—and it required power from behind to push them across the path. It was virtually an extra test in the trial and it certainly showed the strengths and weaknesses of the dogs involved.

Rutherford's Sam was one dog who used his brains to force the sheep across. He came up behind the middle ewe and gave her a gentle yet persuasive nip to send her darting across the path—quickly followed by the rest of the sheep. It was a quiet, controlled nip which was effective without harm to the sheep and it was the sort of assertive shepherding that is required from a collie dog in many circumstances in its daily work on the home farm. A collie which cannot be trusted to use its mouth with sense and without anger or harm to the sheep is useless for practical work, and in trials work should be judged accordingly.

Scotland really had a disastrous International in 1961, though David Moodie and the smooth-coated black and white Nap, out of Fly, the little-sister to Whitehope Nap, salvaged some pride with the Driving title.

Not one of Scotland's collies qualified for the Supreme test and none of us could remember such total eclipse ever happening before. Indeed Scotland's decline in collie matters lasted for some five years, until Wiston Cap's victory at Cardiff in 1965 restored confidence; and England weren't a lot better though from both countries came individual dogs to promise better days.

Scotland had some moments to savour from such collies as William Gordon's 7½-years-old Lad, Shepherds' Champion in 1962; David Shennan's merled Roy, Farmers' Champion in 1963 on his first International appearance; William McMillan's Nap, son of Moodie's champion Nap, from Maybole in 1963; Tom Watson's Jaff of the Mindrum line; John Templeton's reliable Maid, Roy and Nap; and of course David McTeir's white and black Mirk, the outstanding dog at Drymen in 1964; and Thomson McKnight's clever Gael, the greatest sheep bitch of them all.

England had few moments in the successes of Mark Illingworth's Moss and Jim, Brace Champions at York in 1963; Tim Longton's great hill collie Ken, the Farmers' Champion in 1964; and of Don, the 1962 Farmers' Champion, and Scot, Driving Champion in the same year, handled by Welshmen John Evans and Llyr Evans.

Chapter 7

Their craft was supreme

I remember Roy's fantastic record; how Juno became the first bitch in 25 years to win the Supreme; acclaim the success of Gael, the greatest bitch of all; admire the natural easy talents of Ken; and record how Wiston Cap came to create a dynasty.
The years 1961 to 1971.

Apart from the Welsh dominance, Ayr in 1961 is remembered of course as Alan Jones' year. In the place where he made his International debut twelve years before, the Welsh farmer from Pontllyfni handled his strong tricolour Roy to the Supreme and Farmers' Championships, crowning a fantastic year in which the four-years-old dog had won the Welsh National, Farmers', Driving, and with his work-mate Spot, the Brace Championships. Ayr 1961 was another milestone in the Society's progress, being the first time that Northern Ireland was represented by three collies, Lyn McKee's English-bred seven-years-old Snip and his Whitehope Corrie of Scottish line from County Down, and Jim Brady's six-years-old Whin from County Antrim.

Yet another phase in the Society's history was reached at the directors' meeting the following year when the age limits—over two and under eleven years—were removed from collies allowed to compete at the International.

The years 1962 to 1964 were not outstanding in the International trials field and only incidents of those years rather than occasions linger with me. Alan Jones and Roy almost repeated their 1961 Supreme success at Beaumaris in 1962, beaten by Alfred Lloyd's home-bred Garry, a grandson of Harry Greenslade's Glen, in an undistinguished International.

Tim Longton's clever Ken from work with Dalesbreds in the remote North Lancashire fells won Longshaw for the first time in 1963—repeating the win in 1967 to become one of the few collies to take this renowned championship more than once.

That most immaculate of bitches, Thomson McKnight's seven-years-old Gael from Glencartholm finally proved herself Scotland's best in the 1964 National by five clear points. Her experienced method and compelling power produced a shepherding stint on the testing course at Glendoune near Girvan in Ayrshire which was only faulted 2½ points by each of the two judges.

After watching Llyr Evans win the Macclesfield Championship with his International Moss in 1963, followed closely by George Eyre's two-years-old Roy

A master-handler John Richardson who had implicit faith in his three great collies Sweep, Wiston Cap and Mirk.

from Bradway, George Mitchell's little black and tan International Jill, and Leslie Suter's six-years-old Craig, the following year's Supreme Champion, 72-years-old Bill Goodier, a founder member of the Cheshire trials didn't entirely agree with my somewhat despondent view of general collie prowess. Bill said 'The present working sheepdog is a cooler, steadier animal, more suitable for sensible stock management than the speed-merchants of old.'

The fifth consecutive Welsh Supreme success in 1963 was quite an event in itself, inasmuch as the winner, Herbert Worthington's 3½-years-old Juno from Abergavenny was the first collie bitch to win the honour for 25 years. Confident in warm sunny conditions over the flat Knavesmire racecourse at York, the smooth-coated black and tan Juno handled Dalesbred ewes with hard practical skill, finishing the half-hour test with ten minutes to spare, and with a concentration, control, and power worthy of victory. Blue-blooded to Hughes' Jaff and Roberts' Jaff, Juno was from a line of her master's home-grown champions, Hemp, Fly, and Moss.

At York there was just a sign that the Welsh supremacy was being gently prised away, though the Welsh team won one of its rare Shepherds' Championships—to 29-years-old Gordon Lewis from the Breconshire hills and his six-years-old tricolour Meg whose final work in holding an erring ewe at the pen was alone worthy of the championship. Wales had last won at Shepherds' Championship in 1959 to Worthington's Fly, Juno's mother. York, with Mark Illingworth and

Moss and Jim on top for England, also saw the temporary break in Welsh brace supremacy stretching from 1956 and mainly shared between Ivor Hadfield and Herbert Worthington with Juno's sire and dam, Hemp and Fly.

Welsh general standards were back to the top the following year at Drymen on the shores of Loch Lomond where the team shield was regained and Leslie Suter's 7½-years-old Craig, a big rough-coated collie from work with beef cows and Welsh Mountain sheep on the hill farm at Gellifiniog, Cross Keys, Monmouthshire, won the Supreme, though with the lowest pointing—181½ of 225—for many years.

The victory of Wiston Cap at Cardiff in 1965 was the collie's first-ever win in an Open Championship and this was somewhat remarkable for a dog who created so much attention by the quality of his work. But the tall-standing, good-looking dog who was to have such an influence on the breed was still under two years old, and he quickly made up his honours list in subsequent years. The following year he returned to the International scene at Chester to win the Shepherds' Championship whilst it was still run over the big course.

Alert, well-built, fast in thought and deed, Wiston Cap was the ideal Border Collie, and young as he was, he had immense wisdom. He was a son of his master's Cap out of Hetherington's Fly and his line held so much of the qualities of Jim Wilson's great hill-dog Cap from whom he inherited all the best of herding skills and these were brought out to perfection by John Richardson who was a brilliant handler. No other collie had as great an immediate impact on the breed, for he was straight away in demand as a sire. Three of his sons, John Murray's blue-fronted Glen in 1971, John Templeton's 4½-years-old Cap in 1972, and Gwyn Jones' black and white Bill in 1974, and three of his grandsons, Gwyn Jones' white-headed Shep in 1976, Bob Shennan's mottled Mirk in 1978, and Wyn Edwards' Bill in 1981 followed his pattern to win the Supreme Championship—a quite outstanding record.

The 1965 International results were a good example of the success of pedigree breeding, four of the five champion collies being of Whitehope Nap line. Wiston Cap was a great-grandson of Nap, as was one of the Brace Champions pair, Gwilym Jones' 2½-years-old Sweep from Brechfa in South Wales; the Shepherds' Champion, the 3½-years-old blue-coated Sam with Lancashire patrol-shepherd Tom Leedham from the Forest of Bowland, and David Young's tall five-years-old Dusk from Cumnock in Ayrshire, the Driving Champion, were grandsons of Nap. Duck's dam, Thomson McKnight's Gael, a daughter of Nap, ran second to Wiston Cap.

Star to the world at the start of his career, Wiston Cap was to become one of the most famous of working sheepdogs, but my star at Cardiff was a little collie bitch at the close of her career, Gwilym Jones' Nell. Beaten by the clock when on the point of penning the sheep, had she completed her work the eleven-years-old Nell would have beaten Wiston Cap for the Supreme title to add to the Farmers' title and, with her son Sweep, the Brace title already won that weekend. As it was her work in the Supreme test was so good that in spite of failing to pen she finished fourth in order of merit.

Right *Harry Huddleston's Bett, 1969 Supreme Champion from North Lancashire.*

Below *The face of simple courage. Evan Evans' Glen overcame hip surgery in 1978 to add nine open championships within the year to his long list of successes. In August 1980 he won the South Wales Association's open championship at Abergavenny.*

Nell was something special. She had run sixth in the 1962 Supreme at Beaumaris and had represented Wales five times, and in her closing years at Cardiff she came so close to immortality. Gentle and ladylike, her method of stock herding was nevertheless confident and sure, and she had all the power necessary to handle awkward sheep. She had that contented and happy temperament of one who delights in a craft in which she excels—a craft which came from natural wisdom coupled with a lifetime's experience.

Of a line from classical Welsh and Scottish ancestors, from David Stone's Jake and Hughes' Jaff and from Jim Wilson's Glen, Moss, and Mirk, Nell was a bonny bitch with a snow-white chest, narrow white head-blaze, and black coat. Bred in South Wales by J.H. Davies at Llanfynydd, she learned her craft well on Speckled-face ewes over 250 acres of marginal land in the Carmarthenshire hills, and she delighted in showing her prowess at trials. Nell was one of the many good bitches I have known, collies of the ability of Tot Longton's Gyp, reserve Supreme after running the big course twice in 1971; Tim Longton's great-hearted Snip, the 1965 English Champion; Peter Hetherington's consistant Nell, the 1970 Scottish Champion: David Brady's black Meg of television fame; and Thomson McKnight's incomparable Gael, Supreme in 1967—for whilst 'preaching' dogs, I like bitches. Maybe it is a bit of sentiment because I have been fortunate to have two grand bitches, Meg and Gael, which were wise, loving, and kind in all their ways, though 'tis true that I consider the dog Rhaq as the best pal I have ever had.

It is generally accepted in shepherding circles that a dog is more useful by virtue of extra push and power than a bitch, but not everyone would agree and the 'dog versus bitch' issue is one of the many sheepdog topics under discussion.

My colleague on the 'One Man and His Dog' television series, Phil Drabble, and I have discussed the subject often, both publicly in front of the cameras and 'off-stage'. He prefers bitches, and outside sheepdog circles he has far more experience of dogs than I—and there is no more intelligent creature than Tick, Phil's German pointer bitch who has more than once nudged my attention to a grey squirrel hiding at the top of a tall tree.

Considered and far-seeing in all his opinions—even the most provocative!—and probably the best practical naturalist in the country, Phil Drabble's opinion is one I greatly respect, and his German Shepherd Dog Belle and the lurchers have on occasion emphasised to me the reasons for his opinions, but sheepdog-wise the facts are against the female population.

Since World War II in 36 Internationals up to 1981, the 75th anniversary of the International Sheep Dog Society, only four bitches, Herbert Worthington's Juno, Thomson McKnight's Gael, Harry Huddleston's Bett and Tom Watson's Jen, had won the Supreme Championship.

Before the war in the 29 trials held from 1906 the top award went to six bitches,

Left *Thomson McKnight and Gael, 1967 Supreme Champion at Stirling.* **Far left** *Peter Hetherington with Nell, the most regular of Scottish International collies and 1970 National and 1973 International Shepherd's Champion.*

Left *Tim Longton and Ken, 1966 Supreme Champion at Chester.*

Right *Wiston Cap shows controlled temperament and power in the face of a threat of Blackface rams.*

Walter Telfer's twelve-months-old Midge, William Wallace's trim black and white Meg, Jim Wilson's bonnie Fly, John Thorp's tricolour Jess, W. J. Wallace's wise and experienced Jed, and W. B. Telfer's Queen, winner of three English National Championships. Fourteen bitches have won nineteen of England's 53 championships since 1922; eleven have won thirteen of Scotland's National titles; ten have taken ten Welsh Nationals; and seven have scored eight top successes in Ireland's 21 trials since 1961.

All the supreme bitches are readily recalled to mind, either because they were exceptionally good or because there were so few of them. I always recall with pride and the affection of having known them well such bitches as Gael, so efficient, so professional, yet so friendly and so much a part of the McKnight family at Glencartholm in the Borders. She ran in seven successive Internationals for Scotland and won the Supreme title in 1967 to put a fairy-tale finish to a mass of trials championships, yet she was never happier than when herding the Blackfaces in the quietness of the Esk Valley in Dumfriesshire.

Also of Gael's line, Peter Hetherington's Nell, smooth and white, immaculate and precise in her authority over Grey-faced and North Country Cheviot ewes and blue-grey suckler cows on 1,200 upland acres at Balcletchie Farm, Barr, in the Carrick area of Ayrshire, honoured Scotland seven times and won the International Shepherds' title in 1973 at the centenary event, the Scottish National in 1970, and with her son Hemp, the Scottish Brace Championships of 1976 and 1978.

Tot Longton's rough-coated black and white Nell was good-looking and brainy and a marvellous bitch at running brace trials, particularly with Spot to two English Championships. She was followed on the Lee End milk pastures in North Lancashire by Gyp who proved herself to the world in one International alone,

in 1971 when she ran with great honour in all four sections of the event, Supreme, Farmers', Driving, and Brace, and her daughter Jed followed, sometimes wilful and petulant but always reliable as her trials record of 36 Open Championships proved.

Prick-eared and confident in winning honour for Wales and stealing much of the television glamour, Glyn Jones' Bwlch Bracken was not past giving me a timely nip if I trespassed too far on her privacy.

Mel Page's forceful Nell from Brechfa in Carmarthenshire won many trials and Welsh representative honour and championship with strong and decisive work which always kept her in control, yet she always came for a pat of approval at the end of the job.

The brash and assured—and so successful—work in winter weather conditions of Len Greenwood's little tan-coloured Bett from the heights of Ramsden Moor in the East Lancashire Pennines resulted in us having to change the rules of winter nursery trials to give other collies a challenge.

Tim Longton's little Snip never refused a challenge, whether on the storm-tossed heights of Clougha Fell or in the winning of the 1965 English National Championship after twice being beaten into second place. Such was her spirit that in 1965 she shepherded the half-mile Supreme course to complete in 27½ minutes after having to outrun twice following a human mistake at the sheep-pens.

Work aside, I do believe that bitches make better family dogs—I do not say pets, for to have a successful relationship with a dog it must become part of the family. Bitches, and I think this is true of most breeds, become more a part of your family than dogs; they are less independent and more 'with you' on a walk or outing. Border Collies make excellent companions even if you have no sheep to become involved, but be honest and consider their background and nature—as with all breeds of dogs—and judge your ability and responsibility to treat them accordingly and properly. Bored dogs become frustrated, bad-tempered, and they bite. So don't blame the dog without considering your part in its bad manners.

Gwilym Jones and little Nell from Brechfa did Wales proud in 1965. In 1966 it was England's turn when Tim Longton and Ken from the top of Bowland Forest gave Lancashire, a county of proven collies, its first Supreme Championship.

Ken's victory in the prime of life at six years old regained the Supreme title for England after a lapse of eight years, and gave English shepherding prestige a much-needed boost in International competition. His work was not fancy, he was never one for airs and graces, but was of the simple, down-to-earth quality which made it all the more satisfying. It was a stint of good shepherding uncluttered by style so that any blemish was there to see. There was little, for Ken's method of work placed the emphasis on ability and drove the once so important style into obscurity. It is practicalities which count in herding work—or we will be headed for the beauty contests!

His was a natural easy talent—either in the lung-bursting sweep of Rooten Brook's 1,500 feet high sheepruns or in the concentrated test course of the competitive field—which stamped the Border Collie the greatest stock-dog in the world. Handsome, with black and white rough-coated looks, as well as

Below left *Tom Watson and Jen, winners of the 1980 Supreme Championship.* **Below right** *Tot Longton with Lad and Rob, 1969 International Brace Champions.*

productive, he was home-bred of Wilson's Cap hill-line, and he won four English International caps, two International and three English Championships, and such top-class victories as Longshaw, the Royal Lancashire, and the Yorkshire.

In 1967 beneath the grey ramparts of Stirling Castle Ken came very close to repeating his Supreme victory until deemed disqualified when sensibly—and with pure practical shepherding work—controlling a bolting ewe with his mouth.

His crown went to a worthy successor, the collie bitch which I rate the greatest of all time, Thomson McKnight's Gael from Glencartholm. Glencartholm is a place where I have spent so many happy hours, seeing old collies in perfect tune with Blackface sheep, seeing young collies taking their first tentative steps at their craft, watching the roe deer in the woodland, even digging away the snow from the steep track to get out, and always talking 'dogs' in the most hospitable kitchen in Scotland. It is the place from where Thomson and Gael, and her daughter Dot, set out on a misty morning in September 1967 for the road to Stirling. It is the place to which they returned as the toast of Scotland, having won just about everything that was possible at an International. Gael won the Supreme with Dot in second place, Dot won the Farmers' with Gael in third place—behind Tim Longton's Ken—and together they won the Brace Championship.

Gael was one of the few collies to become a legend in her time, and when she died peacefully at home twelve months later at the age of 11½ years she had won almost every honour she could, and more important, had served a beloved master and family faithfully from birth to death. Of her Stirling victory my colleague in agricultural journalism, Matt Mundell wrote 'wonderful old Gael has at last taken her dues—the Supreme accolade of the sheepdog trials world she has for so many years worthily graced'.

For the rest of the sheepdog world Stirling was a frustrating International. I remember sitting in the car in thick mist until lunch time on the first day and how the shepherds' and brace courses had to be reduced in size to national standard for the first time ever—and when the mist lifted to allow the work it was best forgotten apart from the shepherding of Gael and Dot, of Tim Longton's Ken and his son Cap, and of Wyn Edwards' three-years-old prick-eared Jaff from Ruthin.

Gael was home-bred out of her master's Dot sired by the famous Whitehope Nap of whom Thomson thought so much. Gael, like John Richardson's Wiston Cap and Tim Longton's Ken, was of the Wilson's Cap line, indeed she had at least five crosses of his blood, four on her mother's side and one on her sire's side.

Three of the greatest Supreme Champions in three years, Wiston Cap, Ken, and Gael had the one thing in common which marks the champion collie apart from its contemporaries—they had a respect for the sheep they herded. Their stories are told in detail in *Sheepdogs, My faithful friends*.

After some disappointing years in the general standard of work, the shepherding of Welsh Mountain sheep over the vast expanse of flat land beneath the backdrop of Cader Idris on the sea coast at Towyn in 1968 was a great improvement, particularly on the Supreme day when any one of six trials was impressive enough to have won.

All of the twelve dogs in the final gathered successfully at the half-mile pick-up, all but two completed every aspect of the work in warm sunshine. Only 19½ aggregate points from the three judges separated the winner, Llyr Evans' four-years-old Bosworth Coon, and the sixth placed collie, Raymond MacPherson's smooth-coated Tweed, showing the mettle of things to come for his master on his first appearance for England. It was a nostalgic return to his home land for 55-years-old Welshman Llyr Evans who had left the high sheepruns beyond Cardigan Bay thirty years previously to farm Halfbred sheep and beef cows in Leicestershire and Northamptonshire.

He handled Coon, a reliable and adjustable collie of Whitehope Nap breeding, with quiet conviction, gathering well on both hands though missing the fetch-gate with the first ten sheep; the driving was sound, the shedding good, and the penning faultless. It was work to show the quality of Bosworth Coon who won the English National on the Berkshire downlands the following year, went on to win the International Farmers' title, and in his time won over fifty Open Championships.

One of the most experienced handlers in Britain, 53-years-old Harry Huddleston of Arkholm in the Lune Valley of Lancashire, handled one of the most willing of bitches, the clever little 6½-years-old Bett to the Supreme title at Littleton Old Hall near Chester in 1969 in one of the most illustrious collie gatherings in years.

In the final test were six former Supreme Champion handlers and three former Supreme collies—Llyr Evans with Bosworth Coon (1968 champion), winner of the Farmers' Championship; Thomson McKnight (1967) with Jaff, a son of Brocken Robbie; John Richardson with Wiston Cap (1965), so brilliant in his qualifying work; Herbert Worthington with Juno, the top bitch in 1963; Alan Jones (1961) with Lad, tricolour grandson of Brocken Robbie; and Meirion Jones (1959) with the red-coated Craig, twice the winner of the Fylde Championship in Lancashire.

Bett beat them all with the kind of sensible balanced work on Welsh Mountain ewes which had earned her merit registration by the International Sheep Dog Society. She listened to instructions and heeded them in her gathering over tricky terrain, her driving was paced with tight turns at the gates, her shedding in a 6-2-1-1-3-2 sequence well taken, and the pen was good. It earned 406½ of 450 points, eight better than Bosworth Coon on reserve marking. From work with the 'Grassgarth' pedigree Friesian milkers and Dalebred ewes at Arkholme, Bett was a bitch who always gave of her best and on that day at Chester she led the English team to its best International for thirteen years.

England's success at Chester was a 'flash in the pan'. For the next five years English prestige rested on the ability of seven collies to earn single success at each of the Internationals.

In 1970 at rain-lashed Kilmartin it was Michael Perrings' clever Kyle taking the Shepherds' Championship to the Yorkshire Dales; in 1971, Tot Longton's strong working Gyp from Quernmore near Lancaster won the Driving title; Eric Elliott's Bill, English Champion in 1973, from Ashopton retained the Driving honour at Newcastle in 1972; at the centenary event at Bala in 1973 Jim

Cropper's grand shepherding brothers Fleet and Clyde from the East Lancashire Pennines won the Brace Championship; and in 1974, again at Kilmartin, another sound pair of hill collies, George Hutton's Nip and Shona from the Lakeland Fells above Threlkeld held on to the Brace honour. Scotland took England's crown in 1970—and stuck to it with three Supreme wins in succession.

It was the era of the Wiston Cap heritage, although the big dog's son, the black-coated Sweep had already won the 1968 Driving Championship for John Richardson. In 1970 it was Cap's half-brother, David McTeir's black, white and tan Wiston Bill from a Blackface herding in Manor Glen near Peebles, who took the top accolade. Wiston Cap and Wiston Bill were both out of Walter Hetherington's smooth-coated Fly. Cap's son, the big black, white and tan Mirk, a collie who enjoyed the finer points of trial's shepherding, won the qualifying trials.

In 1971 over the close-cropped grass in Trelai Park at Cardiff where sheep were good and manageable in ideal conditions of clear sun-drenched air the first of Wiston Cap's sons, the four-years-old mottled Glen with 66-years-old shepherd John Murray from Sanquhar, emulated his sire's Supreme success. It was a poor International though Glen took his chance of honours with a nineteen points lead over Tot Longton's Gyp in a championship in which two other sons of Wiston - Cap, Chris Todd's white and black six-years-old Pip from Cumbria and John Richardson's Mirk were third and sixth, and the top six were all of Whitehope Nap line.

Other than these six there was little to enthuse over. Only three of the nine collies completed their work in the Shepherds' class; only the winning run to John Campbell's Cap and Nell, with their sprig of lucky white heather from Ross-shire, was worthy of note in the brace contest; and ten of the forty dogs in the qualifying class failed to complete their work.

Trophy-wise, with the Supreme, Farmers', Shepherds', and Brace going north of the Border it was Scotland's most successful International since Gael's International at Stirling in 1967—and it came from the same bloodline. Murray's Glen, a tall black and white merled dog, did not go to his job all that well. Running to the left, he needed instructions to gather the first pack of sheep, and John struggled a bit to get him back for the second ten sheep. But that was the end of his problems and after turning the twenty sheep away on the drive Glen only lost eleven of 150 aggregate points on the rest of his trial, completed under the quiet and calm instructions of one of the most experienced of shepherds on a total of 370 of 450 scored. Glen was home-bred out of John's multi-coloured Katy whose line was to Robert Swan's Jim, the grandsire of the 1967 Supreme Gael.

Chapter 8

100 years on

I see the results of a century of trials shepherding and conclude that Britain's sheep flock is in the safe and capable care of a collie breed which, in intelligence and stamina, is equal to the responsibility.
The years 1972 to 1981.

The Wiston Cap influence continued to the 1972 International at Town Moor, an expanse of rough grassland to the north of the city of Newcastle, where Blackface sheep needed bossing and were strong enough to discern weakness in a dog.

Fourteen per cent of the collies taking part were sired by Wiston Cap, his 4½-year-old rough-coated son Cap with John Templeton at Fenwick, near Kilmarnock, won the Supreme, and his 3½-years-old white-headed son Ben, Scottish National Champion that year with David McTeir at Milton in the Manor Valley near Peebles, won the Shepherds' honour in a section which was the best for many years. John's Cap also joined his workmate Fleet to win the Brace title.

With these three championships and the team shield Scotland were the top country again; England were sound; Wales with nothing to show for their efforts and only one dog—Ivor Hadfield's prick-eared Lad from Prestatyn—through to the Supreme test were as bad as the previous year and in the sheepdog doldrums; and Ireland made sheepdog history when Jim Brady's four-years-old Jim, son of the 1968 Supreme Champion Bosworth Coon, earned their first-ever International Championship, the Farmers'.

Only three of the twelve collies in the final test completed their work, two failing altogether to find their second packet of sheep, and outrunning in general was as bad as the previous year at Cardiff. Trials were again proving their usefulness of purpose and value by bringing out and showing up the faults in some strains of working dogs. Inefficient gathering—the very basic craft of the working dog—was not common to all bloodlines but was serious enough for the sensible breeder to stop and think, to indulge in a bit of self-criticism.

Lighting the general gloom at Newcastle with practical rather than classical work as the sheep and course demanded were collies which used their brains, were capable of initiative when necessary, and had the stamina of hard-working ancestry.

My notes of the weekend were of but a handful though enough to dispel total despondency. John Templeton's Cap and Fleet were just that bit better on contact with the sheep to win the Brace honours than Tot Longton's Gyp and Lad, but there was little wrong with any of the four collies. Jim Brady's Jim had only minor points loss in fetching and driving to be fractionally better than Jim Cropper's Fleet to win the qualifying test. Sire of Brady's Jim, Llyr Evans' Bosworth Coon was virtually faultless in outrun and lift in both qualifying and Supreme.

There was little wrong with the top two shepherds' collies and David McTeir's Ben took the championship in the shedding-ring over Gordon Rogerson's black and white rough-coated Nell from the Chatton Moors of Northumberland. Other collies I noted sound were Harry Huddleston's smooth-coated Sim, the English Champion; David Shennan's Maid; Adrian Bancroft's Anne, slipping on her fetch; Raymond MacPherson's World Champion Nap; and Martin O'Neill's Nell, the first-ever collie from the Republic of Ireland to win a place in the Supreme test. I recall that at least ten of these dogs were Nappers.

Scotland's third successive Supreme Champion Cap had the wisdom, initiative

Pedigree of JEN (93965) 1980 Supreme Champion with Tom Watson

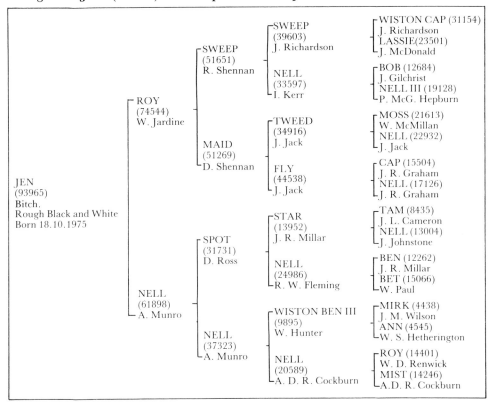

The numbers in brackets are the Stud Book numbers of the International Sheep Dog Society.

and temperament which came from daily work with Ayrshire milk-cows as well as Blackface ewes, and he had the benefit of partnership with a calm unflappable handler in John Templeton. He brightened a dull Saturday afternoon in Newcastle when without a falter he found his first lift of sheep on the ridge of Town Moor, and the light really brimmed when, with a little practical whistled guidance, he raced back to get the second batch of sheep. Driving to the right, he was in full command all the way round to the shedding-ring, reached in fifteen minutes from the start of his first outrun. Coolness from both dog and man finally solved the shedding task with the final sheep going away after twelve minutes and eleven aggregate points had raced by, and a clean pen gave the winning tally of 389 of 450 aggregate points.

It was a popular win, for John Templeton had always graced the trials field with gentlemanly conduct, respect for dog and sheep, and pride in his craft. The following year he took Cap and Fleet to the American World Championship where Cap was placed fifth and Fleet second. Sadly Fleet died in a motel fire during the trip, and Cap stayed in America with Fred Bahnson for work on the plains of North Carolina.

John Templeton earned his trials successes—and they have continued since 1972—by dint of hard work and a knowledge of bloodlines which he put to good use to breed a whole family of successful dogs.

'I started at twelve years old with Moss, a granddaughter of Wilson's Cap, and ten years later I won my first international cap with her son Roy,' John recalls. Indeed Roy, a big smooth-coated dog, won the Scottish National and went on to

five representative honours and 150 Open awards. He was sired by John Purdie's Roy whose line was from Jim Wilson's 1930 Supreme Champion Craig. Once in, John stayed in the Scottish team for eleven successive years and in the first five years Roy was placed first, second, and twice third in the National events. In 1958 Roy partnered his younger brother Hope to win the Scottish Brace Championship. In the next six years Roy II and Maid, son and daughter of Roy, Nap and Fleet, sons of Maid, won Scottish Brace, Scottish Farmers', and Hyde Park honours for John.

In 1972 Cap gave warning that it was to be his season by winning the first four trials of the Open calender; he completed it with the Supreme and Scottish Farmers' titles and, with Fleet, the Scottish and International Brace honours.

In 1979 John was reserve Supreme with Moss, a great-grandson of Wiston Cap; in 1980 he was third with Max, an Irish import by Tim Flood's Scott; and in 1981 he handled Roy, son of Moss, to third placing. John Templeton has won the highest honours; he has also served the trials' cause as secretary of the Sorn Sheep Dog Trials Association since 1963. This was his 'home event' when he lived at Blackbriggs near Mauchline in Ayrshire and was the first trial in which he competed.

Nine times John and his dogs were placed second at Sorn and though they had gone out and won National and International honours it appeared that the honour of winning their local event was to elude them. When they did win—in 1978 for the first time—they did it in style, winning outright the Open trophy with three successive victories.

Above left *We're a great team. Dart reminds 'the boss' Alan Foster of Cartmel Fell in the Lake District after winning the 1979 English driving championship. They went on to win the 1980 English National and International Shepherd's honours.* **Above right** *1980 International Shepherd's champions, Alan Foster and Dart.* **Right** *Jen rests amidst her trophies after winning the Supreme Championship of 1980 for Tom Watson. Eric Halsall records the success. Tim Longton holds the Farmer's cup he won with Tweed.*

When the International went to Bala in North Wales in 1973 to mark the 100th anniversary of the first sheepdog trials ever held, it was happily a great occasion in every way. Shepherding was good with most of the collies up to standard and the five championships went to capable dogs and were shared by all the four countries.

Over a sun-drenched course, faulted only because of its lack of full size on the banks of the River Dee in the centre of the Welsh mountains, two of the greatest hill-dogs in Britain, brothers Fleet and Clyde from a 1,000 bleak acres in the Lancashire Pennines won the Brace title for Jim Cropper and England; one of the finest bitches of her time, Peter Hetherington's slim little Nell from the Ayrshire uplands, gave Scotland the Shepherds' honour; Alan Jones' eight-years-old Lad, winner of 27 Open trials in two years, took the Farmers' Championship to the Lleyn Peninsula of North Wales; and Irish collie, Jim Brady's big rough-coated Bosworth Jim, winner of the previous year's Farmers' title, added to his own and his country's growing prestige by earning the Driving honour.

And on the final day when strong Welsh Mountain ewes disputed authority in the heat of the sun, we saw the emergence of a truly great collie, Glyn Jones' Gel, to win the Supreme Championship at the age of three years. Typical of the best of his breed in herding intelligence, stamina, and temperament, and wearing the bonniest black and white looks, Gel, from Bwlch Isaf in the Clwydian Mountains, had earned his first International cap the previous year when the youngest dog at Newcastle.

He was to go on to another three Internationals, come within one aggregate point of repeating his Supreme victory at York in 1975, and become one of the best-known collies in Britain through immaculate television appearances. There has been no greater collie dog than Gel—of line to Wilson's Cap. At Bala he was young and adding to his wisdom with every outing, but with a master teacher like Glyn Jones at the helm he was confident and assured and he met the great occasion without a flicker of doubt among such illustrious company. He took the big occasion in his stride to win the greatest honour in the sheepdog world by a convincing 29 points with 3½ minutes of work-time to spare.

Pedigree of BILL (78263) 1981 Supreme Champion with Wyn Edwards

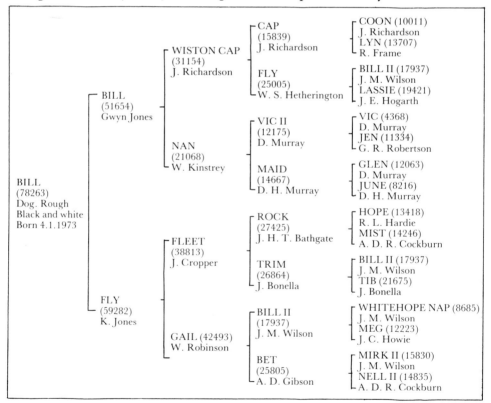

The numbers in brackets are the Stud Book numbers of the International Sheep Dog Society.

Jim Cropper's Clyde from the high Pennines came closest to the Welsh dog. A younger 5½-years-old brother of his master's Fleet, whose doings were legend in the North Country, Clyde was by John Bathgate's Rock out of John Bonella's Trim, a mating of proven results.

The other champions at Bala—Alan Jones' Lad was of similar line to the Welsh farmer's famous Supreme winner Roy; Peter Hetherington raised Nell from a pup on the foundation skills of Supreme Champion Gael; and Jim Brady's Jim inherited the brains of his sire, Supreme Champion Bosworth Coon—so good and wise breeding again proved its value in the 100th year of sheepdog trials.

This trend continued into the 'second century' and the practical dogs won the honours with the International Sheep Dog Society getting perhaps more venturesome in the choice of its courses. These, the rush and bog of storm-lashed Kilmartin in 1974, the adventurous layout of Lockerbie in 1976, the 'blind valleys' of Libanus in the Brecons, the ruggedness of Chatsworth in 1978, brought out the courage and stamina as well as the wisdom of the collie dog, the qualities which are so necessary for the day to day herding of farmstock.

Pedigree of MIRK (67512) 1978 Supreme Champion with Robert Shennan

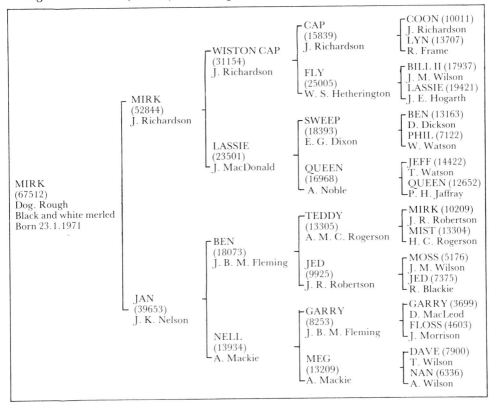

The numbers in brackets are the Stud Book numbers of the International Sheep Dog Society.

Left *Wyn Edwards from the Vale of Clwyd asks Bill, the 1981 Supreme Champion, to look for his sheep.*

Right *Surrounded by his trophy haul, Bill, the 1981 Supreme Champion with Wyn Edwards from North Wales.*

Below *The grandstand and setting of the 1980 International at Bala.*

Gwyn Jones' Bill, a cool and balanced collie from work with Welsh ewes in the mountains of Snowdonia became the third son of Wiston Cap to emulate his sire's Supreme success at Kilmartin, mastering not only the problems of the terrain but also the distractions of a rainstorm. He won the Driving Championship as well, and his son, John Wilson's prick-eared Scott from a Blackface and Cheviot herding at Ashkirk in Selkirkshire won the Shepherds' title.

Another great hill collie of supreme heart and stamina, George Hutton's smooth-coated Nip from the Lakeland Fells ran reserve Supreme to Bill and led the English team to their only overall success in thirteen years. Partnered by his fell-mate Shona, Nip shared the 1974 and 1975 International Brace titles. Both collies were of McKnight's Gael breeding.

The Wiston Cap saga, which is of the realms of fiction in pedigree breeding, continued with three of his grandsons winning the Supreme.

In 1976 at a 'working dogs' International' over a successfully different course at Lockerbie, Gwyn Jones won his second Supreme shield in three years with Shep, the white-headed son of Harry Thomas' Shep and Tamsin from Cornwall.

In 1978 it was Bob Shennan's mottled Mirk from Ayrshire, the 7½-years-old son of John Richardson's Mirk and John Nelson's Jan, who was successful at Chatsworth in the Peak of Derbyshire.

In 1981 over the most testing course of them all at Armathwaite in the Eden Valley in Cumbria, Wyn Edwards' handsome Bill from Ruthin, the son of Gwyn Jones' 1974 champion Bill, was the winner.

Contrasting the roughness of hill slopes were the courses laid down over the flat lands of the Knavesmire racecourse at York in 1975 and of the Castle Kennedy flats near Stranraer in south-west Scotland in 1979. Flat land of this nature has its own peculiar shepherding difficulties, particularly in the gathering of the sheep, invisible at half a mile at collie-eye level, and it is exceptionally difficult terrain on which to judge distances and lines of driving, so that both dog and handler have to balance skill and judgement with sheep pace. It calls for perfect understanding and reaction to control from man and dog.

Raymond MacPherson's white-headed Zac won both York and Stranraer to become only the seventh collie in history to win more than one Supreme. An adaptable dog, Zac was so competent and capable that he could switch his skills from his home environment on the rough moorland of the Tindale Fells to the strange surroundings of unaccustomed flatness.

Similarly adaptable on whatever course he was put to the test, Alan Jones' Craig, a strong, wilful, yet skilful partner to the Welsh farmer, also proved the value of the right parentage in his successive driving victories in 1975 and 1976, his Farmers' Championships in 1977 and 1979 at Libanus and Stranraer, and his

Pedigree of TWEED (96630) 1981 English National and 1980 International Farmers' Champion with Tim Longton

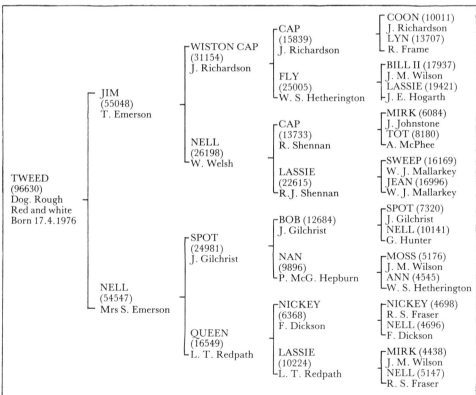

The numbers in brackets are the Stud Book numbers of the International Sheep Dog Society.

Of that elite band of collies which have won the world's greatest sheepdog honour more than once. Raymond MacPherson's Zac after his second victory at Stranraer in 1979. The white-headed collie from Cumbria won his first Supreme Championship at York in 1975.

Brace victory at Bala in 1980 with Spot on his right hand. Craig was bred in Caernarvonshire out of Owen's Nell sired by his master's Moss.

Craig's greatest rival on the International fields of 1976 and 1977 was his namesake John R. Thomas' black and white Craig from work with 1,500 Speckled-face ewes over high grassland in the Mynydd Epynt of South Wales. On North Country Cheviots of Lockerbie in 1976 Thomas' Craig was third in the Supreme with Jones' Craig fourth on equal points; at Libanus the following year Thomas' Craig won the Supreme with Jones' Craig reserve, reversing their order in the qualifying tests of the previous days when Thomas' Craig won the Shepherds' honour and Jones' Craig the Farmers' title.

Over seven years old when he won the top honour, Thomas' Craig had virtually graded himself to championship status over the previous four years. In 1973 at Bala he ran fourth in the Shepherds' Championship, beaten by Hetherington's Nell, Richardson's Mirk, and Fraser's Phil, a redoubtable trio. In 1975 at York—the last time the Shepherds' Championship was run over the double-gather course—Craig had faltered badly on his outrunning though he still finished second to John Richardson's Mirk. In 1976 at Lockerbie he had no difficulty over the short course for the Shepherds' Championship but still found problems on his second gather on the Supreme course. In 1977 he had got it right and went to the top on the last run of the three days. Craig was a practical, strong working collie who learned from experience and he took the big championship test

The successful Scottish team at the Bala International 1980. National President Andrew Beattie holds the shield.

over ground littered with natural obstacles, and often working alone out of sight of his master, as an everyday stint of shepherding, sound, steady, and unflurried, to complete two years' competitive work with three International and three Welsh titles.

Trained by John Thomas since the age of nine months, Craig was a son of Welsh International collie Suter's Chip, out of Hawken's Jill, and his line went back to Greenslade's Glen and Chapman's Garry.

The International Society has never had a better set course in Wales than the one at Libanus with the back-cloth of the Brecons. It was naturally testing with much left to the dogs' own intelligence and ability to work things out unaided— and I watched the work from the platform of a television camera high above the grandstand as this was the first Supreme contest to be fully televised.

Ireland won their first-ever International Brace Championship at Libanus with John McSwiggan from Gortin Glen in Tyrone handling his home-bred brother and sister Chip and Jess, of Whitehope Corrie line, to a nine points victory over their closest rivals John Griffiths' smooth-coated Sam and black and white Nell, also home-bred at Talysarn in Caernarvonshire. It was at Libanus also that Tom Watson, a most capable and popular Scottish shepherd, won the Driving Championship with his home-bred Mirk, the handsome black and white collie which won the 1976 Scottish Shepherds' title, Tom's second such championship.

But the return of the International to Bala in 1980 saw the culmination of all

Above left *A successful National President—England's champion in 1981, Tim Longton from North Lancashire, with the Duchess of Devonshire, a staunch admirer of working collies, who presented the prizes at the Bolton Abbey National event. Tweed lays on the ground after winning the championship, in company with Clun Roy who also earned his International 'cap'.* **Above right** *John R. Thomas and Craig, 1977 Supreme Champion at Libanus.*

Tom's hopes and dreams—the winning of the Supreme Championship after forty years of competitive shepherding. With Jen, a trim, self-assured, black and white bitch taking her trial with a boldness and touch of perfection which was always sound and easy, Tom gave Scotland its 21st Supreme in the 52 years since 1922 when Wales had joined the International fray. England held fifteen Supremes and Wales sixteen. Jen, five years old and of placid temperament, was only the fourth bitch in forty years to win the title.

Tom, 67 years old and a master of the art of shepherding sheep and dogs, was competing at his fourteenth International and he was the most popular winner for many years. It was an emotional occasion and Tom said to Jock Murray who had won the title in 1971 at the age of 66, 'We both left it a bit late but we made it.'

Tom Watson was in charge of one of the finest Blackface flocks in the Borders, 500 top quality ewes running over some 1,000 acres of the Lammermuir Hills from Longcroft and it was essential to his management that he had reliable collies. He had been a shepherd since he was sixteen years old and from an early age had learned the value of good dogs as helpmates and companions. A good stockman, he started to breed a family of dogs which were to serve him faithfully down the years.

Bob Shennan's Mirk starts his driving stint on his way to winning the 1978 Supreme Championship at Chatsworth.

Starting with proven bloodlines, his first collies were half-sister and half-brother, the prick-eared Nell and the mottled Nickey, both mothered by Alex Watson's Bess whose heritage was Dickson's Hemp, Wallace's Loos, and Sandy Millar's Spot, the 1925 Supreme and four times Scottish Champion. Nell was sired by Wilson's Cap, and Nickey's father was William Watson's Kep, son of the 1928 International Shepherds' Champion Brown's Spot II and grandson of Brown's Spot, the 1923 Supreme and founder of the American Stud Book.

'Nell and Nickey taught me a lot,' said Tom Watson, and it was Nell who gave him his first big competitive honour when she won the Scottish Shepherds' title at Musselburgh in 1948. She was bonny and wise, black with a white chest, and the cocked ears of alert understanding. Experience on the Border sheepruns blended with inherent intelligence and the year after her National win, at seven years of age, she won the International Shepherds' Championship, and repeated the win the following year at Ruthin.

But it was on the hill where Tom valued his dogs most, for without them he could not have earned a living, and though he was frequently in Scotland's International team it was not until 28 years later in 1978 at Chatsworth that Tom won his third International Shepherds' honour—with Jen of the lovely temperament. Two years later the clever little collie fulfilled the ambition which Tom had striven so hard and so patiently to attain—the Supreme. Thus she joined an outstanding company of dogs which had partnered Tom throughout his working years. There was Nell and the rough-coated Nickey in the beginning; followed by Nell's daughter Phil, sired by Wilson's Supreme Champion Glen;

Above *Complete authority over sheep is a combination of inbred intelligence, practical experience and the indefinable quality of method—Glyn Jones' Gel, the 1973 Supreme Champion.* **Below** *Bill Smith, chairman of the North Berkshire Society, who assisted me with the course-directing of the 1980 English National at Tackley.*

Phil's son Tam, sired by Wilson's Moss; and in later years there was Craig of the same proven line of ability.

It was at the 1980 International that England came out of the competitive wilderness, for apart from the lone success of Raymond MacPherson's Zac in 1979 English collies had not won an International Championship of any ranking since 1975. Ireland with their limited resources had done better.

Tim Longton's red-coated Tweed and Alan Foster's big black and white Dart, two first class dogs from hill-herdings in the North Country won the Farmers' and Shepherds' titles to restore some balance to the records. The five-years-old rough-coated Dart whose craft came from the herding of 400 Dalesbred ewes and sixty suckler-cows and calves on 300 acres of Cartmel Fell above Lake Windermere also ran second to Tom Watson's Jen in the major test. A moment of doubt on his second gather and a few points dropped in the shedding-ring cost him the title.

A confident and skilful collie, Dart was in great form in 1980. Over the flat lands by the River Dee on the Bala International course he herded the Welsh Mountain ewes to reserve Supreme, top qualifying, and Shepherds' honours;

Pedigree of CRAIG (59425) 1977 Supreme Champion with John R. Thomas

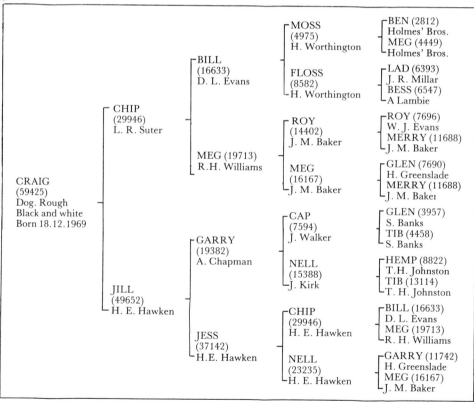

The numbers in brackets are the Stud Book numbers of the International Sheep Dog Society.

Bill, good-looking, strong and forceful, and winner of the 1981 Supreme Championship.

over the rolling Oxfordshire grassland at Tackley in the English National event he shepherded strong crossbred sheep to the National and Shepherds' Championships; and in open trials in the North of England he earned fifteen awards.

Capped for the first time the previous year when he was third in the National and also won England's Driving Championship, Dart was home-bred and trained from puppyhood on the Lakeland fells. He got his initial trials experience on the Pennine nursery fields with eleven awards in the 1976–77 winter season, and his major victories in addition to his International honours were at Kentmere, Lorton, Cockermouth, and Walna Scar in the Lake District, at Park Hall in Lancashire, and at Malham in Yorkshire.

Dart was one of the many successful sons of Fred Coward's Ken, the sire of dual Supreme Champion MacPherson's Zac. In 1979 Ken had four sons and a daughter in the English International team. They were Foster's Dart, MacPherson's Zac, Alan Leak's three-years-old Roy from Gaisgill, Athol Clark's rough-coated Rob from Middleton-in-Lunesdale, and Thomas Longton's four-years-old Lassie from Quernmore.

Zac, Roy, and Rob were brothers, out of John Hadwin's Quen. Quen and her sister Queen were two remarkable bitches with John Hadwin at School House Farm, Backbarrow, near Ulverston in North Lancashire which mothered pups of the highest intelligence, and their progeny were eagerly sought throughout the North Country. Both were daughters of Supreme Champion Bosworth Coon and reserve Supreme Champion Tot Longton's Gyp, Quen born in February 1969 and Queen in February 1970.

Fred Coward's Ken was bred by John Hadwin out of Moss, sired by Tot Longton's Rob, winner of forty Open Championships. Ken won fourteen open trials and numerous other awards but will best be remembered as a sire of champions. He had natural ability, power, and stamina, so necessary for his work on the fells by the celebrated Kirkstone Pass in Lakeland.

England's other success at Bala in 1980, Tim Longton's four-years-old red and white Tweed was a forthright shepherding dog with a determined and steady approach to his craft and the most illustrious of pedigrees. He was bred in Weardale by Mrs S. Emerson out of Nell, the daughter of Scottish Champion Gilchrist's Spot, and his sire was Tom Emerson's prick-eared Jim, a son of Wiston Cap. Tweed was a born hill-dog with an inherent strength and wisdom to Jim Wilson's great hill-dog Cap, and he matured from daily work with Dalesbreds on the bleak, storm-swept runs of Clougha Fell at the head of the Trough of Bowland.

His experience widened from early trials baptism, his temperament was nurtured by the expert teaching of one of Lancashire's leading handlers to bring International recognition at the early age of two years. At his first National trials in 1978 he partnered his fell-mate Bess, the little Lancashire Champion the same year, to the English Brace title. In 1980 Tweed was second to Alan Foster's Dart in the National at Tackley where he won his master's sixth Farmers' Championship and he went on to win the International Farmers' championship a month later. In 1981 Tweed gave Tim his fifth National Championship over the flat lands by the River Wharfe at Bolton Abbey near Skipton, leading an entry of 235 collies to lead England to the International at Armathwaite in the Eden Valley.

There, in September1981, Britain's working collies ran a gruelling test over a Cumbrian fellside to prove without doubt their wisdom and stamina, and general high quality. They came through the most testing work for years with flying colours to show the error of their thinking to those who would deny the trials-proven collie its superior place on Britain's sheepruns.

From England, Wales, Scotland and Ireland, the cream of collie craft faced the double-gather test of the International Sheep Dog Society on twenty sound Swaledale ewes—grey dots in the bracken at half a mile—with courage and intelligence; and their precise and careful approach to every aspect of practical farm work, and under competitive pressure, marked them classically expert—and silenced their critics.

When shepherding on the fellside could be carried out with the clever and ordered skills of the 8½-years-old Bill in complete understanding with Wyn Edwards from Ruthin in North Wales to win the highest pointing for four years for the Supreme Championship; when a young prick-eared dog, Bwlch Taff, the two-years-old champion of Wales with Glyn Jones, could run an even better second gather than the winner; when the handsome black and white Cap under Yorkshireman Norman Darrell could stick to his job with such authority to finally dominate a testy ewe to clinch the Brace Championship, Britain's sheep flock was in safe and capable hands.

Above *Scotland's John Templeton and Fleet in the American World Championship at Maryland, Delaware in May, 1973.* **Below** *Stalwarts in the Welsh international cause, Alan Jones and Craig from Pontllyfni on the Lleyn Peninsula.*

It was undoubtedly Wales' International for in addition to the Supreme, Wyn Edwards and Bill had the Farmers' Championship; Jim Dyson and his 8½ years-old son of Wiston Cap, the tricolour Glen from a herding above the Vale of Llangollen took the Shepherds' honour; and the fifteen Welshmen and their dogs won the team shield. No praise could be too high for Wyn Edwards and Bill, winners of the Supreme. They partnered each other to perfection, Wyn guiding and marshalling, and Bill answering and using his inbred skills at the distance. Only on the return gather for the second packet of sheep could Wyn have had any 'butterflies', but the dog proved capable.

With Welsh ewes and beef cows on a mixed holding near Ruthin in the heart of the Vale of Clwyd, Bill was a good-looking, medium sized, all-round dog who enjoyed his work, and he was the son of Gwyn Jones' Bill, Supreme Champion of 1974, thus adding to the Wiston Cap saga as the third grandson of the 1965 Supreme Champion to emulate his success.

Strong and forceful—and always upstanding—Bill got a lot of his determination from his dam's line. Out of Mrs M. K. Jones' Fly at Lampeter in Cardigan, his maternal ancestry was to Jim Cropper's great Pennine hill-dog Fleet, and through Jim Wilson's Bill II to Whitehope Nap.

Competitively the Welsh Bill had an enviable record. He had four Welsh caps,

Three of the greatest shepherd contestants in the world at the 1973 Bala International. John Richardson with Mirk, second in the contest; Peter Hetherington with Nell, international champions; Bob Fraser with Mindrum Phil, third in the trials.

had been Welsh Farmers' Champion in 1977, and Welsh Brace Champion with workmate Jaff in 1979 and 1981, was the current year's National Driving Champion and held a host of North Wales local championships. Bill's Supreme win came late on the Saturday afternoon, and later the previous evening he had gone to the top of the qualifying list to win the Farmers' trophy by a narrow four aggregate points over Alasdair Mundell's handsome 7½-years-old Cap from hill work in Argyllshire who has stood top from the previous day.

Bill and his workmate at Cefn Coch Farm, the prick-eared tricolour Jaff, were three aggregate points behind Norman Darrell's Cap and Pat from Pickering in North Yorkshire in the brace contest. Welsh team victory came from a united effort with Bill at the top of the qualifying list; Jim Dyson's Glen third: the young Bwlch Taff and Glyn Jones fourth; E. A. Hopkins' Lyn, a seven-years-old daughter of Griffith's Craig, tenth; and Lyn Lewis' black and white Mirk from Penycae in South Wales, eleventh.

English reputation was upheld by Norman Darrell's four-years-old Cap and five-years-old Pat from the Vale of Pickering winning the Brace title; and the driving victory to John Thomas, shepherding in the Cotswolds, with his home-bred Cap, six-years-old son of his 1977 Supreme Champion Craig. Good in partnership and winners of the year's English brace title, the two Yorkshire collies stuck to a far from easy task to take their first international honour. Regularly in the awards in the north-east, Cap was a grandson of Wiston Cap, and Pat, daughter of John Bathgate's Drift out of Alistair McPhee's Jill, was champion of the North Country's nursery fields in 1978–79.

Scotland—with two Supreme Champions in the previous three years—had to go North empty-handed for the first time in 22 years. Though they had five dogs through to the last day they were best served by Alasdair Mundell's good-natured Cap, a great hill-dog with Blackfaces in the Cowal Hills and a most unlucky collie in competition, who was reserve Farmers' Champion, and by John Templeton's young Roy, the two-years-old son of his master's Moss, from Fenwick Moor in Ayrshire who ran third in the Supreme contest.

Adding to the success of the 1981 International was the first contest for young handlers, one chosen from each country, and won by seventeen-years-old Gordon Watt with Irish International collie Chum from Omagh in County Tyrone. Wales were represented in this innovation by Ceri Jones from Bodfari with the four-years-old Gel II, England had John Harrison from Shap with Meg, and Scotland's chosen was eighteen-years-old Alan Campbell and Ben from Lochgoilhead. Reserve Supreme to Edwards' Bill was a young dog which reflected the progressive planning of a man who farmed over 1,500 ewes on 3,800 acres and needed the continuing cooperation of skilful dogs to manage them.

Cap at three years old was the latest of Raymond MacPherson's dogs to prove his qualities on the International field, following such great collies as World, British, and Television Champions Nap, Tweed, and Zac from Tarn House, Hallbankgate, near Brampton. Cap's success in earning representative honours at his first attempt in 1981 gave his master his seventh successive appearance in the English International team and his thirteenth in fourteen years. And before crossing the Border to farm in England, Raymond had represented Scotland three times. So essential to the sheepfarmer is the progressive age-grouping of his dogs, almost on the lines of crop rotation, that he always has young dogs under training and gaining experience to take over the shepherding duties when the current workers get too old for the hard work.

So it was at Tarn House where ten dogs formed the management team and where such youngsters as Cap were waiting to oust the likes of Tweed and Zac on the fell and equally keen to emulate their peers on the competitive field.

Cap, born in Pitlochry in June 1978, had grown into a big, strapping hill-dog. He was black and white with a touch of tan and his stamina and brain power came from an ancestry which included Scottish Champions Jim Millar's Ken, John Richardson's Mirk, and John Gilchrist's Spot, Irish Champion Lyn McKee's Whitehope Corrie, and Supreme Champion Wiston Cap in four generations.

The 1981 International at Armathwaite was one of the best trials ever staged to test the prowess of the modern working collie and so in its 75th anniversary year the International Sheep Dog Society had surely got its planning right, fulfilling its avowed intent to improve the management of stock by improving the efficiency of the herding dog.

Chapter 9

National dilemma

I discuss the popularity of sheepdog trials which led to an embarrassment of national organisation, though I find that collie quality and resilience will overcome the shortcomings of human organisation.

The International in 1981 was the right kind of test, but in all honesty this could not be said of the ISDS' National trials. Since 1979 when the number of entries extended England's event at Penrith to four days, the directors of the Society spent countless hours of verbal controversy in an effort to form a plan to meet what in effect was a reflection of the popularity of trials. Excessive entries had become almost an embarrassment and the Directorate failed to cope. Four days in England's case was decided upon after the farce of trying to adequately test 178 single dogs and twelve brace pairs in three days at Welbeck in 1978 and English directors sought an answer but Scotland, Wales and Ireland were at that time not affected—and quite honestly—not concerned.

When I, and others, suggested what appeared to be the obvious solution of letting each country run its own National as conditions necessitated I was accused of splitting-up the International 'atmosphere'—a sort of sheepdog 'apartheid'. Two years later when Wales and Scotland met the same problems of growing entries that very suggestion was mooted officially! Foolishly—in my opinion— Wales were prevented from experimenting with a scheme to grade collies to their National in 1981 on the argument that what was decided for one National must apply to four.

English entries rose from the highest three-day figure of 195 plus thirteen brace at Chatsworth in 1976 to 235 and nine brace in the four-days programme at Bolton Abbey five years later, and still dogs were having to be retired to get through the event when they fell below standard.

This fault was of course due to dogs of insufficient merit being entered by people who—quite soundly—argued that as members of the Society they were entitled to enter their dog whatever its standard of efficiency. Welsh progress ranged from coping with an entry of 150 singles and eight brace in 1976 at Talsarnau; to struggling with trials running late into the evening on an entry of 172 and nine brace in 1980 at Tywyn; to extending the 199 and nine brace entry of 1981 at Llandeilo over four days. Scotland realised they could not get through their 1981 entry of 179 singles and eight brace at Glamis and added another half-day to the programme. Ireland with their limited entries could of course manage, although they wisely extended their one-day event to 1½ days in 1977 and to two days in 1978 to make for a more relaxed, and thus more efficient, programme.

Theoretically the Nationals are the top trials events in each of the four countries where to win a title or to earn a merit place in the International team is a prestigious result. 'On paper' they should be the meeting place of the top collies in the land. They are, but up to the February 1982 meeting of the ISDS directorate when a qualification system was decided upon for National entry, they were cluttered with a great number of very mediocre collies and even with some collies which were not fit to compete in nursery trials so that instead of a short, sharp clash of the top skills which leaves the blood tingling with excitement they had become long drawn-out events where even the 'fanatics' became a trifle bored and the Border Collie was so often seen at its worst. Many open trials, those of the calibre of Longshaw in Derbyshire, Sorn in Ayrshire, and Ceiriog Valley in Clwyd, were better. There was rarely any fault with the local committee which ran the Nationals, it was the 'system' which was wrong.

For the spectator who did not pretend to know the finer points and whose only interest was to watch clever dogs at work the Nationals of recent years had become a pure bore. Worse, they had become exasperating, almost a mystery in procedure, and contrived to kill interest—and this after so much had been done to interest and educate the man in the street in the role of the working collie in the farming pattern. Of particular concern to me was the bad reputation which the Border Collie was getting from farmers who visited the Nationals, the local farmers who use a dog for their stock herding but who are not interested in competing at trials and who by virtue of the National trials being held in their locality go along for an hour or so to see the 'best collies in the country.'

They have indeed always seen the best but hidden among so many mediocre dogs that, not understanding the system that any dog whose owner had paid his 'subs' could run at the National, they went away thinking that the mediocre was the height of collie ability.

When they discussed what they had seen in the village pub at night they came to the conclusion that the dog they had tied up in their own yard was equally as good and I could readily understand why.

Under a system of unlimited entries the dogs which win can fall into two very distinct categories. They can be the great dogs they are meant to be to earn an international cap by overcoming the stress and strain of the event, or they are lucky dogs, dogs who 'cash in' on the extended amount of good fortune—luck— that must be around. Happily it is ability rather than good fortune which earns the major awards.

The cause of the poor National image was no mystery. It was simply that there were too many entries under rules which permitted any member of the society to

Right *Mutual affection, mutual understanding in their craft—Harold Loates and Wiston Jill from the Trent Vale of Nottingham win England's National Championship in 1979. Two years later they won the famous Longshaw Championship.*

enter any registered dog irrespective of its work ability. Our predecessors in officialdom were much wiser in limiting their trials to proven dogs and this was realised in 1982 with the directors of the ISDS taking perhaps the most important rules decision in the Society's history. Aware for some time that only dogs of proven quality should really be allowed to compete at the National trials, the directors had—so it seemed—been discussing the method of grading them for years and years without finding a solution acceptable to all.

The 'kettle came to the boil' with the excessive 1981 entries and it was obvious that action was needed quickly, and before the collie breed became discredited.

So—at Carlisle on 6th February 1982—it was decided that in order to limit the National trials to three days duration of around 120 to 150 entries the accepted collies would have to prove their working quality beforehand. The qualification for National entry would be based on a dog's success at open trials, and the success or otherwise of the plan would be reviewed in the light of experience.

It was a wise decision, in effect grading-up still further to the honour of international representation and supreme victory.

Basically a system which chooses the International team on merit from the National event cannot be wrong for any other method of selection could lead to an accusation of favouritism and even worse!

For someone in authority to sit down and select a team, as applies to most other sports, would lead to the constant and regular appearance of certain handlers—and for a limited period the same dogs—for a good handler with a

Below *Two of England's best known collies, Tot Longton's Bute and Mossie, 1954 National Brace Champions. Bute ran Reserve Supreme in 1956 and Mossie twice won England's National title.* **Below right** *William Cormack's June, 1973 Scottish National Champion from remote Caithness.*

mediocre dog will invariably give a better show than a poor handler with the best dog in the world.

This method of selection would produce the strongest team but it would kill the enthusiasm and spirit of the hundreds of sheepdog trials now held. The 'new' National method gives each man and dog a thorough and equal chance to show their ability and stake their claim to International recognition and it still allows the 'outsiders' to win through to the International In 1979 at the English National at Penrith 10 newcomers won representation into the 15-strong International team, giving a great boost to the enthusiasm of all who had been trying for years to make the team. Having criticised the Nationals of the late 70s so strongly—self-criticism because I have been a director of the society since 1964—the National championship is still the greatest honour that each country can award and it has been won by some very great collies.

Stuart Davidson's smooth-coated Ben from Sandbank near Dunoon won the 1980 Scottish National at Thornhill with an outstanding score of 215 of 220 points, an average loss of only 2½ points per judge. In 1936 Jim Wilson's little Nell scored 99 out of 100 points to win the Scottish National at Helensburgh, and two years earlier the faultless trial was adjudged when Sandy Millar's smooth black and white Ken from Newmilns won Scotland's Championship at Pitlochry with maximum points.

Today with each of the two judges having 110 points from which to mark, every minor blemish can be more readily reflected than in the 1930s and Stuart Davidson's work with Ben in 1980 was as fine a piece of competitive shepherding as we are likely to see.

Over the Drumlanrig Castle course Ben was assertive, steady and sensible in his management of North Country Cheviot ewes and, never a laggard in his work, he had his test completed in ten of the fifteen allotted minutes. Decisive

action was a feature of Ben's character and a month later at the International at Bala he completed the half-hour Supreme test in seventeen minutes, listed eighth in the contest.

Very much a 'one man dog', he was devoted to his master in their management of 1,000 ewes and 150 beef cows on the hills by Loch Fyne in Argyll, and his daily skills and his competitive craft were applauded by viewers to the sixth series of 'One Man and His Dog'. Almost six years old when he won the Scottish National in 1980, Ben was a medium sized bare-skinned dog who could move like the wind yet hold his temperament to a controlled stalk, and his decisive shedding of sheep was his stamp of authority. He had the brains to match problems and the boldness to take the initiative.

Bred in the Highlands at Muir of Ord by Donald MacKenzie out of his Mist, a black and white daughter of Scottish Champion Gilchrist's Spot, his paternal line was from McKnight's Jaff, a son of Barbara Carpenter's Brocken Robbie.

Though Sandy Millar and Jim Wilson tended to dominate the earlier Scottish Nationals they were followed by men and dogs of equal calibre, David Murray whose Sweep, Toss, Vic, Glen, and Number won two Nationals, five Brace, and six Driving Championships, Jim Millar, son of Sandy, who won four National Championships with Drift, Ben, Tam, and Ken, and Willie Hislop of Gordon with his two Sweeps and Jim.

I had the benefit of Willie's experience and knowledge of the trials scene when, together with Bill Jones for Wales, we course-directed at the Internationals. In sunlit splendour as at York in 1975, or more often it seemed huddled in sparse shelter from downpour as at Kilmartin and Stranraer I have listened to his tales of the days 'when dogs were dogs'.

Willie, who farmed at Coltcrooks, Gordon in Berwickshire, won the 1946 International Farmers' and the 1948 Scottish National and Driving and International Driving Championships with his first Sweep, a black and white son of his own Glen and Kirk's Nell, the mother of champions. Sweep won 187 trials awards in seven years, the first three years of which were limited war years, and he sired Griff Pugh's Don, the 1951 Welsh National Champion, and George Redpath's Moss, the 1956 Supreme Champion.

In 1959 Willie again won the Scottish National and Driving titles with the second Sweep, of line to Jim Wilson's Cap, Mirk, and Moss. In 1961 he won his third Scottish National Championship with Jim, a grandson of his first Sweep.

Scotland has undoubtedly run some of the best Nationals and one of the very best was at Kilmartin in 1966 when two of the best dogs that the country has ever known showed working skills of the very highest order. 'Superb' was the only description which could be used for the work of John Gilchrist's white-headed Spot in repeating his previous year's win by earning 197 of 200 points, and John Richardson's Wiston Cap was only two points behind in second place. Steady on his sheep and always in control Spot, whose fame as a breeding sire became known around the world, was only at blemish in his shedding. Cap, whose fame after his previous year's Supreme win became even greater, was just a little off-line in his driving.

20-years-old Maurice Collin with Kep and Cap from Skeeby in North Yorkshire, winners of the 1951 International Brace championship.

Both shepherds, John Gilchrist at Roslin and John Richardson at Lyne near Peebles, led a Scottish team that year which included seven shepherds, and they set the example at the International at Chester. There, the following month, their personal rivalry continued with the prick-eared Cap scoring a mere half-point more than Spot for the Shepherds' Championship, though Spot had the satisfaction of leading the qualifying tests and running second to Longton's Ken in the Supreme. Cap, in great form as ever, had one sheep determined to tease him throughout his qualifying run and failed to pen and lost his chance of Supreme contest. Both Cap and Spot who improved the Border Collie breed so markedly were never better than in that year of 1966.

So successful on other trials courses throughout his life, John Richardson's Wiston Cap never did win the Scottish National Championship. His son Mirk, the trials specialist, did so in 1975. He was a big rough-coated black, white and tan dog born in April 1968 and mothered by Jackie McDonald's Lassie, of Wilson's Cap and Wallace's Loos line.

Shepherds have always played an important part of Scotland's international trials history just as they have in the country's agricultural economy. Scottish Blackface sheep are known throughout the world for their top quality lamb meat and their speciality wool, the finest for the famous Harris Tweed, and they are Britain's most numerous breed. Similarly the Cheviot sheep is one of the best

Above left *A superb champion, Stuart Davidson's Ben, 1980 Scottish National Champion and television champion at Bala.* **Above** *John Campbell's Cap from Strath Carron.* **Left** *John Campbell's Nell from Strath Carron.*

dual purpose breeds in Britain, known for quality mutton and wool for the weaving of Scottish Tweed, and it has justifiable claim to an important role in Scottish agricultural prosperity. Both Blackface and Cheviot live on the high windswept lands, generally the Blackface to the heather moors and the white-faced Cheviot on the rough grass moors. Their care and management and their contribution to the country's wealth is in the hands of conscientious men and clever dogs. Down the years Scotland, particularly the Border hills where lives the bulk of the sheep population, has of necessity produced good shepherds and good dogs.

When those Blackface sheep looked up from their grazing and saw the likes of John Richardson's Mirk, Willie Rae's Connie, David McTeir's Ben or Peter Hetherington's Nell coming to muster them, they did not argue. They accepted the ways of the collie and meekly did as commanded.

Willie Rae's Connie from a 1,400 feet high herding at Lockenkit, Corsock, won the 1977 National at Doune in Perthshire and had the conviction of Wiston Cap blood on both sides of her pedigree.

David McTeir's white-headed Ben, a son of Wiston Cap, took the 1972 National trophy, and a month later the International Shepherds' award, to his kennel at Milton by Manor Water near Peebles.

Peter Hetherington's forceful Nell, a great-granddaughter of Wiston Cap, from Barr near Girvan enjoyed her victory run at Haddington in 1970 for the top award.

Grey-faced at 7½ years old and a cool worker on Halfbred ewes on the lowlands of Windyedge by the busy Perth to Stirling road, Donald MacDonald's Glen proved his ability to officialdom and merit-registration by the quality of his trials work which gave him the 1974 Scottish Championship in a memorable National of classical shepherding on the riverside course at Earlston in Berwickshire.

One of the most popular of Scottish wins was that of a trim little prick-eared bitch called June who took the National Championship to Caithness in the far north for the first time ever in August 1973. Had the weather been good at home at Wester Dunnet she might never have competed, for her master William Cormack was more concerned with the hay-making. The rains came and she got her chance.

Small but great-hearted, with the blood of the great Loos in her veins, June took that chance over the long gather of Blackfaces on Camperdown Park by Dundee. Unabashed by the tense atmosphere at the biggest gathering of collies

Pedigree of BEN (88284) 1980 Scottish National Champion with Stuart Davidson

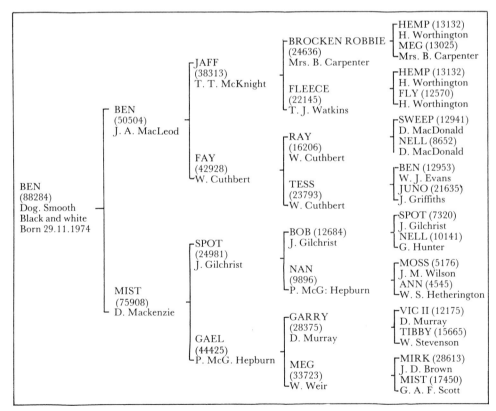

The numbers in brackets are the Stud Book numbers of the International Sheep Dog Society.

Competitors at the English National trials at Rydal in the Lake District 1973.

she had ever joined she settled to the job she did best, the authoritative shepherding of sheep.

Strikingly garbed, white-faced, black and white with a dash of tan, June at four years old had learned her craft the hard way, mastering the 45 cows as well as the 230 North Country Cheviots on the home farm by the Pentland Firth, and she showed a calm yet assertive temperament to have her way. The National was only her fourth competitive trial that season yet she never put a pad seriously wrong. Always she gave the impression that nothing was too much to ask of her, that she would have a go at any problem which could arise.

A month later at Bala in the International she demonstrated lion-hearted enthusiasm when asked by Willie to take an almost impossible chance to single a sheep. She did so in the most practical and positive way, but had to use her mouth to take the sheep. She was disqualified. It was one of the finest pieces of decisive shepherding I—and others—had ever seen, to be applauded rather than disqualified, but rules are rules—to be changed if they lead to faint-hearted interpretation! Collies with June's determination are the type needed in the Highland country—indeed in any country. There you need collies with power to move sheep in the worst of weather conditions, collies with initiative to get among the rocks and stone dykes, with stamina to face the tough heather slopes, and with reliable good health to stand the rigours and extremes of hard country. June was

Thomas Longton of Quernmore wins the English Brace Championship at his first attempt, at Penrith in 1979, and is congratulated by Ray Ollerenshaw, chairman of the International Sheep Dog Society.

of that breed as were John Campbell's dogs which won four Scottish Brace titles in five years from 1970 to 1974 and the International honours of 1971 and 1976.

When you consider that by the very nature of the country and the comparatively small populace trials are far from numerous in the Highland area, the competitive success of these dogs is all the more outstanding. They brought practical skills to Scotland's—and Britain's—leading trials and proved such basics to be right.

John Campbell was used to handling a team of dogs in his management of Blackface sheep and hill cows on the 2,000 windswept hill acres at Gruinards in Strath Carron in Easter Ross so that brace trials were second nature for him. He made the every day hill task into a delightful trials exercise of cooperation and partnership with his collies. Eleven years after he won the young farmers' award at the 1959 Dalmore trials near Evanton on the Cromarty Firth he made the long trip to Haddington in East Lothian for his first National and won his first major honour with the five-years-old tricolour Cap and the older black and white Nell, as 'faithful a bitch as man ever partnered'.

Since 1970 the name of John Campbell has become well-known and highly respected on the International fields, for he went on to win Scotland's Brace titles in 1971, 1973, and 1974 with Cap, a son of Scottish Champion Gilchrist's Spot; Nell, from Wilson's Tweed and Mirk; and Moss and Meg, son and daughter of Cap. Moss and Meg were both home-bred out of John's Jed, a daughter of Wiston Cap. In 1971 Cap and Nell took the International Brace Championship to the far North for the first time ever, and their successors—and kin—at Gruinards,

John Campbell with Cap and Nell, 1971 International and Scottish Brace Champions.

their son Jim and Cap's son Moss repeated the success at Lockerbie in 1976.

Proving the maxim that a good handler can get the best out of every dog, David Shennan, from Knockgerran Farm near Girvan in the Carrick district of Ayrshire, won two Scottish Nationals in three years in 1976 and 1978.

Meg, the smart little bitch which became known to millions of people when she won the first series of 'One Man and His Dog', won the title in 1976. In the forceful and businesslike manner which appealed so much to her fans, she won the National in a run-off decider with Tom Watson's Mirk, mastering North Country Cheviots over the course at Golspie. The previous time that Scotland needed a run-off to decide their championship was in 1946 when Jim Wilson's Glen beat Willie Hislop's Sweep at Stirling.

Trim, prick-eared, and always determined to give of her best, Shennan's Meg was of the most immaculate breeding with McKnight's Gael and Gilchrist's Spot in her make-up as well as Wiston Cap. She passed her qualities to her granddaughter Nan who worked so well under David's guidance to win the top Scottish honour in 1978.

David Shennan's successes in the National and International sphere, and those of his brother Robert who won the Scottish title the following year with Mirk, are of the many instances of handling ability enjoyed by certain individuals and by certain families. They have the knack of getting the very best out of any dog which partners them.

There is no better example of family success than that of the Longton family in North Lancashire. Timothy Longton senior won the English National at

Morecambe in 1949 with the black and white Dot, the three-years-old daughter of Huddleston's Cap, to start the family's success.

Thomas, or Tot to all his friends and thus known throughout the sheepdog world, won the 1950 and 1956 English Nationals with Mossie, home-bred and a descendant of Sandy Millar's champion Ben. He has won three National and two International Driving Championships; one International and nine National Brace Championships; and in 1976 he won the Television Brace honour with Jed and Kerry.

Tot farms in partnership with his son Thomas at Lee End in the village of Quernmore, three miles from Lancaster, where milk production from the pedigree 'Marydale' herd of British Friesians is the main project together with fat lamb production from Dalesbred ewes. In 1980 Thomas followed his father to the winning of the Television Brace honour with Lassie, daughter of Jed, and Bess, daughter of Kerry. At Penrith in 1979 Lassie and Bess won the National Brace title at their first attempt.

Tot's younger brother Tim who farms above the Quernmore valley won the Supreme International Championship in 1966 with Ken; in 1964 Ken won the International Farmers' title; and in 1980 Tim again won the Farmers' honour with the red-coated Tweed. At national level Tim has won five National, seven Farmers', one Shepherds', and four Brace titles. Brother Will from Thwaite Gate Farm at Carnforth won the 1957 English Shepherds' Championship with the tricolour Roy, and another brother, Jack from Low Bank House, Barbon, has represented England on the international field and earned such top Open. Championships as Moorcock, Allandale, Alston, Penrith, Quernmore, Otterburn, and Hornby.

Also related to the Longtons, the Huddleston family from the same area of North Lancashire have written their name into sheepdog history. Harry from Snab Green Farm, Arkholme, won the 1969 Supreme with Bett. Harry from Caton won the 1972 English National with Udale Sim, a hill-type collie whose breeding lines with the same farming family went back to the turn of the century. A nice, easy, happy dog who was always keen to work, Sim represented Britain in New Zealand at the Rotorua Championships.

England's Championships have so often gone to the hill-dogs of the North Country such as Tim Longton's Tweed, Alan Foster's Dart from Lakeland, Ken Brehmer's Ben from the Northumberland moors, and Miss Jean Hardisty's 4½-years-old Flash from the Cumbria–Yorkshire border in recent years.

In 1977 at Swinhoe by the Northumbrian coast Jean made history by becoming the first-ever lady in the four international countries to win a National Championship. Also the first woman ever to be included in an English team, Jean handled Flash, the great-granddaughter of her father's 1961 English Champion Jim, with the calmness and competence that befitted such an historical victory.

One collie bitch which disputed the supremacy of her more northerly

Left Gordon Rogerson and Spot from Northumberland, reserve Supreme Champions in 1978, winners of the county's Trials League, and 'One Man and His Dog' contestants.

contemporaries at Penrith in 1979 was Wiston Jill who partnered Harold Loates in the shepherding of Mule ewes on 500 mixed acres of Poplar Farm at South Leverton in the Trent Vale of Nottingham. Quietly confident in her manner and a good-looking bitch with the wisdom of good breeding, Jill showed that her work on Swaledales to win the first four-day National was not just a flash in the pan when two years later she won the world-famous Longshaw Championship trials in Derbyshire.

Six years old at Penrith, Jill had three Supreme Champions in three generations of her blood, Wiston Cap, Bosworth Coon, and Longton's Ken. Bred in Scotland from Hetherington's Meg, a daughter of Coon, she was sired by Clarence Storey's Roy, the son of Wiston Cap and the grandson of Tot Longton's wise old Rob.

And another bitch from 'down country' and also of Wiston Cap heritage, Gerald Hawkins' home-bred tricolour Trim from Halse near Brackley in Northamptonshire added her blow to northern prestige when she ran second to Jill and won the Shepherds' trophy.

Points do not often finish equal at the top of a big National entry, but this happened in two consecutive years at England's events of 1972 and 1973. Then the ruling is that the collie with the better outfield work gets the decision. In 1972 over ridged and furrowed land in the heart of the famous Pytchley Hunt country on the Northamptonshire–Leicestershire border, it was Harry Huddleston's black-coated Udale Sim who got the decision over Ray Ollerenshaw's Ken, a five-years-old son of Tim Longton's Supreme Champion Ken, from the Derbyshire Peak. In 1973 over flat valley land by the Rothay river between Rydal Water and Lake Windermere two collies from the Derbyshire sheepruns tied on equal 194 out of 200 points and the decision went to Eric Elliott's eight-years-old Bill over Cyril Bostock's 3½-years-old Mick who won the Driving honours held by Bill the previous year.

Bill, the previous year's Yorkshire Champion, was strong and experienced in

hill work. From Crookhill Farm at Ashopton, his duties were with one of the few remaining White-faced Woodland flocks over 2,000 acres above the Ladybower Reservoir in north Derbyshire.

The 1973 English National will be remembered for the closeness of its overall pointings. Only 7½ aggregate points divided the twelve collies in the chosen International team; a mere half-point gave Tim Longton his first Brace title with Cap and Roy over Jim Cropper's Fleet and Clyde; the Shepherds' honour went by three points to Adrian Bancroft's clever 6½-years-old Anne from the upper Ribble Valley in Yorkshire.

Anne was a bonnie bitch and she had brains to match. She was the kind of collie which instilled confidence; you knew she would give of her best whenever she went to sheep, and moreover she was a glad companion for Adrian on the heights of his Pen-y-Ghent sheepruns.

England has never been really strong in its shepherds representation; the most successful have been Mark Hayton's son Arthur from Otley in Wharfedale who won six successive championships, Bob Fraser of Northumberland, also with six titles, and Fred Morgan from the Vale of Evesham who won seven.

Arthur Hayton's black and tan Jock and Pattie, a tricolour daughter of his father's Supreme Champion Glen, monopolised the Shepherds' class between 1934 and 1939 and won two International Shepherds' Championships in 1934 and 1937. Pattie starred with her son Pal Glen in the making of the film *Song of the Plough* in the early 1930s.

Bob Fraser won his six National titles with six different dogs, all of his famous Mindrum breeding which is known throughout the world; and Fred Morgan only missed taking the championship twice in the nine years from 1961 to 1969, winning four times with Moss, a tricolour son of George Redpath's 1956 Supreme Champion of the same name.

Bob Fraser was always a champion of working sheepdogs. He bred them right, he trained them right, he respected them. In return they won him the highest of trials honours and served him with reliability and friendship throughout the whole of his working life as a shepherd in Northumberland. To those of us who know and respect one of the greatest of all 'sheepdog men' it is not surprising that Bob was the founder secretary of the Northumberland Sheepdog Trials League, a system of trials within the county which is actually a model for a national qualification system.

Northumberland gave the country 'One Man and His Dog'; television gave Northumberland its sheepdog league, for it was after seeing the programme in 1976 that John Metcalf, an agricultural merchant at Alnwick, was so impressed that he approached Bob Fraser with the league idea to stimulate interest. Simply, each Northumbrian dog which wins a place in the county's twenty trials earns points and the collie with the most points at season's end is the winner. So successful was the open league that there is now a winter nursery league.

Not only did Bob Fraser take up the pen on behalf of his beloved sheepdogs but he emphasised the quality of his lifetime's work by winning top place in the first year of the league with Mindrum Phil, his television bitch, winning at Eglingham, Lowick and Whitley Chapel.

In 1978 another dog seen by the millions of viewers of 'One Man and His Dog', Gordon Rogerson's little prick-eared Spot, won the league. So vital to the herding of 1,000 Blackface ewes over 1,800 acres of high ground on the Chatton Moors, Spot was a good strong, adaptable dog who inherited the brains and stamina of his mother, Nell, the clever black and white bitch which won the 1972 English Shepherds' Championship and represented England three times.

Over the International course at Newcastle in 1972 Nell ran second to David McTeir's Ben, Spot's grandsire, and with the class and power of his Scottish ancestry Spot came within thirteen aggregate points of winning the Supreme at Chatsworth, second to Bob Shennan's Mirk.

North-eastern collies are blessed with good trials management and among the best of courses are those set by the Northern Sheep Dog Association in Durham and North Yorkshire. Stalwart of these events, seven of which are held every summer with nurseries in winter, has been Maurice Collin who returned to trials competition after a lapse of fifteen years with a full-marks win at Thirsk 1975 with Spot, a collie he also handled into the International team.

In 1951 when he was only twenty years old, Maurice handled his Cap and Kep, a pair of collies with power, pace and intelligence, to the International Brace Championship at Blackpool, beating such renowned men and dogs as David Murray with the legendary Vic and Number and John Evans and Coon and Nell. It was a year when brace running was at its best and Cap and Kep lost only an average of 6½ points from each of the three judges. From Skeeby by Richmond in the entrance to Swaledale, Maurice was one of really few Yorkshiremen to earn International honours, though a single honour is held by one of the county's farming families. Allan Heaton, who farms at Catterick and at Brandsby by the Howardian Hills, won the Longshaw Championship in 1976 and his son Mark won this major English Championship in 1979.

Allan, England's International president since 1981, won with Ken who has

One of the greatest of all 'sheepdog men'. Bob Fraser, in retirement at Wooler, relaxes with his television finalist Phil.

represented England and won over ten Open Championships. A strong, leggy bare-skinned dog, Ken was another successful son of Griffiths' Craig and his maternal line went back to Raymond MacPherson's Nap, the 1971 English National Champion and the 1973 world title winner in America.

Mark, at 24 years of age the youngest winner of Longshaw, handled Cap, a black and white rough-coated son of Jack Tully's Glen, the 1977 English Shepherds' Champion and a collie of Fraser blood. Longshaw is perhaps the best known and most prestigious of the hundreds of local trials held in Britain. Supported by the Ducal families of Rutland and Devonshire since first held in 1898, Longshaw takes place in early September amid the wild and lovely moorland countryside of North Derbyshire and attracts crowds of spectators from the industrial areas of Sheffield and Manchester. To win Longshaw is a great triumph and only the best come through the elimination process to the championship.

International Sheep Dog Society chairman, and former chairman of the Longshaw Society, Ray Ollerenshaw who farms sheep and beef cows on some twenty square miles of the High Peak of Derbyshire won the Longshaw Championship in 1977 with Tweed.

In that year 143 collies from England and Wales contested Longshaw and the long-legged Tweed ran fifth in the qualifying trials, two points behind the leader George Hutton's black-coated Nip from Threlkeld in Cumbria. He was drawn last to run in the final and was set the task of beating Bill Little's four-years-old Lassie from Goosnargh in Lancashire who had scored 144 of 160 points. The Halfbred ewes were strong and Tweed, with nine years' experience on his home herding, liked to test his mettle on such unwilling sheep, so he faced them in a manner which immediately mastered their stubbornness. He moved them with purpose, they surrendered to his confidence, and the Championship was his by three hard-earned but decisive points.

One of a team of ten dogs which managed some 5,000 sheep from Old House at Derwent on the 2,000 feet high Howden Moors above the valley of the Ladybower Reservoir, Tweed was a rough-coated black and white dog who had been bred on Salisbury Plain out of Coward's Bess sired by Christ Winterton's International Spot. He represented England in the home International and in 1978 was one of Britain's representatives in the New Zealand Championships. Mist, torrential rain, and windstorm, conditions which a collie meets in its daily life of shepherding the hills, have affected trials in summer but rarely does snowfall limit activities in the open season as at the Fylde Sheepdog Society's event in April 1981.

Not that the course itself over the flat lands of Goosnargh near Preston was affected, but a sudden and fierce fall of snow on the high country from Wales to Scotland meant that collies were at the more important task of rescuing sheep from under the snow. Throughout the country they did a marvellous job of rescue, and sheep deaths, which in my area reached five per cent with lamb losses as high as 33 per cent, would have been much higher but for their scenting powers which marked the buried sheep and effected their rescue. Normally a mini-national with collies from England and Wales and often from Scotland and the first major contest of the year, the unseasonal weather cut the normal entry of over 100 to 39.

Scotland's International team chosen at the 1980 National at Thornhill.

I have a particular interest in the Fylde Society. I judged their first nursery trials in November 1965 and their first open and novice trials the following April. Both trials were held on flat land at Wyndyke Farm, Marton, in sight of Blackpool's famous tower.

Bill Miller's little smooth-coated Jed from Brock near Garstang who became the season's champion led 21 youngsters in the nursery trials; Herbert Hargreaves' black and white Meg of Harden near Bingley won the novice trials; and Tot Longton's clever four-years-old Rob from Quernmore won the Open Championship, his sixth of forty such championships in his lifetime. Since 1966 Tot Longton has won the championship with Jed in 1972 and with Jess in 1977; Meirion Jones' red-coated Craig and John Squires' blue-coated Mirk have each won the championship twice; and Scotland's sole winner was Thomson McKnight's tricolour Jaff from Canonbie in 1970.

Tot Longton, Tim Longton with Clun Roy in 1980, Bob Singleton with Meg in 1981, Bill Little with Tweed in 1978, and Vincent Fox with Roy in 1976 have kept the championship in the home area against strong outside competition. Wherever I go in the country sheepmen take a pride in their local trials and listed at the back of the book are the trials I know personally or those which I have been told of by friends and officials. I make no attempt to rate them—it is much more fun to find out for oneself either as competitor or spectator.

I do like the enthusiasm which fires so many men and women to stage nothing but the best. I like the good-natured and challenging comments of Ted Hope of Godmersham near Canterbury on the so-called Northern supremacy. 'The sheep up north are usually better to work than those in our area of Kent. I would like to see some of the northern collies on our Romney Marsh sheep,' he says.

Ted applauds the interest and growing ability of his contemporaries in Kent but deplores their lack of courage to enter the National. He started the Hundred of Hoo Society to cater for the interests round the Thames and Medway area in north Kent in 1951 and was also responsible for the formation of the Thanet Society in 1959, and both have been responsible for an improvement in local collies and the quality of shepherding in the area.

There are three societies, the Thanet, the Romney Marsh, and the Sussex which together form the South Eastern Sheep Dog Societies and publish a joint itinerary of twenty trials.

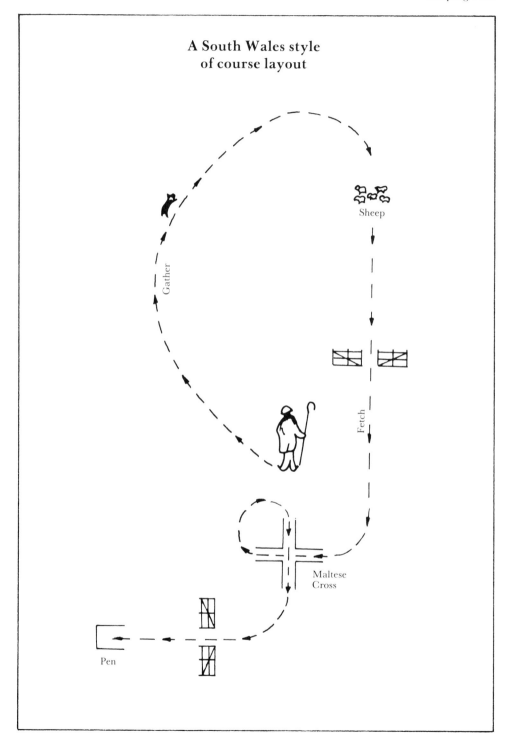

**A South Wales style
of course layout**

Sheep

Gather

Fetch

Maltese
Cross

Pen

Chapter 10

No frontiers for excellence

Gael and I linger in the tranquillity of the mountains from whence came the best of Welsh collies and my thoughts wander—from the hard-earned and established prestige of the collies of north and south Wales to the growing competitive calibre of the dogs of Ireland and the Isle of Man.

Gael, my little collie, pricked her ears to the unfamiliar Welsh commands. She lay by my side in the golden bracken on the mountainside high above the Vale of Clwyd and up above the trials course of Bwlch Isaf. It was interesting to see her reactions to the unknown words, her puzzled look as she angled her head, ears pricked as she questioned each shout. The whistles she could follow, the words were too strange but no doubt her fertile brain would soon have mastered them. Whatever else, a collie is an intelligent creature and so understanding and adaptable that it can change masters and instructions within days.

The Welsh commands came clearly through the thin frosty air to my lofty seat, and though I had no more understanding of the words than Gael, I could see every response of dog and subsequently sheep as on a plan-board below me. Ever since I sat in the comparative luxury of First Division press-boxes to report football matches during my sporting journalistic days, I have maintained that to look down on the action rather than to see it sideways-on from the 'touchline' is the best way to correctly assess it. Would that this were possible at sheepdog trials when every angle of movement, every distance of a flanking turn, every deviation of sheep would be so clearly seen. Only at trials in hill country, from the top row of the grandstand at the International, or through the lense of a high-positioned television camera is this usually possible.

Binoculars as visual aids are a big help over such as the International course, though when used by judges they have sometimes led to controversy. Handlers have argued that the judge should not be able to see more than they; judges have argued that they are judging the dog's initiative and action when it is out of unaided eye-sight and working alone as at the lift on the half-mile International course. Course-directors have often been thankful that they had binoculars to hand. On more than one occasion has frantic word come down the telephone link from the shepherds at the sheep release pens reporting 'ungentlemanly' conduct by a collie on meeting its sheep!

However, at Bwlch Isaf I took the rare opportunity to look down on the course

Above *Harford Logan and Jim, representing Ireland in 1978, approach the pen at the Chatsworth International.* **Above right** *The forceful dominance of Glyn Jones' Gel II puts sheep in the pen at Riddlesden.*

which in early November was only of nursery size though 'different' and interesting across the deep-cut stream below the farm buildings. Even the top sheepdog handlers have to start at the beginning with a young dog, and nursery trials held on Saturday afternoons throughout the winter are now common to the major sheepruns of Britain.

It was a glorious afternoon at Bwlch Isaf. Sunbeams gladdened Gael's sable coat as she lay at my side, small cloud shadows raced each other across the higher mountain, a kestrel hung in the clean air, head down, yellow-rimmed eyes watching the unfamiliar happenings over the ground below. The beauty of autumn brushed the trees with reds, yellows, and browns in intriguing patterns.

'Come Gael,' I interrupted her Welsh lesson. With her following at my heel I walked down to the trials field. Nursery trials are particularly friendly affairs. With new dogs having their first run away from home even the National and International Champion handlers can have their egos deflated to much leg-pulling and ribbing. Not that sheepdog men get swelled-headed—except for a few!—for there is nothing like three truculent sheep and a collie wanting a 'rest-day' to cut one down to size. At nursery trials with a very raw dog just starting the chances of the unexpected occurring are even greater.

The dogs never get 'big-headed', a little temperamental sometimes perhaps, but their nature is too placid and friendly to resist the advances of even the merest beginner. Doing the menial work for the beginners at Bwlch Isaf on that Saturday afternoon were the famous. International Champions and television 'stars' Gel and Bracken, as hosts on their home ground, were 'fagging' for the youngsters by

fetching and taking away the sheep for the trials—never too high and mighty to twitch a tail for a friend.

At the end of that afternoon the form-book had run true. Selwyn Jones and Alan Jones, two household names in Welsh 'sheep-doggery', finished first and third from 39 entries. They were divided by Llew Roberts from Bala and his prick-eared Spot, the eighteen-months-old grandson of Wiston Cap. Selwyn won with a well-grown bitch called Meg, an eleven-months-old granddaughter of Scottish Champion Gilchrist's Spot which he had trained since puppyhood; and Alan's success was with Nell, a shy little eighteen-months-old granddaughter of Wiston Cap and mothered by Dick Nicholl's Jill.

Alan Jones is a 'crowd-puller'—whenever he goes to the post the crowd gathers to watch, for by manner and repute he is one of the best handlers there has ever been, winning championships for Wales since he first stepped on to a trials field at the age of sixteen in 1945. Selwyn Jones also has honoured his country since he first took a dog to the post at Trawsfynydd when he was fifteen years old. Shepherding the Migneint Mountain at Bron Erw, Ffestiniog with 1,000 Welsh ewes and 130 Welsh Black cows is his business and the test of his dogs which have won National singles and brace honours, and such top championships as Vivod, Glyn Ceiriog, and Longshaw. Selwyn has judged the International trials four times.

A land of legend and romance, of high mist-enshrouded summits and scarred industrial valleys, of rich productive farmland and bleak buzzard-flown crags, of lively white-faced sheep and hardy jet-black cows, Wales has seen romance on the trials field. No writer of fiction would dare to tell of the winning of two successive National Championships by a collie barely clear of puppyhood as did Bwlch Taff for Glyn Jones in 1980 and 1981. And Taff was the son of Glen, the collie which was tragically killed on the Clwydian Mountains after training before four million viewers on television.

A few seconds on the stop-watch robbed Gwilym Jones' little Nell from Brechfa of the Supreme Championship in 1965; and time in favour gave John Thomas' Craig from the Brecon Beacons the honour in 1977. Alan Jones' big tricolour Roy from the Lleyn Peninsular took the National, Farmers', and Driving honours from Dolgellau in 1961 and went on to glorious success in the Supreme at Ayr.

A spontaneous burst of Welsh voices marked in song the victory of 26-years-old Meirion Jones and Ben at Cardiff in 1959 to delight his father who had won the Supreme title in 1935; Wyn Edwards' handsome Bill from the Vale of Clwyd won the top placing at Armathwaite in 1981 to the great joy of Wyn's ailing father who received the news by telephone as they travelled home.

Wales can be very proud of its sheepdogs and their masters. Much of their doings I have already recorded and we have discussed how Eurwyn Daniel from above the mining valleys of South Wales emulated the success of his father David William to win Supreme honours with Ken at Blackpool; of how Herbert Worthington's Juno from Abergavenny became the first Welsh bitch to win the Supreme in 1963; of how Gwyn Jones from Snowdonia won two Supremes in three years with Bill and Shep. Add to the roll of honour in recent years such Welsh Champions as Norman Davies from Snowdonia with the rough-coated Cymro, a grandson of Alan Jones' Roy; Captain Grant Jones' 4½-years-old black and white Tos, a son of Griffiths' Craig; and Dick Nichols from high ground at Llananno in the heart of Radnorshire whose black, tan and white Moss, a grand hill-dog with plenty of initiative from Mrs Carpenter's Brocken Robbie, won the 1972 National Championship and fifty first prizes.

Welsh prestige was founded on the likes of Bill Miles, farmer at Berthlwyd at Treharris in the centre of the mining valleys, who won the novice Championship at Manmoel near Crumlin in 1921 when he was fifteen years old with Lass. Twelve years later he felt competent enough to enter the Welsh National at Margam with his Rock, a son of Wilson's Craig and Nell, and he handled the four-years-old black and white dog into the Welsh International team at his first attempt. Since then Bill Miles has been a regular member, his experience adding confidence to the team.

A founder-member of the South Wales Sheepdog Trials Association with Bill Miles, Frank Price of Llandew in the Brecon Beacons has devoted much of his time and abilities to the organisation of the International Sheep Dog Society in Wales as well as finding time to run his dogs and to become chairman of Brecknock Rural District and mayor of Brecon.

One of the earliest stars at the National events in Wales was L. J. Humphrey's Toss, a black and white rough-coated grandson of Dickson's Hemp, who was selected for the Welsh team on ten occasions between 1923 and 1933, the first time when he was only twelve months old. In work at Rhoslefain Farm, Towyn, in Merioneth, Toss won two National Championships and with his kennel-mate Lad won the first two Welsh Brace titles in 1931 and 1932.

Toss was a dog who could quickly assess the temperament of the sheep he

Right *An opportunist, Lyn McKee's Irish Champion, White-hope Corrie cools off with a sly lick.*

Below *Matt Graham from the Isle of Man handles Gay and Spy in the 1979 Manx Brace Championship. Gay won the 1976 Irish National Championship.*

herded. Often seen in the top collies when they meet their sheep at the start of a trial, the use of both brain-power and experience enables them to immediately sense the mood of the sheep. If sheep tend to be unruly and wild the dog will 'lay off' and control them from a distance until they settle down; if sheep are steady and slow the dog will move up close. The way a collie thinks out its problems is seen in so many ways, even in its play and relaxation. My Gael quickly learned that pressing her paw on the side of a tennis ball would send it bouncing away for her to chase.

Humphrey's Toss at six years old failed by a single point to win the Supreme Championship at Llandudno in 1928 to Jim Wilson's Fly but his kin, George Whiting's eight-years-old Chip won the top accolade at Ayr in 1933. Toss was a son and Chip a grandson of Thomas Hunter's Sweep, 1924 International Shepherds' Champion and exported to New Zealand two years later. George Whiting brought Chip from Scotland to his home at Llwydcoed, Aberdare at eight weeks old and his first outing was to round up the chickens in the farmyard.

L. J. Humphrey won six Welsh Nationals, two with Toss, two with the black and white rough-coated Lad, and two with Moss, all of Dickson's Hemp line. Such collies of traditional and proven line laid the foundations of Welsh sheepdog prestige, and after World War II the Welsh reputation was built up by such dogs as Hughes' Jaff, Williams' Lad, John Evans' Sweep, Griff Pugh's Don and Laddie, and Harry Greenslade's Glen, all of which won the National title.

Only two dogs have ever 'swept the National board clean' in the same year. At the first National after the war at Llanfairfechan in 1946 Dick Hughes brought Jaff from his milk and sheep farm in the centre of the Isle of Anglesey to win the National, Driving, and Brace titles. A wise and clever tricoloured dog, Jaff, who was to become world-famous for his driving qualities, was partnered by his son Ben in the brace contest, and it was his great-grandson, Alan Jones' Roy who repeated the 'grand slam' in 1961 at Dolgellau.

Jaff had the method to control sheep with an easy relaxed manner, a concentration that was intense, and a nature that was powerfully balanced. He won three International and six National Championships and he was a true Welshman, sired by Lord Mostyn's Coon. Lord Mostyn was a great supporter of Welsh sheepdogs, he ran his own collies into two Welsh International teams, and for many years held the presidency of the International Sheep Dog Society. His faith in Welsh sheepdogs was well justified, for though there have been the lean years, Welsh collies and their handlers have always been formidable opponents on the International field. Among themselves they have differing opinions as to ways to test a dog's capabilities and it was at the 1928 International at Llandudno that Lord Mostyn urged his countrymen to standardise their courses at local trials 'to enhance the chances of Wales in the International event'.

In North Wales the trials course will invariably be laid out according to the accepted national style though the beauty of many of the Welsh trials, both north and south, is the use made of the available land and the rural glory of the setting. In the south they test to the 'South Wales style' which is mainly a gathering test with hurdle lay-out different to National and involving a maltese-cross, a narrow fenced passage through which the sheep have to be driven. Often there is a championship for both South Wales and National styles. Two 'parent' associations, the South Wales Sheepdog Trials Association and the North Wales Sheepdog Society, consider the interests of the many trials societies and both produce a useful fixture list of the year's events.

The day that Ireland really and truly pronounced its emergence as a 'sheepdog nation' must be the day when an Irishman, Harford Logan with his three-years-old Star, but recently resident in Scottish territory, won the Scottish National Championship.

On Thursday, 20 August 1981 Harford and Star, albeit a Scottish-bred dog but taken at five months old by the Irishman, beat the cream of Scottish men and collies in the record 179-entry at the 3½-day National at Glamis in Strathmore. Moving from Millisle in County Down after winning the Irish National in 1980 to farm at Lagnaha, Duror in the romantic country of Appin in Argyllshire, Harford took the three-coloured Star, winner of six open events in Ireland, to the Scottish Championship with a decisive 6½ points.

Further emphasising the quality to which Irish trained dogs had risen,

Below left *Second in the 1979 Irish National Championship at the age of 15, Gordon Watt of Omagh with Chum. Gordon and Chum also won the first young-handlers contest at the International in 1981.*
Below right *Gael, of Shetland descent and my faithful friend over many years.*

Harford's seven-years-old Sweep, winner of the 1980 Irish National, also won a place in the Scottish team, placed fourteenth. Scotland could take consolation in that Sweep was also bred in Ayrshire, a grandson of Wiston Cap.

Signs of Ireland's growing strength in international affairs, which the country had only entered in 1961, came when Jim Brady from Ballyclare made history by winning Ireland's first International Championship, the Farmers' trophy, at Newcastle with Bosworth Jim in 1972.

The following year Bosworth Jim, a good-natured son of Llyr Evans' Supreme Champion Bosworth Coon, won the International Driving Championship; Martin O'Neill's Risp from the richest of farmland in County Meath won the 1976 International Farmers' Championship; John McSwiggan of Gortin Glen in Tyrone won the 1977 International Brace title with Chip and Jess; and Harford Logan took the 1980 International Driving honour with Sweep. Bosworth Jim was English-bred and Sweep Scottish-bred, but Risp, Chip and Jess were bred in Ireland, and this was the most encouraging aspect of Irish sheepdog affairs— that Irishmen were working Irish-bred dogs. For long enough and for a country which was ninety per cent agricultural, Irish farmers relied on stock herding with the brown and white native collie which had no Border Collie blood and no 'eye'.

Martin O'Neill, whose international appearances with Nell and Risp had always been impressive since 1968, used 'rough working dogs' and had never seen a Border Collie until 1961.

Lionel Pennefather, who worked so hard and so successfully for Ireland to improve its standards and become accepted in International competition, believed that tradition in remote farming areas and that perhaps the sea barrier had some inhibiting effect on progress but was still a little baffled as to why the standards of the native collie did not improve as the years passed.

Even today in the west of Ireland which is a big sheep-rearing area there are very few trials to create interest and encourage improvement in working dog standards. Yet Ireland ran its first sheepdog trial in 1888 at Dublin, though the standard of the Irish dogs is reported as being 'deemed unworthy of any prize'. In 1898 the North East Agricultural Association held a trial at their Balmoral showground, Belfast, but no Irish dogs competed, the entrants all coming from England, and in 1908 the North of Ireland Sheep Dog Trials Association was formed at Londonderry but there is no record of its events, if any.

It was not until 1924 that trials in Ireland really got 'off the ground' and this was due to the foresight of the Clonmel Kennel Club in County Tipperary who invited James Reid, the secretary of the International Sheep Dog Society, and Sandy Millar, Scottish National Champion, to judge their event of eleven competitors over a well-laid course in the Golden Vale of Munster. Jess, handled by M. Kiely from nearby Cloghern in Waterford won the Donoughmore cup and £5 first prize money. Clonmel had taken the step which stirred the interest and at their trials the following year 26 dogs competed and it was said that the standards of shepherding had already improved.

Other trials were held at the Carlow agricultural show in the Barrow Valley, at Delgany by the Wicklow Mountains, at Mitchelstown in the Ballyhoura Hills,

The most successful Manx competitor at International level, Ronnie Kinrade from Glascoe, with Cap,
International, Manx National Champion, and Manx 'dog of the year'.

and at Enniscorthy by the Slaney River in Wexford.

Clonmel further suggested the formation of the Irish Sheep Dog Society which held its first trial on the racecourse at Clonmel in September 1926. Lionel Pennefather, to be Ireland's national president for fifteen years, attended that trial as a spectator and was to build on the pioneering work of Clonmel when he moved north to farm hill sheep on 2,000 acres of County Londonderry. In 1961 the Northern Irish contingent was accepted into the International contest.

The Republic of Ireland joined the North in 1965 to form a team known as Ireland and including the collies from the Isle of Man.

Between 1926 and 1961 were 35 years of almost imperceptible growth, the enthusiasm kept alive by the visits of such English and Scottish handlers as Mark Hayton, John B. Bagshaw, and Sandy Millar, and by the determination of such trials societies as those at Tallaght and Phoenix Park in the Dublin area, Fethard in Tipperary, Fermoy in Cork, Glenelly at Plumbridge in Tyrone, and

Cairncastle, Cushendall, and Ballycastle in Antrim. Typical of the spirit of those that were interested was the door to door collection taken from the farmers of the Larne area to raise funds to form the Cairncastle Sheepdog Society in 1936. Except for a break in the war years the trials have been held ever since and now have a reputation as one of the best in Ireland. At the first event in 1936 there were twelve novice dogs, fourteen in the confined Antrim class, and eighteen in the open contest. Today the entry in one open class is near the 100 mark with many Scottish dogs crossing the water to compete.

Jim Brady's Antrim-bred Risp, a son of Scottish Champion Gilchrist's Spot, won Cairncastle three times, and David Brady's black-coated Meg of television fame won the Championship in 1976 and 1979. Risp, a maternal grandson of Wilson Hardisty's English Champion Jim, ran in the Irish National twice in 1969 and 1970 and was reserve champion on both occasions and Driving Champion in 1970. He was the father of Martin O'Neill's better-known dog of the same name which won the television trials at Loweswater in 1976.

The first Irish National was held at Glenarm in County Antrim with fifteen single entries and four brace entries in a one-day programme in 1961 and was won by Lyn McKee's English-bred Snip from Hillsborough in County Down. Lyn won again in 1963 with Whitehope Corrie, a handsome collie of clever breeding from Wilson's Cap, who had a marked influence on Irish bloodlines. His son, Jim Brady's red-coated Buff won the Irish National in 1964 and 1967, one of four collies to win the honour twice.

Lionel Pennefather's rough-coated black and white Bess won in 1962 and 1966; Jim Brady's Bosworth Jim in 1972 and 1973; and Harford Logan's Scottish-bred Jim in 1974 and 1977.

One of the most satisfying National victories was that of Scott, Tim Flood's friendly tricolour winner in Newtownstewart in 1978. 'He was going on ten years at the time and after a lot of bad luck in Nationals he made it with a great run,' Tim told me after Scott had scored 210 out of 220 aggregate points from the two judges.

Scott, a smooth-coated son of Brady's Risp and O'Neill's great-hearted Nell, was one of the Irish-bred collies which had a big influence on the collies of the south, and his daughter Cosy in 1975 and his son Flash in 1979 won the Irish National for Tim. Nell—'the best collie I ever owned,' said Martin O'Neill—ran second four times at the Irish National and never won once. She was probably the most popular collie ever to run the International field for Ireland and it is typical of her master that he blames himself for what he calls her lack of success. 'Her failings were my lack of experience and she was never properly trained for internationals.'

The great spirit she always showed was Nell's success.

In 1976 when the Irish National was held at Knockaloe near Peel in the Isle of Man a collie from the island made history by winning the championship. Leading the entry of fifty which included thirteen Manx collies by a narrow half-point over Harford Logan's Jim, Matthew Graham's Gay from an upland farm on the island scored 177½ of the 200 points. She was calm and in steady control throughout her work which reflected the strength of character she had inherited from her sire Wiston Cap, and from her maternal grandsire Jim Cropper's Fleet. Gay also won the Manx Championship that year.

Also winning a place for the island in the Irish team in 1976, Ronnie Kinrade, who farmed sheep, beef, and milk cows on the fertile northern lands of Glascoe, had his Ben, a grandson of Wiston Cap, in fifth place. Ronnie has been the most successful Manx competitor at International level with five appearances in the Irish team with Hemp, a son of Alan Jones' Supreme Champion Roy, with Cap, a son of Wiston Cap, and with Ben. Cap and Ben and their younger kennel-mate Tam, a great-grandson of Wiston Cap, won the Manx 'dog of the year' for six successive years.

This 'dog of the year' idea is based on the aggregate points from the local trials on the island, ten at the time.

The leading trials are the Manx National trials which are a sound test with qualifying trials and a double-gather Championship held at Port-e-chee Meadow near Quarter Bridge at Douglas usually in the second week of July. In the past ten years the Manx Championship has been won by Ronnie Kinrade four times with Cap in 1975 and 1978, Ben in 1977, and Glen, another grandson of Wiston Cap, in 1972; Arthur Quayle with Bess of Whitehope Nap line in 1973; Doug Little and Moss from Port St Mary in 1974; Matthew Graham with Gay three times in 1976, 1979 and 1980; and George Quirk's Ross from Ballaquine won in 1981.

From these results can be seen the influence of the Whitehope Nap line from Scotland on the Island's collies and John Bregazzi of the Knockaloe Experimental Farm at Peel and the Manx Society's secretary believes that Wiston Cap blood has had a marked influence on the gathering ability of Manx dogs. John said that trials competitions and the introduction of new blood had greatly improved the Island's collies in the last thirty years.

Chapter 11

The big experiment

Will it work is the question as sheepdog trials go on television and the 'butterflies' begin to flutter until the skills and personalities of the Welsh Gel and Bracken, Spot and Craig turn them into instant stars for millions of people.

'Hope' I whispered. Answering his name with a flip of his tongue over my face, the handsome black and white collie dog pricked his ears, turned his wise almond eyes over the white screes of Norber and, his alert interest caught by the cameras, immediately became a star of 'One Man and His Dog'.

Never work with animals; they always steal the show. Not that I have any aspirations of stardom for I prefer my country peace and all my life I have known the appeal which makes these working collies the natural stars of the programme. Nor was I the only one being up-staged in the making of the 1977–78 series of the television sheepdog trials. Atop the limestone rocks of the fell beyond the village of Austwick in Ribblesdale Hope's father, Kyle—the wisest collie in Yorkshire on his day and the winner of the 1970 International Shepherds' Championship—was over-shadowing his master, Michael Perrings, in the making of the programme's title shots.

Minor cogs in a team of highly skilled technicians, Mike and I had no complaints, for working collies were what the programme was all about, and Hope and Kyle, together with their contemporaries representing England, Scotland, Wales and Ireland were truly the stars in a competitive International programme. And these dogs created a programme which became compulsive viewing for an audience which reached eight million people—eighty times more people than fill Wembley Stadium on Cup Final day!

The success of 'One Man and His Dog' has been due to the simple but satisfying composition of clever dogs in skilful craft, honest countrymen with no false airs nor graces, and fair competition set amidst the grandeur of Britain's countryside. It is a mixture which has made for pleasant and relaxed television viewing. Eric Roberts in the Yorkshire Post wrote 'The main attraction must be the satisfaction of watching anyone do anything excellently. There also is the outside chance that something will go wrong and provide an hilarious sequence such as the sight of sheep scattering over the countryside while a shepherd frantically waves his crook.'

Whilst on the subject of review, I have made my commentary bloomers but my

The master of Austwick. Alan Jones won both the singles and brace trophies with Spot and Craig.

favourite personal treasure referring to my 'unorthodox and off the cuff remarks' is Dorothy Johnson's comment in the Glasgow Daily Record 'I doubt if David Coleman, Harry Carpenter or Bill McLaren could get away with a comment like "Oh calm down . . . the bitch is getting too excited!" '

As a test of sheepdog ability the television trials could not be better—in some respects more exacting than the International—for there are three trials to be won on a knock-out basis to earn the BBC trophy. A collie has to prove itself the best in its national section, meet the best of another section in the semi-final, and beat the other semi-finalist in the final. With the cream of sheepdogs from the four countries taking part, the Television Trophy is second only to the International in the list of coveted awards. Indeed in some circles it is regarded even more highly than an International Championship because of the wider exposure and more general interest to the public.

The courses have been extremely stiff, utilising natural features on the land, and even more down to earth in work requirements than the accepted trials layouts. Though difficult, the temptation to introduce what might be termed gimmicks to attract the viewing public has been resisted and never have the demands on the dog strayed from practical requirements. We have seen collie intelligence at its very peak. We saw the handsome black and white Hope use wisdom and experience to ease wily Swaledale ewes off a potentially dangerous crag without hurt at Rannerdale; Dick Fortune's 8½-years-old tricolour Jill leap a six-foot high stone wall to anticipate and cut off erring Dalesbreds in Ribblesdale.

We praised the power and authority of David Carlton's rough-coated Tony in pushing his sheep against all their instincts into the unsettling blackness of a trailer which replaced the pen at Austwick; the agelessness of Martin O'Neill's 9½-years-old Risp in driving Swaledales up the steep Lakeland slopes by Crummock Water. We admired the gentle efficiency of Glyn Jones' clever Gel when driving sheep quietly down through the tall bracken in Rannerdale; the effortless and total control shown by Raymond MacPherson's Tweed on a course which took Beulah Halfbreds down the hill, over the stream, through the woodland and across the pasture at Cilycwm for a loss of only three of 110 points.

As far as publicising trials and bringing a knowledge of the sheepdog's craft to the general public, the programmes have been totally successful, showing the townsman the essential role which the collie dog plays in the production of his food and clothing—in sheepmeat and wool. And the whole idea, like so much that has been good for sheepdogs, sprung from the wet Northumbrian countryside. BBC producer Philip Gilbert was watching a local trial near Alnwick when the germ of the idea of putting sheepdogs on television came to him. He brought his idea to the English National trials in Leek in 1974, discussed it with International Sheep Dog Society chairman Frank Tarn and secretary Lance Alderson, and sat with me on the course-director's bench through three days of torrential rain.

Left *The family of a famous collie bitch receives loving care. Cuddled by Mrs Beryl Jones and well-fed by Bwlch Bracken at Bodfari in North Wales.*

Right *Unbeaten after five brace trials on the television screen—perfect partners and idols of the viewing public—Glyn Jones' Gel and Bwlch Bracken from Bodfari.*

Leek was enough to put off even the most ardent sheepdog fan let alone a newcomer with what at the time seemed to be an outrageous idea. With that most uninspiring introduction to the International scene Philip was a brave man to go ahead with his idea. Into such a series of programmmes as 'One Man and His Dog' goes almost twelve months of planning so that with the initial venture it was not until 1976 that the first trials at Buttermere in the Lake District reached the television screens.

The procedure has been to run the trials in September and after the necessary technical work has been completed to screen them in the following Spring. Of extreme importance is the site. It must be scenic, a good test of shepherding skills, a suitable access for the BBC mobile 'village', yet away from traffic lanes with their unwanted noise. There are times when one almost despairs of finding such a site.

Typical of the requirements was Norber at Austwick in 1977. Here we used two high sheep pastures, one scattered with boulders and criss-crossed by tiny streams on undulating ground, the other steep and split by a typical dry limestone wall; both fields running up to the white screes and rocks of the fell. The first field was used for the heats of the programme in which each of the four countries decided their own champion; the second was used for the semi-finals and final and for the brace tests when one pair of dogs from each country competed. Both made testing courses of shepherding prowess.

To reach such places down the years we have required police escort along

One Man and His Dog BBC2 Televison Trials at Buttermere. Sept. 1975. Screened 1976

SINGLES COMPETITION	Heats	Points	Semi-Finals	Points	Final	Points	WINNER
ENGLAND—WEST	Maximum: 100						
Raymond MacPherson (Hallbankgate)	ZAC	92	Raymond MacPherson. ZAC 94	100			
Tim Longton (Quernmore)	ROY	89			David Shennan. MEG 95	100	
George Hutton (Threlkeld)	NIP	86					
SCOTLAND							David Shennan. MEG
David Shennan (Girvan)	MEG	91	David Shennan. MEG 97				
John Templeton (Fenwick)	BUFF	85					
John Gilchrist (Roslin)	ROY	83					
ENGLAND—EAST							
Llyr Evans (Whittlebury)	CHIP	89	Bob Fraser. PHIL 90				
Chris Winterton (Barkby)	LAD	87			Bob Fraser. PHIL 94		
Bob Fraser (Wooler)	PHIL	91					
WALES							
Gwyn Jones (Penmachno)	BILL	73	Glyn Jones. GEL 89				
Meirion Jones (Pwllglas)	MOSS	77					
Glyn Jones (Bodfari)	GEL	83					

Judged by: Norman Seamark (Bedford): Gwynfor Pritchard (Pwllheli): Bill Merchant (Dingwell): BBC Producer: Philip S. Gilbert.

BRACE COMPETITION		Points	Final	Points	WINNER
ENGLAND—WEST		Maximum 110			
George Hutton (Threlkeld)	NIP & SHONA	83	John Gilchrist. ROY & BOB 92		
SCOTLAND				110	
John Gilchrist (Roslin)	ROY & BOB	89			Glyn Jones. GEL & BRACKEN
ENGLAND—EAST					
Bob Fraser (Wooler)	PHIL & BETTY	69	Glyn Jones. GEL & BRACKEN 101		
WALES					
Glyn Jones (Bodfari)	GEL & BRACKEN	99			

A tense moment at Austwick as Harford Logan with Jim and Sweep puts sheep into the trailer.

single-track country roads, had to trim back hedges in narrow lanes, take sharp corners out of farm roads, remove lengths of dry stone walls, strengthen stream bridges to take the weight of the heavy trucks, and when trapped in the mire, call upon the local tractor force to get us moving again. Always we have been made welcome. Farming folk are so obliging and have always cooperated in supplying our wants. At Austwick we arrived in the middle of a bread strike—but our large company of competitors and technicians—and dogs—never went unfed.

When the site has been found and the competing teams of handlers and collies chosen, the local farmers form the team for running the actual trials, for providing and caring for the sheep, and for providing the field equipment. In this respect, the likes of Lakeland Farmers George Hutton and Chris Todd in Cumbria, Michael Perrings at Austwick, Eurwyn Daniel at Cilycwm, and Huw Roberts at Bala have made excellent team leaders. Success or failure of the programme depends entirely on teamwork, the technical expertise of the BBC men—and women—in conjunction with the trials knowledge of the field staff. In all there will be some sixty people working for success.

When the heavy and bulky technical equipment has been sited, the six cameras rigged, shelter marquees with adjacent 'mod-cons' erected, and the trials course laid out, there is always the final and chilling thought 'Will it work?'

The final preparation at the end of construction day and before every series of 'One Man and His Dog' starts is the proving of the course—to assure the trials staff that every section of the test is practical and workable, and to give the cameramen a chance to flex their muscles in following the action.

The first man ever to test a BBC trials course was Cumbrian farmer Chris Todd who worked his International collie Pete on seven of the wildest Herdwick sheep ever to come before a camera at Buttermere. Over the pasture of Gatesgarth Farm at the eastern end of the lake Pete needed all the stamina and skill of his daily herding on nearby Mellbreak Fell to win the tussle. After following those wily ewes round the course in his lense, one of the cameramen was heard to exclaim that the ball at Old Trafford never moved as unpredictably as those sheep.

Choosing the teams of men and dogs to take part is not as easy as one would think. There are other qualities besides competent handling to be considered for it is not always easy to give of one's best under the critical lense of a television camera. Few handlers can honestly claim to be without 'butterflies' in the stomach when they go to the post in an open trial with perhaps a few hundred spectators, or a few thousand at the most, ready to criticise. But then short-comings are quickly forgotten and the next trial within days offers a chance to redeem one's self-respect. Sheepdog trials are the finest cure known for big-headedness! Today you win the Supreme Championship; tomorrow you slink from your mistakes tail between legs!

But to take the risk of disaster on permanent record and before millions of viewers is another matter and not for the faint-hearted. I take my hat off to my

Pedigree of BWLCH TAFF (113243) 1980 and 1981 Welsh National Champion with Glyn Jones

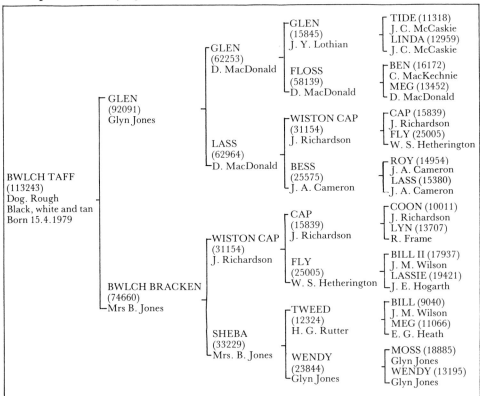

The numbers in brackets are the Stud Book numbers of the International Sheep Dog Society

The end of the first 'One Man and His Dog'—Lance Alderson, then secretary of the International Sheep Dog Society, presents the television Brace trophy to Glyn Jones at Buttermere in 1975.

colleagues who accepted just such a risk with the first series. None of us really knew what would happen when in September 1975 the pattern was set at Buttermere. Nor had the Lakeland weather boosted our morale during 'digging in' operations. Heavy rain pelted down from a grey cloud that seemed but a few feet above our heads and the glorious vista of towering crags which was to be the backcloth for rivetting pictures was but a memory. It was certainly a good omen when even the infamous Lakeland weather relented to give us rain-washed Lakeland crags with tumbling water cascades, a fresh trials carpet spattered with colourful wild flowers and the grey waters of the lake lapping gently on the edge, and visibility that was crystal-clear.

All the times we were to run trials in the Lake District on this and subsequent series the weather-gods were on our side and we only ever lost half an hour's recording time.

To offset the degree of experimentation to some extent and to level the odds for the 'doggy beginners'—the technicians had surmounted far more difficult 'firsts'—the course at Buttermere was the conventional type with gathering and driving tests set over flat ground and the men selected to compete were the best. They knew dogs and sheep intimately and were prepared to put their reputations on the line and stand by their skill.

Four teams of three handlers and dogs representing England West, England East, Scotland, and Wales—Ireland came into a later series—contested Buttermere for the single-dog trophy, with one pair of dogs from each area vying for the Brace honour. Every handler had represented his country in International competition, eight of them had won the Supreme Championship. There were

One Man and His Dog BBC2 Television Trials at Loweswater. Sept. 1976. Screened 1977.

SINGLES COMPETITION	Heats	Points	Semi-Finals	Points	Final	Points	WINNER
SCOTLAND	Maximum: 100						
Peter Hetherington (Girvan)	NELL.	86					
David Mc'Teir (Manor)	GARRY	87	David McTeir. GARRY 95	100			
Tom Watson (Lauder)	MIRK	78					
WALES							
Wyn Edwards (Ruthin)	BILL.	91			Mervyn Williams. GAIL. 94	100	
Mel Page (Brechfa)	NELL.	93	Mervyn Williams. GAIL 96				
Mervyn Williams (Gladestry)	GAIL	96					Martin O'Neill. RISP
ENGLAND							
Tot Longton (Quernmore)	JED	91					
Michael Perrings (Giggleswick)	KYLE	92	Michael Perrings. KYLE 89				
Gordon Rogerson (Chathill)	SPOT	88			Martin O'Neill. RISP 96		
IRELAND							
Jim Brady (Ballyclare)	JIM	79					
Tim Flood (Clonroche)	SCOTT	72	Martin O'Neill. RISP 93	96			
Martin O'Neill (Summerhill)	RISP	84					

Judged by: Tim Longton (Quernmore): Selwyn Jones (Ffestiniog): Willie Hislop (Gordon): BBC Producer: Philip S. Gilbert

BRACE COMPETITION		Points	Final	Points	WINNER
SCOTLAND	Maximum 140				
Peter Hetherington (Girvan)	NELL & HEMP	118	Peter Hetherington. NELL & HEMP 119	140	
WALES					
Wyn Edwards (Ruthin)	TOSS & JAFF	117			Tot Longton. JED & KERRY
ENGLAND					
Tot Longton (Quernmore)	JED & KERRY	114	Tot Longton. JED & KERRY 132		
IRELAND					
Tim Flood (Clonroche)	COSY & NELL	99			

three Supreme Champion collies and two International Champions involved.

The sheep were Swaledale ewes from high ground and they found the delicacies of the lush pasture course irresistible, their grazing interests adding to the difficulties of the dogs. They only moved from their grass-banquet when the dog insisted.

Three judges, Norman Seamark from Bedford, Gwynfor Pritchard from North Wales, and Bill Merchant of Dingwall in Ross-shire made the decisions, and Bill Jones of Anglesey was course-director.

Only one of 100 points divided the single finalists, David Shennan's little prick-eared Meg from Girvan in Ayrshire and Bob Fraser's clever 5½-years-old Phil from Wooler in Northumberland at the end of the series.

Phil, representing the England East team, slipped at the end of her cross-drive to finish with 94 points, giving Meg, the five-years-old granddaughter of Supreme Champion Wiston Cap, the opportunity to snatch the television trophy and the Blue Ribband presented by the International Sheep Dog Society for Scotland.

Scotland's National Champion in 1976, Meg worked her sheep with the adventurous and dominant spirit which, controlled and manipulated by her master, made her a popular 'star'—for much of the appeal of the television events has been the way that viewers have taken a particular dog to their hearts. The style which typified the power of her line gave Meg the unique honour of winning the first-ever television trials. She was a hardy, useful bitch, smooth-coated, quick and adaptable, and ever a tryer, taking pleasure from assisting her master either in the winning of trials' trophies or with the management of the 400 Blackface ewes and 100 beef cows on the home farm at Knockgerran in the Carrick district of south-west Ayrshire.

Sired by Thomson McKnight's Drift, the 1970 International Driving Champion, she was the great-granddaughter of Scotland's great Supreme bitch McKnight's Gael; and on her mother's side she went back to Supreme Champion Wiston Cap and Scottish National Champion Gilchrist's Spot. Ever true to such famous heritage, she won four caps for Scotland and at Buttermere she averaged a pointing of 94 of 100 in her three trials. She furthered the reputation of her bloodline when her granddaughter Nan won the 1978 Scottish National Championship.

Bob Fraser's Phil, a daughter of the famous Mindrum line of Northumberland, improved as the Buttermere trials progressed. She won the English East heat, scoring 91 of 100 points to lead Llyr Evans' 5½-years-old Chip who later won the 1976 English National Championship, and Chris Winterton's rough-coated Laddie who slipped after immaculate gathering; and in the semi-final against the Welsh Gel, Supreme Champion of 1973, she earned a one-point victory at the pen.

Black and white and quite tall in stature, Phil was steady and sure, always on her feet, and always dominant until that fatal slip in the final. The sheep unhurried and under her complete control, her work was pure artistry until the split-second at the cross-drive gate when, suddenly too low for the hurdle, her reaction to command forced the sheep to a bad turn. A nice bitch, easy to work and of a lovely temperament, Phil nevertheless credited the breeding and training of one of the nicest and best-known of sheepdog men, Bob Fraser.

Known wherever shepherds gather, Bob was kind-hearted and helpful, understanding in his ways with dogs and sheep, knowledgeable in his counsel and always with that Northumbrian twinkle of merriment in his eye—and he created a bloodline, started by his Moss, a close descendant of Old Hemp, in 1923 which has become world famous for its reliability and integrity. Bob was one of the many nice human characters which 'One Man and His Dog' has introduced to the British public.

There was Martin O'Neill whose soft Irish brogue was as rich as the lands he farmed in County Meath; there was Dick Fortune, a cheery and canny Scot who never revealed his true age though we all knew he had farmed in New Zealand for over twenty years; Lionel Pennefather reflected the quiet determination in voice and manner which had put Ireland on the sheepdog map in 1961; and there was Evan Evans from Trawscoed who somehow managed to defy the laws of gravity in the wearing of his cap. Experienced in the ways of the countryside, of its human and wild inhabitants, and the ideal colleague in the pleasures and traumas of presenting the trials, Phil Drabble, who gave much of his own personality to the programme, was quickly accepted into the 'shepherds' club'. Tim Flood of

The hub of the whole field operation, the scanner where Philip Gilbert, the producer of the first three series, chooses his pictures with Geoff Lomas, engineering manager on his left, and Gerry Cole, producer's assistant, on his right.

the twinkling eyes entertained us with his queer-looking nose-whistle though his competitive luck always ran out when he crossed the water from Ireland; George Hutton was a droll comedian with his straw hay-time hat and always with the black-coated Nip at his heel; and after Chris Todd told us in his quiet unassuming way that he would not be able to earn a living from the Lakeland Fells without the help of his dogs there was no doubt in anyone's mind that collie dogs were truly beloved of these men.

All were honest and modest countrymen, speaking with a heart-warming frankness which reflected the philosophical attitude so essential to a life involved with the whims of nature. Adversity or a touch of ill-luck in the competition was, as Lancashire farmer Tot Longton said 'Just one of those things', to be quickly forgotten as the next day dawned.

All praised their dogs when things went right, blamed themselves as handlers when things went wrong. Even seventeen-years-old David Bristow from Murton in Yorkshire in the first junior competition in 1980–81 credited his 3½-years-old Tweed with all the skill which mastered an awkward sheep that was running victory away.

One of the most modest of modest men was Glyn Jones whose clever twosome of Gel and Bracken was unbeaten after five brace trials on the screen. He called competitive brace running a 'bit of a lark'—even though he is a master at the art of working two dogs together. At home on the mountain at Bwlch Isaf in the Clwydian Range he will take two and even more collies in the very practical gather of his white-faced flock, able to command each individual dog with its own set of commands. From the very first television programme at Buttermere the good-looking Gel and the clever little Bracken became idols of the viewing public. On their last appearance to win the 1979–80 Brace trophy at Rannerdale they had become the best known dogs in Britain. Their immaculate partnership was uncanny, they seemed to know exactly what the other was thinking, each relied totally on the other to master any sheep stupidity and they had a perfect understanding with 'the boss'.

Glyn Jones was a considerate boss. He taught Gel from the age of ten months old to win the Supreme Championship of the International Sheep Dog Society in 1973 and he moulded Bracken from a puppy to International status. Glyn's consideration for his dogs, and he has handled many sheepdogs, comes from really knowing them, knowing and accepting that each is an individual with its own particular characteristics, some good, some bad, but all very much a part of its make-up. That he tolerates the whims which so often go with genius comes from such understanding of the collie mind. Wise dogs respond to such treatment, find they can respect and trust the man who shares, indeed orders, their lives.

Gel and Bracken were of this mould. Neither was an angel—Gel could disagree with Glyn, and Bracken had her moments—but few collies with the trait of genius ever are. Individually they were masters of the craft of shepherding sheep; together they turned a workaday craft into a form of art. Their flowing rhythm, their precise pacing, their sweeping turns, moving together on measured distance to keep sheep going away all the time set them apart from others, and they were recipients of a fan-mail from a viewing public which thrilled to their skills.

Broad headed, gentle eyed, handsomely black and white rough-coated, Gel was partner to Glyn Jones in triumph and adversity. Together in sunshine or snowstorm they shepherded the 800 acres of bracken covered mountain, assisting the ewes with their white woolly lambs in springtime, driving them from drifting snow in winter. Together they won most of the trials trophies of any count including the greatest, the Supreme. Gel was more of an individual than Bracken and was never happier than with Glyn Jones. He died naturally from a heart attack in March 1981 at the age of 10½ years.

He was of Welsh breeding from Caernarfon, the son of W. T. Williams' Nell and Elwyn Griffith's Craig and his shepherding life enhanced the most aristocratic of lines through Wilson's Cap, Dickson's Hemp to Tommy and Old Hemp.

Bwlch Bracken, her registered name, was 1½ years younger than Gel and was also from Wilson's Cap. She was born at Bwlch Isaf out of Beryl Jones' Sheba and sired by the 1965 Supreme Champion Wiston Cap. When she joined Gel in competitive partnership the brace honours which went to Bwlch Isaf were numerous, including the Welsh National title in 1974, though the International Championship always eluded them. They were second by only five aggregate points from three judges to another good Welsh trio, Gwilym Jones and Queen and Glyn in the Chatsworth International in 1978.

Seen for the first time on television at Buttermere Gel and Bracken, then five and 3½ years old, were confident winners for Wales. After the then (1974 and 1975) reigning International Champions, George Hutton with Nip and Shona, strong black-coated hill collies from the Helvellyn fells above Threlkeld in Cumbria, had slipped rather surprisingly in their first trial, there was little to trouble the Welsh dogs. In the final they scored a sound 101 of 110 points to lead by nine points over 71-years-old John Gilchrist from Roslin with Roy and Bob, both sons of his famous Scottish Champion Spot—the grandsire of Gel.

The following year at Loweswater Glyn was invited to bring Gel and Bracken to meet the champion pair of that series, Tot Longton's mother and daughter team of Jed and Kerry, two good North Lancashire bitches from the milk lands of the Conder Valley. Glyn had never beaten Tot, one of the best of international brace handlers, and so the contest promised much in the way of top-class brace work.

Nor were viewers disappointed. Kerry at only 21 months of age lacked experience, though it was her mother, the clever little Jed who slipped a vital three points in driving in their final workmanlike score of 130 of 140 points. But Gel and Bracken, always at their best on the big occasion, barely put a paw wrong. Gel over-ran on his outrun to drop three points but then, gathering his concentration, he matched his splendid partner to finish the test only faulted another one point. Their work from the lift was the finest piece of brace shepherding seen on the television screen.

With their reputation on the line they contested the fourth series over the most difficult of courses among the rocks and bracken of the Lakeland valley of

Rannerdale. Though Gel was hampered by a slight leg strain, they made shepherding look easy even over such demanding terrain, beating Donald McDonald's 11½-years-old Gael and the big smooth-coated Mirk from Perthshire low ground by thirteen points in their first contest, and finishing ten points clear of George Hutton's clever Nip and his four-years-old son Roy who failed badly on the gather, in the final.

The perfect partnership was finally broken by the death of Gel in 1981, undoubtedly the finest of a fine breed of collies to come down the mountain from Bwlch Isaf.

Glyn Jones will always have good dogs for he takes the trouble to use their inherent qualities and mould them to blend with his own. In 1980 he won the Welsh National Championship with the sixteen-months-old Bwlch Taff, and almost of the realms of fiction Taff repeated the victory the following year. Taff was the tricolour rough-coated son of Bracken and of Glen—whom Glyn trained before the cameras in the second series of 'One Man and His Dog' and who won his first Welsh International cap in 1977 before his tragic death when only four years old. Also in the 1980 Welsh team Glyn ran the younger Gel, a three-years-old relation of the old champion and the handsome black and white collie which Glyn's daughter Ceri ran with success in the first junior contest of 'One Man and His Dog' at Cilycwm, and at the 1981 International at Armathwaite.

The Buttermere television event, being the first, opened up a whole new dimension on sheepdogs for me though the actual trials runs were no different to any others—but in those early days it was good to get them over and Phil and I moved quickly to the local hostelry to discuss our efforts and relax the pressure over a most welcome and refreshing pint of Lakeland hospitality!

Hay-time comes late amid the high fells of Lakeland and the second series of 'One Man and His Dog' at Loweswater in September 1976 (screened 1977) was looking sadly towards postponement at one time.

It was a rainy spot we had chosen over the stone wall, hedge and fence-divided fields of Waterside and High Nook farms on the southern end of the lake. Even in early summer when Philip and myself and my wife and Gael—for 'canine opinion'—together with Chris Todd and George Hutton surveyed the site for course layout it was pouring with rain. Highnook Beck was racing water and the heights of Carling Knott and Mellbreak disappeared into cloud cap. Whilst drying-out in the local pub we decided that an amalgamation of the fields with a few gaps made as natural hurdles in the stone walls could make two interesting trials courses.

September did indeed come with the grass safely harvested and some classical collies gathered. Davie McTeir's uncapped hill dog Garry surprised Scottish Champions Peter Hetherington's wise old Nell and Tom Watson's handsome Mirk to lead Scotland; Welsh victory went to Mervyn Williams' experienced Gail, three points clear of Mel Page's Nell and Wyn Edwards' upstanding Bill, both of whom were unlucky in the shedding-ring; Michael Perrings' 9½-years-old Kyle, the wisest of collies at the end of a great career, was better than either

Above *Winners of the television trials at Loweswater. Tot Longton with Jed and Kerry and Martin O'Neill with Risp.* **Right** *'Are you my famous dad?' Puppy Lyn greets her father Bwlch Taff, the collie which won the Welsh National Championship in 1980 at the age of 16 months and repeated the success the following year—a record of the realms of fiction.*

Tot Longton's clever Jed or Gordon Rogerson's young Spot for England; and the tireless black and white Risp with Martin O'Neill was easily in front of Jim Brady's Jim, top of the Irish success list, and Tim Flood's Driving Champion Scott in the Irish heat. Better driving gave the Welsh Gail a one-point lead over McTeir's Garry in the first semi-final; and Kyle lost everything to O'Neill's Risp on a slip in outrunning though he only dropped three points in the rest of his trial. Risp, the 1976 International Farmers' Champion and a sound, happy work dog with sheep and beef cows over 300 rich acres in County Meath, won the final for Ireland with crisp forceful work on the Swaledale ewes, though only two points divided his work from the nice easy, though not quite as assertive, shepherding of the 5½-years-old Gail.

Risp, at six years old, was probably the best collie in Ireland at the time for not only had he proved himself in home-country trials but on each of the four occasions he came to represent his country against the English, Scottish, and Welsh, he was always to be counted at the end. A good-tempered yet assertive rough-coated dog, and tireless and willing as he showed when he came back to the television trials on Rannerdale's rocks, he finished fourth in the Supreme International contest in 1973, and fifth in 1976 after leading the cream of British collies in the qualifying tests at Lockerbie to win the International Farmers' title.

One Man and His Dog BBC2 Television Trials at Austwick. Sept. 1977. Screened 1978

SINGLES COMPETITION	Heats	Points	Semi-Finals	Points	Final	Points	WINNER
WALES	Maximum 110			110		110	
Alan Jones (Pontllyfni)	SPOT	95	Alan Jones. SPOT 98				
Garnet Jones (Llanfair D.C.)	CRAIG	90			Alan Jones. SPOT 96		Alan Jones. SPOT
Selwyn Jones (Ffestiniog)	JILL	94					
ENGLAND							
David Carlton (Chipping)	TONY	100	David Carlton. TONY 95				
John James (Kingsland)	MIRK	92					
Chris Todd (Loweswater)	TOT	97					
SCOTLAND							
John Bathgate (Peebles)	DRIFT	87	Dick Fortune. GLEN 83				
Dick Fortune (Edinburgh)	GLEN	98			Lionel Pennefather. BILLY 85		
Douglas Lamb (Roslin)	GLEN	88					
IRELAND							
Harford Logan (Millisle)	JIM	73	Lionel Pennefather. BILLY 84				
John McSwiggan (Omagh)	CHIP	89					
Lionel Pennefather (Carrigaline)	BILLY	90					

Judged by: Bob Fraser (Wooler): Glyn Jones (Bodfari): Thomson McKnight (Canonbie): BBC Producer: Philip S. Gilbert.

BRACE COMPETITION	Points	Final	Points	WINNER
WALES	Maximum 140		140	
Alan Jones (Pontllyfni)	CRAIG & SPOT 120	Alan Jones. CRAIG & SPOT 131		Alan Jones. CRAIG & SPOT
ENGLAND				
Chris Todd (Loweswater)	PETE & BOB 107			
SCOTLAND				
Dick Fortune (Edinburgh)	GLEN & JILL 120	Dick Fortune. GLEN & JILL 115		
IRELAND				
Harford Logan (Millisle)	JIM & SWEEP 108			

On that day as far as Ireland was concerned he was priceless, yet he and Martin had almost parted company for the give-away price of £60 three years earlier. They were just not getting on together, but making the best of each other to become the best of pals, they finally clinched their partnership with an Irish International cap just six months after the threatened parting.

As Glyn Jones's Gel, Risp was also a grandson of Scottish Champion Gilchrist's Spot, though it was his maternal grandmother who gave him his particular character. She was Nell, the black-coated bitch whose cheerful, happy-go-lucky, yet professional shepherding made her such a favourite with the International crowds in six appearances in the Irish team. That she was at the top of her profession was proved by the merit registration which put her in the International Sheep Dog Society's Stud Book. Her sire was Deacon's Flash, her dam Flood's Lassie, and her line was to Scottish Champion Whitehope Nap.

Nell can claim a place in sheepdog history as the first collie from Eire to win through to the Supreme Championship trials of the ISDS—at Newcastle in 1972.

Beaten by two points by Risp in the Loweswater final when a particularly awkward ewe teased her on the drive, Mervyn Williams' black, white and tan Gail was from work with Speckled-face and Clun-cross ewes on hill grazing at Gladestry, Kington on the border with Hereford. Very even tempered at $5\frac{1}{2}$ years old, she was kind with sheep and had a good understanding with her master.

Peter Hetherington's mother and son team Nell and Hemp, the 1976 Scottish Brace Champions, were well set for the Brace Championship until they got to the close work when for some unaccountable reason Nell, one of the finest bitches in Britain, made some shocking mistakes in the ring and at the pen.

Their opponents, Tot Longton's mother and daughter team Jed and Kerry were not the partnership to lose such opportunity, though Kerry's 21-months-old lack of experience wanted helping by a handler who is among the best brace men in the world. Jed, eight-years-old experienced daughter of Supreme Champion Llyr Evans' Bosworth Coon and her master's reserve Supreme Champion Gyp, won 36 Open Singles Championships before she retired in 1978.

When 'One Man and His Dog' went to Wales to Cilycwm in 1980 Tot Longton's son Thomas won the Brace contest with Lassie, daughter of Jed, and Bess, daughter of Kerry.

Of necessity in a sheepdog trial so many of the farm 'obstacles' have to be represented by 'props', such as the gates used on both fetch and drive to represent openings through which sheep have to be herded, and the pen made specially of hurles to represent a building or transport trailer into which sheep have to be driven.

The third series of the programme at Austwick in 1977–78 was the one when Philip Gilbert said, 'Why assimilate these tests, why not use the real thing?' And so we did—using the natural rocks on the land and gaps in the stone walls, actually using a small livestock-trailer in which to 'pen' the sheep.

In the field used for the heats when each of the four countries decided its own champion, ten sheep were gathered from under the steep rocks and brought down the slope over a rock-littered field and driven to negotiate the specified rock-gaps, taken three times over a stream, persuaded down an alley-like passage as often seen in South Wales style trials, and finally herded into a farm trailer. This was more like the real work on the home fell. In the semi-final and final tests the course was re-set on the adjoining field so that there was a steeper and more demanding gather, and gaps in the stone field-wall were used as 'obstacles' so that everything became more akin to the real thing.

A bitterly cold and biting wind which swept from the fells is a lasting memory of Austwick for it made the strangers to our part of the world realise just how valuable are the stone field-walls to our farming in the North Country. They are the vital shelter for our stock, and we humans took refuge in their lee during the running of the trials. We crouched and talked, and many a good impromptu discussion on dogs and sheep took place whilst waiting to be called to action.

Willie Hislop and John Bathgate extolled the virtues of their Suffolks, Cheviots and Blackfaces as sheep of quality mutton and strong-wearing wool for warm clothing, whilst David Carlton, Chris Todd, and I argued for the toughness of our Lonk, Swaledale, and Gritstone breeds. Glyn Jones and Selwyn Jones said there was nothing better than Welsh Mountain lamb for tenderness and flavour. Lionel Pennefather and Harford Logan told us of the rising quality of Irish collies, and Alan Jones talked of the concentration as well as the ability which a collie dog needed to win in top trials competition.

Austwick of course, over the high limestone pastures of the Dales country, belonged simply to that one man and his two dogs, to North Wales farmer Alan Jones and his International Champion Craig and the young unproven Spot who won both the singles and the brace trophies. Here we saw the making of a champion when Alan, wise and experienced in the ways of sheepdogs, decided to put his faith in the three-years-old Spot over the tricky and testing slopes of Norber, relying on the inbred intelligence of the young dog and his legginess and stamina to master both Dalesbred sheep and wind-swept course.

In the first test it was touch and go with Spot a little too strong on the fetch, but with encouraging conversation from his master he steadied and settled his zest to correct his pace on the drive. His thoughts wholly concentrated on the sheep, he then established the partnership which was to take him and Alan to victory and he saved the one point which won the Welsh heat over Selwyn Jones' much more experienced eight-years-old Jill from Ffestiniog and Garnet Jones' somewhat excitable Craig from Llanfair Dyffryn.

In the semi-final against the English pair, David Carlton and his reliable Tony whose driving was great after a poor start, Spot settled to his work like a veteran, took the right time to contact and order his sheep, and alert and never off his feet, finished with a lead of three points. It was in the final that Spot really came of age, finding a flair for the big time, and so precise in his driving work over the difficult terrain that he dropped only three of thirty points.

Ireland's four-years-old Billy with Lionel Pennefather from County Cork could not match it, losing half the drive points, and Spot became a worthy champion.

Alan found in those three trials that Spot had the right temperament, the stamina, the intelligence, and signs of the total commitment to his shepherding that is absolutely necessary for a collie to win the Supreme Championship of the ISDS. The following year Spot did win through to the Supreme Championship and finished third to Bob Shennan's Mirk and Gordon Rogerson's Spot, and in 1980 he won his first International Championship, partnering Craig to the Brace title at Bala. Partnered by his older and much more experienced kennel-mate Craig at Austwick, Spot took his full share of work in the two brace tests in which they beat the 1976 and 1977 English Brace Champions, Chris Todd's litter-brothers Pete and Bob from the Cumbrian fells and, their partnership running like a well-oiled machine, taking a convincing sixteen points lead over Scotland's Jill and Glen with Dick Fortune of Edinburgh for the final. Alan's handling of the two dogs in all the trials of that television series was a very controlled and skilful display of the shepherd's art. It was not unexpected. I have watched Alan Jones many times, have judged him on occasion, and he is a master at the craft of handling sheepdogs.

But first he must have the right collie—and he is prepared to spend the time and the many disappointments in finding it. He travels some 15,000 miles in a season to visit around fifty trials. He does not breed, he prefers to buy a likely candidate and put on the championship polish, and he prefers dogs to bitches.

Spot at Austwick was three years old, a great-grandson of Gilchrist's Spot, and taught his initial job by James Sandilands in Lanarkshire. Craig was proven and skilful. The prick-eared son of his master's Moss, he had won the 1976 Welsh National, three Welsh and two International Driving Championships, and subsequently won the International Farmers' Championships in 1977 and 1979. From work with 600 Welsh ewes and 200 Welsh Black cows on 300 acres of the Lleyn Peninsular at Lleuar Bach Farm, Pontllyfni, Craig was a great-great-grandson of Roy, Alan's most famous collie.

In 1961 Roy created the fantastic trials record of winning the Supreme, the International Farmers', the Welsh National, Farmers', and Driving Championships, and the Welsh Brace Championship in partnership with the ten-years-old Spot, his workmate at the time and a son of Gilchrist's Spot. The most relaxed of collies, Roy had the method which gave confidence to the stock he herded. He was strong and commanding, fast and supremely intelligent, and he was one of the most famous collies ever to represent Wales.

Since his first trial when he was sixteen years old Alan Jones has represented Wales on thirty occasions, winning nine International and twenty National titles.

Chapter 12

Shepherding to public acclaim

Eight million viewers warm to the prowess of clever collies as we test their shepherding ability over more and more difficult courses on the rocks of Rannerdale, the steep slopes of Cilycwm, and the changing pattern of Rhiwlas.

Every dog has its day—a day of inspiration or the luck to have everything go right, the right frame of mind, the right sheep, the right conditions, but it is the true champion—or his progeny—who comes back time and time again to prove his superiority.

Championships of the standard of the Supreme International when a collie has to pass through three trials, or the television events when three trials have to be won outright illustrate this most effectively. A collie can have everything go right in a single trial to win an accepted, even coveted, society trial championship, but if the dog has to prove himself over more than one course then the element of luck is dispatched.

I have recorded the many successes of Glyn Jones' Gel and Bracken; David Shennan's trim little Meg and Martin O'Neill's hard-working Risp, both television singles winners, won National and International Championships; and Alan Jones' Craig and Spot won the International Brace title.

So it was with Bob Shennan's mottled Mirk from Ayrshire, the winner of the fourth television series at Rannerdale. One of the best collies that Scotland has produced, a dog of unflappable temperament who knew sheep as well as his master, Mirk won five International caps for Scotland, won the 1979 Supreme Championship, the 1979 Scottish National, and the National and International Driving titles the same year.

Reared and trained by Bob and his companion and help-mate from puppyhood, Mirk was the dog for the big occasion. Rannerdale was the big occasion with the course close by Crummock Water straddling a lively clear-running stream in a deep-cut Lakeland valley of steep sided, bracken covered and rocky slopes, often swept by cold rainstorm.

It was a test of every sheepdog characteristic, stamina and courage, common-sense and intelligence, power and patience, to herd seven Swaledale ewes to competition standard over the roughest possible terrain. It was also a test of engineering ingenuity to televise and the success of the whole operation which brought super shots to the screen of collies working in such natural environment

Above left *The 'Brandsby Pup' who worked so well for Allan Heaton at Cilycwm.* **Above right** *Stuart Davidson and Ben from Scotland, winners of the television singles trophy at Bala 1981.*

was due to the expertise and leadership of Ian Smith who had taken over the production of the programme from Philip Gilbert.

The Lakeland weather had not been kind and when the television crew arrived on that Saturday morning in September they found that the ground was too wet to get all their heavy vehicles to the planned positions. But BBC Outside Broadcast crews thrive on problems and by dint of much pushing and pulling, wall removal, and tractor manipulation the essential equipment was put in place. Cameras were man-handled up the rocks together with their power cables; the commentary box and control centre was balanced on scaffolding poles; and George Hutton and his merry band laid out the trials course so that every obstacle and problem was beaten in time for the planned start.

Sitting by the fresh clear stream in the valley with George Hutton's Nip nosing under my arm I even had time to admire the beauty of the place to which we had come, the wild rocky fells which were home to the tough little Herdwick sheep. It was country which Nip knew well for, a great old trouper in England's trials cause, the black-coated dog spent his working life in those high places. The cold clear water of Lakeland was however not so welcome when on later days it was coming from above, spattering on the microphone, and seeping in icy rivulets down my neck.

Such were the conditions when the good understanding between Bob Shennan and Mirk took the 8½-years-old Scottish collie to a two points lead in his first trial. Mirk was a little impetuous and had to be held back on the steep downhill fetch where, though balancing his movements, his power zig-zagged his sheep from line for his major fault of six points. He steadied to drive up the opposite fellside and round the rocks at the top, showing that absolute trust and respect for Bob's guiding commands which made them such a formidable partnership. Shedding and penning were easily carried out and Mirk went into the semi-final against the renowned nine-years-old Gel with Glyn Jones, winner of the Welsh heat by five clear points.

It was a fascinating prospect for the watchers, perhaps the two finest collies in Britain at the time, both Supreme International Champions, on the most rugged of tests. Mirk won it by his immediate response to command, listening to obey every instruction over the blustering wind which blew through the valley. He steadied and coaxed the Swaledales, taking his time and suppressing every urge to push too hard.

Gel took a bone-shaking leap over the stream at the start of his outrun and with previous ligament trouble in a leg may have felt the effects in following quick-moving sheep, but in typical sporting fashion, Glyn made no excuses for work that came well below the dog's usual standard.

The Irish Risp, Martin O'Neill's 9½-years-old veteran of many top trials, was

Pedigree of MEG (81598) Irish International with David Brady

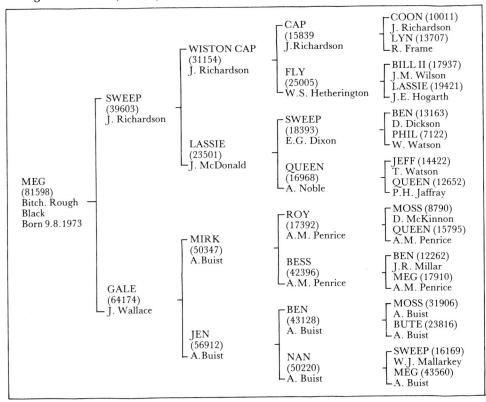

The numbers in brackets are the Stud Book numbers of the International Sheep Dog Society.

Power personified—Raymond MacPherson's Tweed from the Tindale Fells, World Champion in 1976, Television Champion at Cilycwm, 1980 English Driving Champion, 1972 Welsh Driving Champion.

Mirk's final challenger and, used to the flat lands of County Meath, he ran into immediate trouble on the hill. He had great difficulty in finding his sheep among the rocks though his tenacity and spirit finally brought them away and the strength of character for which he was known kept him gamely at their heels to the final penning. But his pointing was disastrous, and profiting from Risp's experience at the gather, Bob Shennan sent Mirk in a wide sweep of the fellside so that he came easily to his sheep and the championship was won at that point.

Admired for his reliability and intelligent knowledge of his craft, Mirk honoured Scotland on many occasions, never better than at Rannerdale. He was one of those dogs which make shepherding a pleasure, a dog to take all the hard work out of gathering a hill. 'He gives me confidence. I thought he could do it,' was his master's comment after winning the Television Trophy.

In Scotland's International team on five occasions—he ran second, first, and third in three successive Scottish Nationals—Mirk's daily duties were in the management of 550 Blackface and crossbred ewes and 150 beef cows at Farden, Turnberry, near Girvan on Scotland's west coast. Well-bred, he was a son of John Richardson's Mirk, the 1975 International Shepherds' and Scottish National Champion. His grandsire was the famous Supreme Champion of 1965, Wiston Cap, and his dam's line took his blood back to Jim Wilson's Mirk and Moss. The mottled Mirk, winner of Rannerdale, was of that line of Border

Collies which have made Scotland famous in pastoral circles.

Rannerdale took the whole Border Collie breed to test and every one of its seventeen representatives came through with honour. Ivor Jones' 4½-years-old Spot from lowland farming in the Vale of Clwyd found the hills strange but stuck to his task to finish his work, and Eurwyn Daniel's trim little prick-eared Meg from the Black Mountains of South Wales showed that willingness to tackle any shepherding problem which has made the breed so indispensible to flock management. Scotland's dogs ran through heavy rainstorm and both David McTeir's Garry of the cool temperament and Donald McDonald's big smooth-coated Mirk showed complete disregard for conditions which were so often their daily lot.

England's 1977 National Champion Flash, well handled by Jean Bousfield, the first lady to compete in 'One Man and His Dog', honoured her title; the handsome black and white Hope, the glad companion under Michael Perrings, showed true enjoyment in mastering the Swaledales on the rocks; and Alan Foster's four-years-old Dart from the Cumbrian fells used the skilful persuasion that was to take him to the 1980 International Shepherds' victory.

Ireland's adaptable Lad with Willie Watt from Omagh, and Max under Lyn McKee from Banbridge, beaten in the heat by O'Neill's Risp gave the old campaigner a run for his victory. Max, only three years old and inexperienced in competition, was the speediest creature on the fellside, his sleek willingness to work impressing us all and taking him within one point of the experienced Risp.

Phil Drabble discusses the Cilycwm 'One Man and His Dog' television final between Raymond MacPherson with Tweed for England and David Brady with Meg for Ireland.

Our impression of Max proved correct. The following May he left Ireland to work with Blackface ewes and pedigree Ayrshire milk cows at Airtnoch Farm on the edge of Fenwick Moor for John Templeton, one of the judges at Rannerdale, and on his first entry to the Scottish National trials later that year won an International cap.

Max thrived in adverse conditions, running on the first day of the Scottish National when heavy rainfall lashed the Thornhill course in Dumfriesshire, and at the end of the third day after Scotland's 157 top collies had competed he was on the twelfth marking—and in the Scottish International team. Bred by W. Hallinan in County Tipperary, and a grandson of Martin O'Neill's Nell, Max quickly enhanced his reputation by passing the qualifying tests at the International at Bala—third of the 53 collies—and when in the Supreme contest he won third placing he had really made his mark on the sheepdog scene. His meteoric rise to fame extended to America when Etroy McCaslin of Ohio persuaded John to let him cross the Atlantic.

Countrywise, England had had a lean time in the way of honours when we went outside the national boundary to run the fifth series of 'One Man and His Dog' in Wales at Cilycwm in September 1980. Only Tot Longton from Quernmore with his home-bred Jed and Kerry had prevented a complete 'whitewash' in the four series by winning the Brace trophy at Loweswater.

Wales had been easily the most successful, winning three Brace titles and the Austwick singles victory to Alan Jones' Spot, and on their home ground were

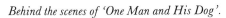

Behind the scenes of 'One Man and His Dog'.

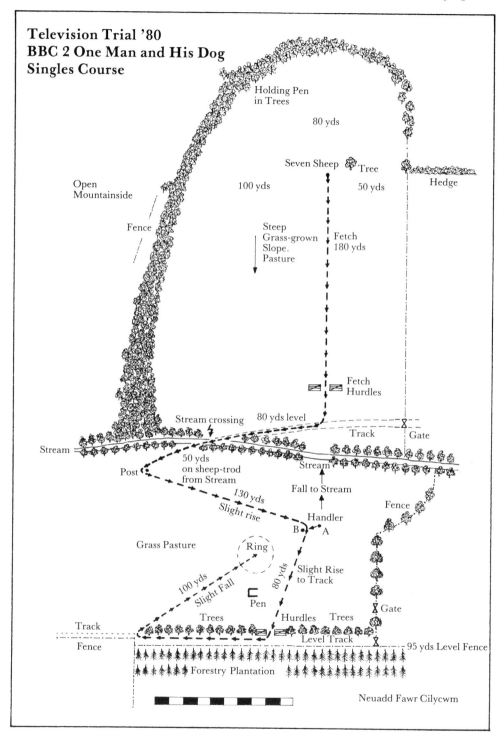

**Television Trial '80
BBC 2 One Man and His Dog
Singles Course**

Holding Pen
in Trees

80 yds

Seven Sheep · Tree

Hedge

Open
Mountainside

100 yds

50 yds

Fence

Steep
Grass-grown
Slope.
Pasture

Fetch
180 yds

Fetch
Hurdles

Stream crossing

80 yds level

Track

Gate

Stream

50 yds
on sheep-trod
from Stream

Stream

Post

Fall to Stream

130 yds

Slight rise

Handler

B · A

Fence

Grass Pasture

Ring

100 yds

80 yds

Slight Rise
to Track

Slight Fall

Pen

Track

Trees

Hurdles

Trees

Gate

Fence

Level Track

95 yds Level Fence

Forestry Plantation

Neuadd Fawr Cilycwm

Above left *A jump for joy as winners of the first junior television trophy at Cilycwm—17-years-old David Bristow from Murton in the Vale of York and his 3½-years-old Tweed.* **Above right** *Evan Evans and Glen, a collie whose simple courage and stamina reflects the personality of the working dog. After plastic hip surgery Glen continued work at the Trawscoed Ministry farm and on the trials field won over 50 open trials championships.*

undoubtedly the favourites to add to their successes with collies of the calibre of Gwilym Jones' 1978 International Brace winners, the bonny smooth-coated Queen and her son Glyn; Evan Evans' indestructable Glen whose hip-joint was plastic; and Wyn Edwards' experienced champion Bill.

It was not to be and England tasted the fruits of total victory, including success in the first junior competition, over a most testing and contrasting course in a competition which, so enthralling and compelling in its keenness, raised the audience to six million. Set in the mountainous land of the red kite and the buzzard at the head of the valley at Neuadd Fawr just outside the village of Cilycwm, four miles north of Llandovery, the tests called for stamina in gathering sheep from the steep slope, initiative in working them through tree-fringed lines out of sight of the handlers, and patience and adaptability on undulating sheep drives.

Off over a tree-screened stream in the valley, the collie had to run the steep hillside to find the sheep, gentle them straight down the hill for some 200 yards, turn them along 130 yards of sheep-trod to cross the stream without guidance

from the handler, and pace a final fetch of 130 yards up a slight rise. Driving over 300 yards included 100 yards hidden from the handler where the collie had to match its own pace. Shedding and penning took the standard procedure. Strategically placed cameras put the viewer right in with the dog, creating the atmosphere of total involvement with the problems, doubts, and decisions of a contest in which any slight mistake could cost vital points.

It was as tough a test of shepherding as could be planned and viewers warmed to the skills—and failings—of the collies which faced it. Autumn sunshine warmed the land and the white sheep moved lazily from my path when I first walked the mountainside to look down with a birds-eye view of the site. The contrast of green cultivated fields laid a bright patchwork against the darker green of the forestry plantation and the brown ruggedness of the mountain was split by a white spume of water where it danced down the rocks to flow in more tranquil pace between the trees in the valley. Swallows and martins hawked insects, a buzzard floated easily on broad wings against the domed and distant backcloth of the Brecons.

Scotland went first to choose their champion and story-book planning could not have produced a tighter contest. Sandy McMorran's nice-tempered Scott, who cost the shepherd a mere £6, was encouraged with a hand-pat of confidence to score 100 of 110 points; Alisdair Mundell's brave hill-dog Cap faced a rain deluge to win 101 points; and Dick Fortune's handsome young Bill took the unfamiliar mountainside in his stride for 100½ points.

Almost as tight in its outcome, the Welsh heat had Wyn Edwards' stylish and powerful Bill from the Vale of Clwyd one point in front of Gwilym Jones' six-years-old Queen from Brechfa in Carmarthen, herself one point in front of Evan

Above left *Commentator, Eric Halsall, with the judges, Peter Hetherington and Bill Jones, Bala, 1981.* **Above** *Meirion Jones' Jill, 'One Man and His Dog' Junior Champion at Bala 1981.* **Below** *Eric Halsall with Geoffrey Billingham (brace champion, with Trim and Jed), Mel Page, and Stuart Davidson (singles champion, with Ben) at Bala, 1981. The commentary box and television cameras are in the background.*

Evans' clever Glen from work with 1,000 ewes at Trawscoed. If ever a collie dog reflected the spirit, courage and sheer guts of his breed it was Glen. In April 1978 he had a serious accident which resulted in an operation to save his life and the installation of a plastic hip-joint in his right hind leg; four months later he won nine open trials in South Wales and at Cilycwm he faced the tough hillside without qualm and with every confidence.

A fantastic stint of shepherding which quashed any notion of senile deterioration or age retirement from his duties on the fells of Cumbria won the English heat for Raymond MacPherson's ten-years-old Tweed. Taking the testing gather in his stride, he dropped one point on line on his fetch, one on his fetch turn, and one on his drive turn to finish on 107 of 110 points. Is it any wonder that Raymond says of the bare-skinned collie, 'He saves me a lot of work'?

Had Tweed, who won the 1976 American World Championship for Britain, not been in such great condition, a collie at the start of his career, the 2½-years-old black and tan Bransby would have been a worthy winner. Taken as a 'service-pup'—in lieu of a stud fee—by Allan Heaton who at the time Brandsby was born

Pedigree of TWEED (62981) 1980-81 T.V. Champion with Raymond MacPherson

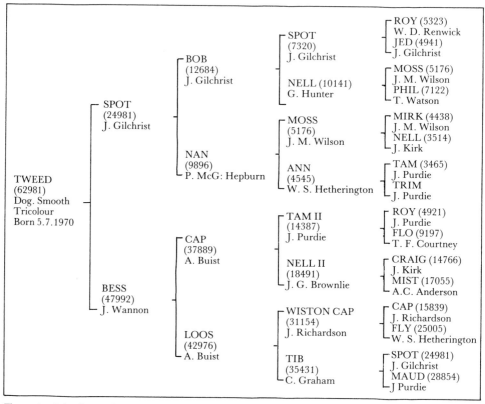

The numbers in brackets are the Stud Book numbers of the International Sheep Dog Society.

Mel Page's Nell at 1981 filming of 'One Man and His Dog' at Bala.

farmed Holstein milk cows and Mule ewes at Peel Park, Brandsby, the young collie became known as the 'Brandsby pup'. The unusual name stuck and has since been recorded in the award lists of many trials, including the 1979–80 Nursery Championship of the Northern Sheepdog Association.

At Cilycwm Brandsby, a happy son of his master's International Ken, romped to the starting post to score 105 of 110 points, the second highest score of the whole contest. It was unfortunate for the youngster that he met the experienced Tweed at his best, as did the third English competitor Thomas Longton's International Lassie from North Lancashire. Joined by her workmate Bess from the milk pastures of the Conder Valley at Lee End near Lancashire, Lassie did however earn her moments of glory in the Welsh mountains.

A strong, balanced collie bitch, Lassie, who liked to be in the action, and the younger Bess, who often liked her own way, and their master Thomas had much to live up to at Cilycwm. Thomas' father Tot won the 1976–77 'One Man and His Dog' contest with Jed and Kerry, mothers of Lassie and Bess. It was a responsibility which did not weigh heavily on the trio who together won the 1979 English Brace Championship at their first attempt. In their first trial to beat the Scottish representatives, Dick Fortune with Bill and Glen from Edinburgh, they had a marvellous trial of coordinated shepherding with both dogs doing their correct share of the work and answering the commands of their master immediately.

Lassie dropped two points on her outrun for cutting in, but once hold of their sheep the two bitches only lost another five points round the course, and Lassie finished her part of the job with a dominant mastery of an awkward sheep to win her pen. In the brace final they met the Welsh favourites, the 1978 International Brace champions Gwilym Jones with Queen and Glyn, and their sound work in every section of the trial again triumphed—only nine of 150 points being lost.

Ireland's champion at Cilycwm, David Brady's black-coated Meg from a mixed holding in the Antrim Hills became one of the stars of the show. Her almost feline grace as she appeared to glide over the ground in balanced control of her sheep, her statuesque concentration when waiting to shed, her placid intelligent eyes which reflected the pleasure in her work, marked a character which was totally appealing. When not at work she forgets all her authority and is kind and gentle in an enjoyable romp with the children.

Wholly devoted to David—when he went on a tour of New Zealand she went missing for two days—Meg was wisely bred. The daughter of John Richardson's International Driving Champion Sweep, she was of Scottish line from Fife and went to David when she was three years old in 1976. He handled her to two Irish caps in 1979 and 1980 and her growing skill at seven years old earned a clear 13½ points victory over Jim McConnell's mottled Dot from County Cork and Tim Flood's Irish Champion Flash in the Irish heat of the television trials.

Meg's controlled and delicate attitude to her sheep led Wyn Edwards' Bill by four points in the semi-final; but the England versus Scotland semi-final produced the drama. Alisdair Mundell's International Cap, the 6½-years-old son of Supreme International Champion Wiston Cap, did little wrong apart from faulty line of outrun to set a sound standard of 99½ of 110 points and when England's Tweed ran into trouble at the stream crossing when out of sight from his handler, Raymond MacPherson, Scotland appeared set for the final. But Tweed was not beaten though he was faced with quite a problem. One of his seven sheep had suddenly, and for no apparent reason, darted in among the trees of the river bank when crossing the stream. Tweed knew he could not leave it and yet was conscious of the 'come-on' whistles which he was hearing from Raymond who could not see that a sheep had left the small flock.

The hidden camera saw Tweed's dilemma: he pointed the missing sheep and knew he should retrieve it, yet had to hesitate to the insistent instructions of his master to bring on the small flock. The wise dog knew it was wrong to leave the single sheep. It was also wrong to disobey his master's instructions. Reluctantly he turned to the six sheep and drove them into sight of his master. It was then that Raymond saw the cause for Tweed's apparent lethargy in bringing the sheep and as he did so the straying ewe, suddenly fearful of losing company, came into sight from between the trees.

It was a time for quick decision. Raymond knew that instinct would draw the single sheep back to the group. Tweed knew it too. Raymond let nature take its

Right *Out in the open field the link between the producer and Eric Halsall and Phil Drabble (right) is stage manager, Keith Hatton—with the sound technician in the foreground.*

The singles finalists in Bala, 1981—Stuart Davidson and Ron Bailey—admire the BBC trophy.

course; Tweed stopped still on his feet so as not to interfere. It was a piece of good stocksmanship which solved a disastrous situation and averted certain trials defeat. The temporarily 'lost sheep' cost them seven points on the judges' book for, however unfortunate, it was a major slip but the clever retrieval of the situation kept them in competition. With the pressure on as the points gap between himself and Alisdair's Cap had dramatically narrowed to 2½, Tweed moved in behind the seven sheep and, head low, eyes burning with concentration, his action purposeful and precise, and his will dominant, he dropped only another point in driving them to the shedding-ring. His shed of a single sheep was decisive, his penning faultless, and he had snatched victory by 1½ points.

Lesser collies and less experienced handlers would have faltered, shepherding faults growing on such a major set-back, but Tweed had reserve of wisdom and character to draw upon after years of shepherding the high fells and Raymond—who has implicit faith in the old dog—is never beaten until he has lost. Such a partnership makes life very difficult for their opponents on the trials fields yet their final against the less experienced David Brady and the loyal Meg was open to the last shedding test.

Though another classical trial had given the Cumbrian pair 104 of 110 points, David and Meg were on the way to beating them with only four points lost into the shedding-ring. Here, with the change of tempo from sweet flowing movement to sudden tense action, and nerves stretched to the extreme, everything suddenly went wrong. Possibly too eager, David asked Meg to come through at a half-chance and sheep erupted. Things went from bad to worse and when the shed was eventually accomplished nine of the ten points had been lost and with them the victory chance.

Stuart Davidson receives his television trophy from Ray Ollerenshaw, chairman of the International Sheep Dog Society, Bala, 1981.

And so Tweed gave Raymond MacPherson his complete 'set' of top trials victories, adding the Television Trophy to his National, Supreme Internatinal, and World titles. It was very apt for no man has greater respect for collie dogs. Farmer of towards 2,000 breeding ewes on 3,800 acres of peat hags, moss and heather moor rising to 2,000 feet in the Tindale Fells to the east of Carlisle, Raymond is wholly dependent on the herding skills of his dogs to make a living.

In a lifetime of farming in bleak and lonely places, he has come to know collie dogs better than most, yet he is 'constantly amazed at their ability in everyday work on the hill'. Such farming conditions as his require the basic qualities of the collie—power, courage, wisdom, and initiative. It is these qualities which Raymond demands of his dogs and it is these qualities, polished to precise perfection, which have brought his complete successes on the trials fields of the world.

When they fail, he—and his wife Margaret who is no mean handler herself—is his own biggest critic, accepting like all good handlers the degree of fault in himself. That they don't often fail is due to the care which Raymond takes in getting to know each of his dogs as an individual. His trials dog must have the finer basic characteristics and qualities, the right amount of power coupled with good nature, be well-balanced and always on its feet and ready for any eventuality.

Tweed is a good example. A strong, well-coupled, smooth-coated collie with black, white and tan markings, Tweed delights in the mastery of his craft. His style and approach to sheep is purposeful and commanding, his actions disciplined, his commitment total. Never happier than when at work, his purpose

One Man and His Dog BBC2 Television Trials at Rannerdale. Sept. 1979. Screened 1980.

SINGLES COMPETITION	Heats	Points	Semi-Finals	Points	Final	Points	WINNER
		Maximum: 100					
WALES							
Ivor Jones (St. Asaph)	SPOT	61					
Eurwyn Daniel (Ystradgynlais)	MEG	77	Glyn Jones. GEL 75	100			
Glyn Jones (Bodfari)	GEL	82			Bob Shennan. MIRK 87	100	Bob Shennan. MIRK
SCOTLAND							
David McTeir (Manor)	GARRY	85					
Donald MacDonald (Windyedge)	MIRK	84	Bob Shennan. MIRK 86				
Bob Shennan (Girvan)	MIRK	87					
ENGLAND							
Jean Bousfield (Cautley)	FLASH	76					
Michael Perrings (Giggleswick)	HOPE	72	Alan Foster. DART 81				
Alan Foster (Cartmel Fell)	DART	82			Martin O'Neill. RISP 66		
IRELAND							
William Watt (Omagh)	LAD	70					
Martin O'Neill (Summerhill)	RISP	81	Martin O'Neill. RISP 82				
Lyn McKee (Banbridge)	MAX	80					

Judged by: Gordon Rogerson (Chathill): Alan Jones (Pontllyfni): John Templeton (Fenwick): BBC Producer: Ian W.B. Smith.

BRACE COMPETITION		Points	Final	Points	WINNER
		Maximum 140			
WALES					
Glyn Jones (Bodfari)	GEL & BRACKEN	129	Glyn Jones. GEL & BRACKEN 119	140	
SCOTLAND					Glyn Jones. GEL & BRACKEN
Donald MacDonald (Windyedge)	MIRK & GAEL	116			
ENGLAND					
George Hutton (Threlkeld)	NIP & ROY	125	George Hutton. NIP & ROY 109		
IRELAND					
Martin O'Neill (Summerhill)	RISP & SCOTT	106			

in life is to carry out the wishes of his master and his value to the shepherding of sheep is beyond measure. Of ideal temperament and good manners, he shows his pleasure with a tail twitch which is contagious.

Raymond's first trials dog was Judy which he handled to victory in 1944 when he was eleven years old at his local trials at Newtonmore, for Raymond is a Highland Scot. Since Judy's victory and her second placing a fortnight later at Kincraig in the first flush of 'beginner's luck' as Raymond calls it, he has worked hard for his International reputation. Whilst farming in Scotland, in the Grampians and then at Dalangwell in Sutherland, he won a place in the Scottish International team three times and in 1957 he won the Scottish Brace title with Lark, a sister of the famous Whitehope Nap, and Bill.

In 1965 he moved to Tarn House at Hallbankgate near Brampton and had thus, under the rules of the International Sheep Dog Society, to change his 'nationality' and compete in the English National. He has since taken England and Britain to the top in competitive shepherding by winning the Supreme International Championship in 1975 and 1979, both times with the white-headed Zac, and winning both American World Championships, in 1973 with Nap, the black-coated winner of the 1971 English National, and in 1976 with Tweed, then six years old.

Equally applauded in America as in Britain, Raymond has judged regularly on the other side of the Atlantic and in 1980 was made an honorary citizen of Alabama. His greatest honour was to receive the MBE for services to British agriculture in the Queen's 1979 list. He is one of only nine men since 1906 to have

Phil Drabble and Eric Halsall at Rannerdale, 1979.

One Man and His Dog BBC2 Television Trials at Cilycwm. Sept. 1980. Screened 1981

SINGLES COMPETITION	Heats	Points	Semi-Finals	Points	Final	Points	WINNER
	Maximum: 110						
SCOTLAND							
Sandy McMorran (Yetholm)	SCOTT	100					
Alasdair Mundell (Toward)	CAP	101	Alasdair Mundell. CAP 99½				
Dick Fortune (Edinburgh)	BILL	100½			Raymond MacPherson. TWEED 104	110	Raymond MacPherson. TWEED
ENGLAND							
Raymond MacPherson (Hallbankgate)	TWEED	107	Raymond MacPherson. TWEED 101	110			
Thomas Longton (Quernmore)	LASSIE	97					
Allan Heaton (Catterick)	BRANDSBY	105					
WALES							
Gwilym Jones (Brechfa)	QUEEN	102	Wyn Edwards. BILL 97				
Evan Evans (Llanafan)	GLEN	101			David Brady. MEG 97		
Wyn Edwards (Ruthin)	BILL	103					
IRELAND							
Jim McConnell (Youghal)	DOT	87½	David Brady. MEG 101				
Tim Flood (Clonroche)	FLASH	85½					
David Brady (Ballyclare)	MEG	101					

Judged by: Ray Ollerenshaw (Derwent); Lyn McKee (Banbridge): BBC Producer: Ian W. B. Smith

BRACE COMPETITION	Points	Final	Points	WINNER
	Maximum: 150			
SCOTLAND				
Dick Fortune (Edinburgh)	BILL & GLEN 131	Thomas Longton. LASSIE & BESS 141	150	Thomas Longton. LASSIE & BESS.
ENGLAND				
Thomas Longton (Quernmore)	LASSIE & BESS 140			
WALES				
Gwilym Jones (Brechfa)	QUEEN & GLYN 135	Gwilym Jones. QUEEN & GLYN 136		
IRELAND				
Jim McConnell (Youghal)	DOT & NAN 121			

won the British Supreme Championship more than once. It was the champion Zac which Raymond planned should compete for him in the Cilycwm BBC2 trials but the clever rough-coated collie injured his leg. Tweed stepped in to give his master the unique honour of holding World, International, National, and Television Trophies.

And Tweed is no respector of national boundaries for he also holds in addition to his World and television titles, the 1980 English Driving Championship and the 1972 Welsh Driving title, the latter won when he was only two years old and with Alan Jones at Pontllyfni. Scottish bred, by Jim Wannon at Freuchie in Fife, Tweed is line-bred to John Gilchrist's champion Spot. Sired by the 1965 and 1966 Scottish Champion, his bloodline is back to Whitehope Nap, a power line which Raymond favours.

The Cilycwm trials were the start of the junior Television Championship and though we introduced it with just a little foreboding as to whether the 'youngsters' could cope under such exposure and pressure, it was perhaps my greatest sheepdog pleasure to be able to present the prize and say 'well done' to all of the four contestants, one from each country. All gave of their best and that was good

Pedigree of NELL (65799) 1973 Welsh National and 1973, 1974, 1978 Shepherds' Champion with Mel Page

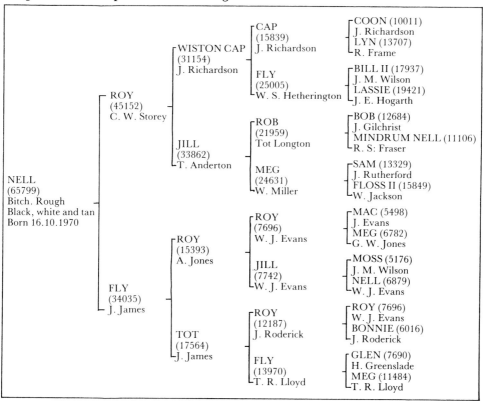

Left *Brace champions at Bala's television trials in 1981, Geoffrey Billingham with Trim and Jed from the Bowmont Valley in the Cheviots. Litter-sisters, Trim and Jed won the 1980 Scottish Brace Championship and the 1981 'Champion of Champions' contest at the Royal Welsh Show.*

Right *Eric Halsall and Phil Drabble discuss the points of an Old English Sheepdog at Bala, 1981.*

enough to have given their older contemporaries a run for their money although we removed the hill gather from the test.

David Bristow, seventeen-years-old assistant to his father at Rose Farm, Murton in the Vale of York, and the 3½-years-old Tweed gave England the 'hat-trick' of trophies. With that 'feeling for sheep' and experienced in nursery trials, and no stranger to the open events, David handled the clever dog to the immaculate total of 108 of 110 points. A top class trial by any standard, the victory hinged on Tweed's dominance of a particularly awkward ewe on the fetch.

Willie Welsh from Lanarkshire, eighteen-years-old nephew of Scotland's International handler of the same name, dropped six points in his driving but worked the handsome 5½-years-old Craig to second placing. Confident and competent in her handling of the cool-natured Gel II who 'reads sheep better than me', nineteen-years-old Ceri Jones, 'general dogsbody' and helpmate—and most efficient pupil—to her father Glyn Jones at Bwlch Isaf, Bodfari, was just another point down in third place, and sixteen-years-old Gordon Watt from County Tyrone, who has represented Ireland in International competition with the clever five-years-old Chum, slipped the cross-drive hurdle after a great drive-away.

In September 1981 'One Man and His Dog' went back to Wales, to Bala in North Wales where sheepdog history had been made over 100 years earlier by the holding of the first-ever sheepdog trials. We were to stage the first televised trials in Bala and there to greet us and to become the perfect host was Robin Price, the great-grandson of the man who had started it all. Robin and his father took part in the programme and gave the viewing public a first-hand account of the Bala scene.

On good fertile farmland of the Rhiwlas Estate where the Prices raised top-quality Welsh sheep and pedigree Welsh Black cattle the course was as testing as ever. The sheep were gathered from the top of a gradual and undulating, tree-dotted slope, turned at right-angles and driven away along a sheep-trod across the face of a steep pasture down to a stream in the valley. They were then pushed

across the water and up the opposite banking, then cross-driven along the top of the bank for some 200 yards before dropping back to the valley and through a field-gate up into the shedding-ring. It was a very practical piece of shepherding with immediate and close cooperation required between man and dog to manage strong Welsh Mountain sheep which were always prepared to test a dog's calibre yet ready to accept controlled authority.

It was always a delight, and many, many people told us so, to watch top-quality dogs at work in their natural environment. It was always a particular pleasure for me to meet dogs for which I had the highest regard.

Of this category was Nell, the wise old campaigner who had served Welsh shepherd Mel Page for eleven faithful years in his work with Speckled-face Halfbreds and beef cows at Brechfa in the Carmarthenshire hills. Nell was one of the collies I tended to get sentimental over—'tis possible you know—even hard-bitten farmers can get sentimental over a collie which has been their constant companion for years.

Nell was eight weeks old when Mel took her from a mating between Clarence Storey's Roy, son of Wiston Cap, and John James' Fly, daughter of Alan Jones' famous Supreme Roy; she started to work at eighteen months old and she had been faithful to her master and to her craft for ten years. Her life had been one of service and she was 'battle-scarred' with a damaged right ear and on her recreational outings she had won the Welsh National trials Championship and three Welsh Shepherds' Championships. She was at Bala to run in the brace contest with her daughter Fly with whom she had won the 1980 National Brace title. I had seen her at work many times and come to recognise her strong and forceful yet controlled and persuasive character which manipulated stock to their ease and I borrowed her from my old friend to partner me in the opening title shots of that Bala television series and I was the one who was proud to walk with her.

As a fitting gesture to the historical aura of Bala, Wales started the programme,

One Man and His Dog BBC2 Television Trials at Rhiwlas, Bala. Sept. 1981. Screened 1982

SINGLES COMPETITION	Heats	Points	Semi-Finals	Points	Final	Points	WINNER
	Maximum: 110			110		110	
WALES							
Robert Pritchard (Pwllheli)	SCOT	82					
Eifion Owen (Penygroes)	JESS	94	Eifion Owen. JESS 96				
Mel Page (Brechfa)	CAP	90			Ron Bailey. SPOT 95		
ENGLAND							
Ron Bailey (Ponteland)	SPOT	102	Ron Bailey. SPOT 97				Stuart Davidson. BEN.
Harry Huddleston (Arkholme)	CAP	96					
Gerald Hawkins (Brackley)	TRIM	77					
IRELAND							
William Murphy (Tallaght)	ALBERT	81	Arthur Mawhinney. CINDY 96				
David Brady (Ballyclare)	MEG	100			Stuart Davidson. BEN 105		
Arthur Mawhinney (Ladyhill)	CINDY	101					
SCOTLAND							
Stuart Davidson (Sandbank)	BEN	100	Stuart Davidson. BEN 106				
Geoffrey Billingham (Yetholm)	JED	95					
Tom Watson (Lauder)	JEN	99					

Judged by: W.J. Jones (Llanfair); Peter Hetherington (Girvan); BBC Producer: Ian W.B. Smith.

BRACE COMPETITION	Heats	Points	Final	Points	WINNER
	Maximum	150		150	
WALES					
Mel Page (Brechfa)	NELL & FLY	140	Mel Page. NELL & FLY 137		
ENGLAND					Geoffrey Billingham. JED & TRIM.
Ron Bailey (Ponteland)	SPOT & ED	121			
IRELAND			Geoffrey Billingham. JED & TRIM 140		
William Murphy (Tallaght)	ALBERT & ROY	Ret			
SCOTLAND					
Geoffrey Billingham (Yetholm)	JED & TRIM	120			

and their heat winner, Eifion Owen's 9½-years-old Jess from Snowdonia and fourth in the 1980 Bala Supreme Championship, set Welsh minds brimming with confidence for the inter-country contest to come. Jess, a prick-eared daughter of Wiston Cap, was just that bit better—four points in total—in every stage of her work than Mel Page's three-years-old Cap, a smooth-coated son of old Nell.

With Robert Pritchard who was in his sixtieth year of trials competition since winning his first novice trial at the age of fourteen, the Welsh International Scot was not at all happy on his gather and pushed too fast round the course. Good sound work from a northern dog, Ron Bailey's tricolour Spot from the Northumberland College of Agriculture, beat Harry Huddleston's thrice-capped Cap from the Lune Valley and Gerald Hawkins' 1979 Shepherds' Champion Trim fromBrackley in Northants to lead England.

The Irish heat saw the surprise downfall of the previous series' great favourite David Brady's black-coated Meg by an equally eye-catching bitch from the same county of Antrim. By a single point picked up in the close work, Arthur Mawhinney's fox-like Cindy, a trim little red-coated bitch from Ladyhill went to the top. William Murphy, known for his ploughing competition skills in Eire, had his work cut out to hold back the keenness of his Albert dog who was far too strong.

When Scotland ran in a windstorm we watched Stuart Davidson from Loch Fyne-side in Argyll quietly handle the strong working Ben, Scottish National Champion in 1980, in what could almost be described as an over-cautious run as though he was feeling his way round the course, gentling the sheep to his way and a one-point lead over Tom Watson's Supreme Champion Jen from the Lammermuirs. Stuart and Ben were to benefit from their exploratory method later in the contest. Scotland's third representative, Geoffrey Billingham's prick-eared Jed from the Cheviots did a good job of work too fast.

When Wales with the medium-coated tricolour Jess under former Welsh guardsman Eifion Owen and England's six-years-old Spot, a placid dog of quiet authority with Ron Bailey, came together in the first semi-final the decision could not have been closer, judges Bill Jones, the Welsh president of the ISDS, and Peter Hetherington, Scottish International, preferring Spot by one point after Jess had started badly though she gathered her composure for a thrilling finish.

Scotland's Ben cleverly remembered the faults of his earlier trial and reached near-perfection in the second semi-final with Stuart Davidson guiding his route over the demanding course and countering his earlier mistakes with good handling. He lost only four of 110 points and the Irish Cindy was unlucky to contest the smooth-coated dog on that form for her own showing was worthy of better things. A great little character with a heart like a lion, Cindy under Arthur Mawhinney was determined to make it a contest and she faced the Welsh ewes with calm confidence. Only when they slipped her down the hedgeside on the drive-away was she beaten. Her efforts brought instant stardom for all the world loves a game loser and Cindy ran into everyone's heart. A granddaughter of Wiston Cap and registered by the ISDS on merit, Cindy enjoyed work with 200 crossbred ewes and milk and beef cows on a mixed holding in Antrim.

Stuart's Ben was equally dominant in the final. In control from the lift, he got the pace of work absolutely right over each of the differing sections of the trial, never allowing his sheep to stop to question his authority, and his method was so relaxed yet dominant that the ewes never offered to rebel. With what was almost a flourish of triumph he shed with copybook precision and penning was little more than a formality. Devoted to Stuart Davidson in his management of 1,000 ewes and 150 store cows in Scotland, Ben showed the true potential of the modern working dog at the right time—in front of a vast audience of non-technical viewers—and proved himself one of the best of collies ever to grace the competition field.

Good as Ben was, he had no easy victory in the final and Ron Bailey's dependable Spot balanced his sheep better at the end of his outrun and was in front on the pointings at the start of the driving work. Only when his pacing went wrong on the cross-drive and he turned the sheep too soon did his fortunes falter and a mix-up in shedding saw the end of a brave attempt to match the Scottish winner.

The brace contest which entailed some steep and tricky downhill work where sheep had to be 'nursed' to prevent bolting got off to a poor start with William Murphy's Irish-bred Albert too exuberant for his older partner and half-brother, the eight-years-old Roy, so that they never really got together and the 67-years-old Irishman from the Wicklow mountains wisely retired to concede victory to Geoffrey Billingham's handsome litter-sisters Trim and Jed, capable ten-year-olds from a South Country Cheviot flock in the Bowmont Valley of Roxburghshire.

Blending right at the start into the partnership which brings doubles' success with each collie doing his fair share of the work, Mel Page's mother and daughter, Nell and Fly, were faultless in outrunning and lift and were absolutely in charge down the steep pasture where controlled restraint was so vital to pace the sheep correctly. Points were lost for line on fetch and drive and minor blemishes which finally added to ten but over such a course their partnership was grand with Nell setting the example yet never interfering with her three-years-old daughter's responsibilities. Only once was the youngster out of touch and she took the responsibility of shedding the sheep and penned her packet cleanly. Out of Nell, Fly was a rather shy, good-tempered daughter of Watkins' Robbie, the son of the wise mating of Barbara Carpenter's Brocken Robbie and Watkins' Fleece.

Against the Welsh trio England's Ron Bailey with Spot and Ed, a six-years-old son of Fred Coward's Ken, had everything right at the start, then went badly wrong on the driving.

Final day came cold and a little breezy with both handlers, Mel Page for Wales and Geoffrey Billingham for Scotland, knowing that hard practical shepherding would win the day, for the course was really too exacting for the text-book stuff. Page's Nell didn't really agree and with her daughter of similar mind, they came down the field and were half-way through the driving test with only two points marked against them. Then Fly slipped badly. She came too far down the cross-drive banking, lost sight of the sheep and in something of a panic darted blindly

Rannerdale 1979. Phil Drabble, Eric Halsall and Ian Smith.

back to where she thought they were. She was too quick and came up in front of the sheep and the rhythm erupted.

Unabashed at her daughter's folly, Nell kept coolly to her job, though, momentarily frightened, the sheep bolted and too many points were lost before she could restore order. The shedding and the penning of both collies was faultless but the damage had been done with a total of thirteen points lost.

Nevertheless the final still had to be won for though faultless on their outrunning, Geoffrey Billingham's Trim and Jed, as reliable a pair of collies in the whole of Britain, came much too fast down the slope and five points had gone before the driving was started. It made for a thrilling contest, won in the end by three points after some first-class partnership driving from the Scottish pair.

Strong and fit, medium-sized and rough black and white coated, with energy that belied their ten years of age, Trim and Jed were an invaluable pair of helpmates for Geoffrey Billingham in his shepherding of the third oldest flock of South Country Cheviot sheep in Scotland at Swindon near Yetholm in the Borders. Daily they were on the 1,400 feet high sheepruns of Cheviot, their unbounded energy coming from an inbred vigour, and from the care and devotion of a master who knew their worth to his profession.

Home-bred in December 1971, they inherited the power and wisdom of their mother Meg whom Geoffrey ran in the English team when he was shepherding in County Durham in 1969. In 1980 Jed and Trim won the Scottish Brace Championship at Thornhill and in 1975 and 1981 were reserve champions.

Matrons by age alone, their fame had spread to New Zealand to where their sons had gone, and Geoffrey's wife Vivien, as capable as her husband in trials, had won with Jed's son Garry.

Scotland thus won both Singles and Brace trophies in the 1981 series of 'One Man and His Dog'—and just failed in the junior contest when twenty-years-old Meirion Jones and his clever 4½-years-old tricolour Jill from Llechwedd near Conway scored a single point victory over the home-bred Mirk with Alan Wilkie, a twenty-years-old trainee shepherd on the Dunecht Estate near Aberdeen. The youngest handler, sixteen-years-old Richard Harrison from Tailbert, Shap, in Cumbria and his smooth-coated Spy worked difficult sheep for third marking; and eighteen-years-old John Murphy and Lassie, a granddaughter of Wiston Cap, from the shores of Lough Neagh in Antrim were only another point down.

The whole contest was noteworthy for the general skill of the young handlers and the quality of their collies over an extremely difficult course. Meirion Jones, who always wears a smile, and Jill, who worships him, showed extraordinary strength of character and temperament when on television again to my commentary in March 1982 they herded the most stubborn Jacob lambs over the tiny Blue Peter garden at the BBC's Wood Lane studios in London.

Leaving behind the white-faced ewes of the Welsh mountains on my way up to Ruthin, I considered that the Bala site had given us all the contrasts of terrain and weather conditions to test the wisdom, temperament, and adaptability of the modern collie.

Through the many series of 'One Man and His Dog' and its varying trials Britain's collies had brought pleasure to millions of people. They had shown the 'man in the street' the importance of their role in the agricultural economy of the United Kingdom—their vital contribution to the management of farmstock in the matter-of-fact business of producing food and clothing for the nation.

Appendix 1

The Supreme Champions

The Supreme Championship of the International Sheep Dog Society is the highest accolade in the world of sheepdogs. It is awarded to the winner of the Society's annual Championship after a revealing process of elimination and it is a very great collie indeed which takes it. (The numbers in brackets are the Stud Book numbers of the International Sheep Dog Society.)

1906 Richard Sandilands (South Queensferry), Don (11)
1907 William Wallace (Otterburn), Moss (22)
1908 James Scott (Ancrum), Kep (13)
1909 James Scott (Ancrum), Kep (13)
1910 Adam Telfer (Cambo), Sweep (21)
1911 Thomas Armstrong (Otterburn), Don (17)
1912 Thomas Armstrong (Otterburn), Sweep (21)
1913 T. P. Brown (Oxton), Lad (19)
1914 Thomas Armstrong (Otterburn), Don (17)
1915–1918 Trials not held
1919 Walter Telfer (Morpeth), Midge (152)
1920 S. E. Batty (Sheffield), Hemp (307)
1921 Adam Telfer (Stamfordham), Haig (252)
1922 William Wallace (Otterburn), Meg (306)
1923 George P. Brown (Oxton), Spot (308)
1924 Thomas Roberts (Corwen), Jaff (379)
1925 Alex Millar (Newmilns), Spot (303)
1926 Mark Hayton (Otley), Glen (698)
1927 J. B. Bagshaw (Blyth), Lad (305)
1928 J. M. Wilson (Moffat), Fly (824)
1929 S. E. Batty (Worksop), Corby (338)
1930 J. M. Wilson (Moffat), Craig (1048)
1931 John Thorp (Derwent), Jess (1007)
1932 W. B. Telfer (Cambo), Queen (533)
1933 George Whiting (Aberdare), Chip (672)
1934 J. M. Wilson (Moffat), Roy (1665)
1935 John Jones (Corwen), Jaff (2199)
1936 J.M. Wilson (Innerleithen), Roy (1665)
1937 J. M. Wilson (Innerleithen), Roy (1665)
1938 W. J. Wallace (Otterburn), Jed (1492)
1939–1945 Trials not held
1946 J. M. Wilson (Innerleithen), Glen (3940)
1947 John Gilchrist (Haddington), Spot (3624)
1948 J. M. Wilson (Innerleithen), Glen (3940)
1949 David William Daniel (Ystradgynlais), Chip (4924)

1950 J. M. Wilson (Innerleithen), Mirk (4438)
1951 Ashton Priestley (Bamford), Pat (4203)
1952 David William Daniel (Ystradgynlais), Chip (4924)
1953 W. J. Evans (Magor), Roy (7696)
1954 Jack McDonald (Lauder), Mirk (5444)
1955 J. M. Wilson (Innerleithen), Bill (9040)
1956 G. R. Redpath (Jedburgh), Moss (6805)
1957 J. H. Holliday (Pateley Bridge), Moss (11029)
1958 W. J. Evans (Tidenham), Tweed (9601)
1959 Meirion Jones (Llandrillo), Ben (13879)
1960 Eurwyn Daniel (Ystradgynlais), Ken (13306)
1961 Alan Jones (Pontllyfni), Roy (15393)
1962 A. T. Lloyd (Builth Wells), Garry (17690)
1963 H. J. Worthington (Mardy), Juno (17815)
1964 Leslie Suter (Cross Keys), Craig (15445)
1965 John Richardson (Lyne), Wiston Cap (31154)
1966 Tim Longton (Quernmore), Ken (17166)
1967 Thomson McKnight (Canonbie), Gael (14463)
1968 Llyr Evans (Whittlebury), Bosworth Coon (34186)
1969 Harry Huddleston (Arkholme), Bett (40428)
1970 David McTeir (Manor), Wiston Bill (36391)
1971 John Murray (Sanquhar), Glen (47241)
1972 John Templeton (Fenwick), Cap (50543)
1973 Glyn Jones (Bodfari), Gel (63023)
1974 Gwyn Jones (Penmachno), Bill (51654)
1975 Raymond MacPherson (Hallbankgate), Zac (66166)
1976 Gwyn Jones (Penmachno), Shep (73360)
1977 John R. Thomas (Llandovery), Craig (59425)
1978 Robert Shennan (Turnberry), Mirk (67512)
1979 Raymond MacPherson (Hallbankgate), Zac (66166)
1980 Tom Watson (Lauder), Jen (93965)
1981 Wyn Edwards (Ruthin), Bill (78263)

Appendix 2

The National Champions

The highest award which any of the four countries of England, Scotland, Wales, and Ireland (which comprise the International Sheep Dog Society) can award to their top collie is the National Championship. (The numbers in brackets are the Stud Book numbers of the International Sheep Dog Society.)

England—National Championship
1922 Ernest Priestley (Hathersage), Moss (233)
1923 Ernest Priestley (Hathersage), Moss (233)
1924 A. Telfer (Stamfordham), Haig (252)
1925 J. B. Bagshaw (Blyth), Lad (305)
1926 W. Telfer (Cambo), Queen (533)
1927 W. Telfer (Cambo), Queen (533)
1928 W. B. Bagshaw (Blyth), Jess (818)
1929 W. Telfer (Cambo), Queen (533)
1930 Ernest Priestley (Hathersage), Hemp (1006)
1931 J. B. Bagshaw (Blyth), Moss (569)
1932 W. B. Bagshaw (Worksop), Jess (818)
1933 W. J. Wallace (Otterburn), Jed (1492)
1934 A. G. Liddle (Darley), Fly (1764)
1935 J. M. Renwick (Alston), Kep (1654)
1936 A. G. Liddle (Darley), Fly (1764)
1937 Mark Hayton (Otley), Pat (2219)
1938 J. M. Renwick (Alston), Kep (1654)
1939 J. M. Renwick (Alston), Bet (2398)
1940–1945 Trials not held
1946 W. B. Bagshaw (Worksop), Mac (4418)
1947 Arthur Hayton (Otley), Barney (4365)
1948 J. H. Thorpe (Nuneaton), Fan (4424)
1949 Tim Longton Snr (Quernmore), Dot (4844)
1950 Tot Longton (Quernmore), Mossie (6235)
1951 J. H. Holliday (Pateley Bridge), Roy (5406)
1952 Cecil Holmes (Ripponden), Lad (4453)
1953 J. K. Gorst (Wennington), Bet (6260)
1954 J. H. Denniff (Dore), Sweep (5594)
1955 Ashton Priestley (Bamford), Jim (10071)
1956 Tot Longton (Quernmore), Mossie (6235)
1957 J. K. Gorst (Wennington), Queen (8810)
1958 W. J. Evans (Tidenham), Moss (7971)
1959 W. J. Evans (Tidenham), Tweed (9601)
1960 Ashton Priestley (Bamford), Sweep (11115)
1961 Wilson Hardisty (Cautley), Jim (12967)
1962 W. J. Evans (Tidenham), Don (13392)
1963 W. J. Evans (Tidenham), Ben (12953)
1964 Fred Morgan (Pershore), Moss (14902)
1965 Tim Longton (Quernmore), Snip (16879)

1966 Tim Longton (Quernmore), Ken (17166)
1967 Miles Cook (Kildale), Maid (28779)
1968 J. H. Holliday (Pateley Bridge), Moss (28996)
1969 Llyr Evans (Whittlebury), Bosworth Coon (34186)
1970 Tim Longton (Quernmore), Glen (48637)
1971 Raymond MacPherson (Hallbankgate), Nap (43986)
1972 Harry Huddleston (Brookhouse), Udale Sim (52690)
1973 Eric Elliott (Ashopton), Bill (39521)
1974 Tim Longton (Quernmore), Roy (54175)
1975 John James (Kingsland), Mirk (68102)
1976 Llyr Evans (Whittlebury), Chip (62102)
1977 Jean Hardisty (Cautley), Flash (79000)
1978 Ken Brehmer (Tarset), Ben (92094)
1979 Harold Loates (Retford), Wiston Jill (79096)
1980 Alan Foster (Cartmel Fell), Dart (92163)
1981 Tim Longton (Quernmore), Tweed (96630)

Scotland—National Championship
1922 Alex Millar (Darvel), Spot (303)
1923 George P. Brown (Oxton), Spot (308)
1924 Alex Millar (Newmilns), Tot (155)
1925 Alex Millar (Newmilns), Spot (303)
1926 Alex Millar (Newmilns), Spot (303)
1927 Alex Millar (Newmilns), Spot (303)
1928 Alex Millar (Newmilns), Mirk (836)
1929 Alex Millar (Newmilns), Mirk (836)
1930 Alex Millar (Newmilns), Ben (891)
1931 J. M. Wilson (Moffat), Craig (1048)
1932 J. M. Wilson (Moffat), Craig (1048)
1933 J. M. Wilson (Moffat), Nickey (1823)
1934 Alex Millar (Newmilns), Ken (1477)
1935 J. M. Wilson (Innerleithen), Nell (1627)
1936 J. M. Wilson (Innerleithen), Nell (1627)
1937 J. M. Wilson (Innerleithen), Roy (1665)
1938 David Murray (Peebles), Sweep (1962)
1939 J. M. Wilson (Innerleithen), Nell (1627)
1940–1945 Trials not held

1946 J. M. Wilson (Innerleithen), Glen (3940)
1947 J. R. Millar (Dalry), Drift (4380)
1948 W. J. Hislop (Gordon), Sweep (3834)
1949 J. R. Millar (Dalry), Ben (4391)
1950 J. M. Wilson (Innerleithen), Mirk (4438)
1951 J. M. Wilson (Innerleithen), Tib (6903)
1952 David Murray (Peebles), Vic (4368)
1953 J. R. Millar (Dalry), Tam (7032)
1954 W. R. Little (Walkerburn), Spot (6775)
1955 J. M. Wilson (Innerleithen), Whitehope Nap (8685)
1956 T. T. Bonella (Kinross), Moss (6805)
1957 John Templeton (Mauchline), Roy (8993)
1958 W. Goodfellow (Newcastleton), Laddie (8049)
1959 W. J. Hislop (Gordon), Sweep (13146)
1960 R. Short (Duns), Nell (12743)
1961 W. J. Hislop (Gordon), Jim (12572)
1962 T. T. Bonella (Kinross), Ben (16449)
1963 J. Hogarth (Selkirk), Laddie (13204)
1964 Thomson McKnight (Canonbie), Gael (14463)
1965 John Gilchrist (Midlothian), Spot (24981)
1966 John Gilchrist (Midlothian), Spot (24981)
1967 A.M. McMillan (Dalrymple), Jock (21994)
1968 J. M. C. Kerr (Maybole), Queen (24078)
1969 J. R. Millar (Dalry), Ken (18754)
1970 Peter Hetherington (Girvan), Nell (53708)
1971 Thomson McKnight (Canonbie), Mirk (28776)
1972 David McTeir (Manor), Ben (56646)
1973 William Cormack (Wester Dunnet), June (59734)
1974 Donald McDonald (Windyedge), Glen (62253)
1975 John Richardson (Duns), Mirk (52844)
1976 David Shennan (Girvan), Meg (63230)
1977 Willie Rae (Corsock), Connie (84203)
1978 David Shennan (Girvan), Nan (85606)
1979 Robert Shennan (Girvan), Mirk (67512)
1980 Stuart Davidson (Sandbank), Ben (88284)
1981 Harford Logan (Duror), Star (109497)

Wales—National Championship
1922 John Pritchard (Pwllheli), Laddie (406)
1923 Thomas Roberts (Corwen), Jaff (379)
1924 Thomas Roberts (Corwen), Jaff (379)
1925 E. Pritchard (Pwllheli), Juno (618)
1926 Edward Morris (Bethesda), Spot (615)
1927 Edward Morris (Bethesda), Spot (615)
1928 R. J. Hughes (Anglesey), Laddie (867)
1929 L. J. Humphreys (Towyn), Toss (464)
1930 L. J. Humphreys (Towyn), Toss (464)
1931 L. J. Humphreys (Towyn), Lad (476)
1932 John Jones (Trawsfynydd), Blackie (1635)
1933 L. J. Humphreys (Towyn), Moss (2206)
1934 L. J. Humphreys (Towyn), Lad (990)
1935 John Jones (Trawsfynydd), Fly (1574)
1936 D. W. Davies (Pontypridd), Nett (989)
1937 R. H. Williams (St Asaph), Jaff (2598)
1938 W. F. Miles (Treharris), Kate (2601)
1939 L. J. Humphreys (Towyn), Moss (2206)
1940–1945 Trials not held
1946 R. J. Hughes (Anglesey), Jaff (4313)

1947 R. O. Williams (Trescawen), Lad (5051)
1948 R. J. Hughes (Anglesey), Jaff (4313)
1949 W. J. Evans (Magor), Sweep (4204)
1950 W. J. Harris (Ynysybwl), Sweep (5096)
1951 Griff Pugh (Sealand), Don (6644)
1952 W. F. Miles (Treharris), Wally (4361)
1953 Griff Pugh (Sealand), Laddie (4362)
1954 G. J. Owen (Sennybridge), Nell (8739)
1955 Harry Greenslade (Cwmcarn), Glen (7690)
1956 Harry Greenslade (Cwmcarn), Glen (7690)
1957 W. J. Thomas (Brynmawr), Glen (7395)
1958 W. Jones (Llanferres), Ben (11401)
1959 Alan Jones (Pontllyfni), Roy (15393)
1960 W. J. Thomas (Brynmawr), Glen (7395)
1961 Alan Jones (Pontllyfni), Roy (15393)
1962 Alan Jones (Pontllyfni), Glen (17251)
1963 Selwyn Jones (Ffestiniog), Vicky (15968)
1964 E. N. Davies (Yspytty), Gwen (19455)
1965 Wyn Edwards (Ruthin), Nip (17278)
1966 W. H. Goodwin (Llandyrnog), Nap (18186)
1967 H. J. Worthington (Mardy), Juno (17815)
1968 J. M. Baker (Cowbridge), Roy (38227)
1969 Leslie Suter (Cross Keys), Sally (46413)
1970 Mel Page (Llangadog), Sweep (23470)
1971 Alan Jones (Pontllyfni), Lad (44675)
1972 R. E. Nicholls (Llananno), Moss (41957)
1973 Mel Page (Brechfa), Nell (65799)
1974 A. Grant Jones (Bryncroes), Tos (61152)
1975 H. J. Worthington (Mardy), Lad (54209)
1976 Alan Jones (Pontllyfni), Craig (72737)
1977 John Thomas (Llandovery), Craig (59425)
1978 Norman Davies (Penmachno), Cymro (82447)
1979 Meirion Jones (Pwllglas), Craig (67343)
1980 Glyn Jones (Bodfari), Bwlch Taff (113243)
1981 Glyn Jones (Bodfari), Bwlch Taff (113243)

Ireland—National Championship
1961 J. W. L. McKee (Hillsborough), Snip (10677)
1962 Lionel Pennefather (Ardmore), Bess (17145)
1963 J. W. L. McKee (Dromore), Whitehope Corrie (13706)
1964 James Brady (Ballynure), Buff (23069)
1965 J. F. Mullen (Swatragh), Nell (16949)
1966 Lionel Pennefather (Ardmore), Bess (17145)
1967 James Brady (Ballynure), Buff (23069)
1968 Harford Logan (Saintfield), Moy (42363)
1969 Harford Logan (Saintfield), Cap (24328)
1970 James Brady (Ballynure), Gyp (33128)
1971 J. J. McSwiggan (Gortiscastle), Rock (36024)
1972 James Brady (Ballyboley), Bosworth Jim (52007)
1973 James Brady (Ballyboley), Bosworth Jim (52007)
1974 Harford Logan (Millisle), Jim (67676)
1975 Tim Flood (Clonroche), Cosy (70560)
1976 Matthew Graham (Isle of Man), Gay (69947)
1977 Harford Logan (Millisle), Jim (67676)
1978 Tim Flood (Clonroche), Scott (57965)
1979 Tim Flood (Clonroche), Flash (106580)
1980 Harford Logan (Millisle), Sweep (87666)
1981 D. O'Sullivan (Clogheen), Nell (99019)

Appendix 3

Where to see trials

The list of sheepdog trials which are held in Britain is extensive and sometimes changeable, subject to both local and national conditions—such as a conflict of dates with the National and International trials—and it is not possible (or wise) to be adamant about the exact date of a trial from year to year.

The following list is as complete as it is possible to get—thanks to the interest of local officials in the various areas—but bear in mind that date-changes do take place though usually not to any great extent as traditional dates do count.

The open trials season generally runs from April to September when the competitions are for collies of every degree of ability, and the winter season is for nursery trials when young collies are blooded to competition. The International Sheep Dog Society, whose offices are at 64, St Loyes Street, Bedford, lists annual dates of local trials in its Newsletter as well as the major National and International events.

Ireland usually holds its National towards the end of July or early August, and the English, Scottish and Welsh Nationals take place in August, with the International in early September.

Local societies often change their dates so as not to clash with the major trials: and some societies hold a confined area competition on the previous evening to their open event.

April
First Saturday—Nelson Agricultural Society, Gisburn Park, Gisburn, near Clitheroe. Rising 250 yards gather of hill sheep in Parkland setting.
Second Saturday—Bodfari, near Denbigh. The first, and one of the most challenging trials in North Wales over a testing National-style course of 350 yards gather of Welsh Mountain hoggs in the Vale of Clwyd, North Wales.
Easter Monday—Littleborough Cricket Club, near Rochdale, Lancashire. Flat cricket-field course with limited distances to work hill sheep.
Third Saturday—Yorkshire Sheepdog Society (1950), Riddlesden Hall, near Keighley, Yorkshire. Novice Championship on extensive flat grassland by the River Aire on National-style layout.
Glasbury-on-Wye (1973), Wye valley, Welsh–English border. A good open 25-acre flat field at Castle

Farm, Boughrood. First trials of South Wales Association. Crossbred—Clun × Speckled-face shearlings on a 300 yards gather.
Last Saturday—Fylde Sheepdog Society (1966), Lancashire. 400 yards gather of hill hoggs over flat undulating grassland with National-style driving at Eaves Green Hall Farm, Goosnargh, near Preston. Top collies from England and Wales competing.

May
First week—Limited trial at *Dublin Spring Show.*
First Saturday—Amberley (1978) in Cirencester Park near Nailsworth, Gloucestershire. Three days of National-style trials over large level field in conjunction with Amberley Horse Show.
Tackley (1975), Oxford. National-style course of 300 yards gather on old ridge and furrow pasture at Field Barn Farm, Tackley, ten miles north of Oxford. Site of 1980 English National trials.
Marple Bridge, Cheshire. Testing course set on difficult sloping and undulating grassland on Cheshire–Derbyshire border.
Cilcain. West of Mold in the Clwydian Range in North Wales.
Neilston Agricultural Society, near Barrhead, south-west of Glasgow in Renfrewshire. Blackface hoggs on awkward little course.
Bank Holiday Monday—Boylestone (1976). Good site in South Derbyshire—west of Derby—with dogs running to cross a driveway and broken fence to work Mule gimmers over a flat area of 250 yards.
Thame. North of the Chiltern Hills in Oxfordshire.
Udimore at Court Lodge Farm near Rye in Sussex.
Fermoy. Blackwater country in County Cork, Eire.
Second Saturday—Yorkshire Sheepdog Society (1950). Open Championship at Riddlesden Hall, near Keighley, Yorkshire. Top quality National-style trials over extensive flat grassland by River Aire with qualifying tests in two fields and final contested by leading dogs on hill sheep.
Sussex in Eridge Park near Frant south of Royal Tunbridge Wells.
Felindre. A downhill fetch on a National-style course in The Teme Valley at Pantycarrigle Farm by B435 road on the Radnor–Shropshire border in Powys.

Second Sunday—Rickney, near Pevensey north of Eastbourne in Sussex.

Summerhill, south of Trim on good land in County Meath, Eire.

Third Saturday—Quernmore in the Conder Valley near Lancaster. Hill sheep worked over a good sized flat grassland course of National style. Usually held in conjunction with village sports.

Standean Sheepdog Society. 400 yards gather, 350 yards drive of Romney Halfbreds on the undulating South Downs at Patcham, Brighton in Sussex.

Cockermouth. A 300 yards uphill fetch of Swaledale hoggs over meadow ground at Prospect Farm, Setmurthy, in the Derwent Valley by Bassenthwaite Lake in Cumbria.

Humberside Agricultural Show. 300 yards gather and good driving of Mule hoggs on level grassland at the Racecourse Showfield at Beverley near Hull. Qualifying trials on Friday: Championship on Saturday.

Llaneglwys. Speckled-face hoggs in open and novice National-styles over a remote and steep course set in a field of the Eppynt Mountains in South Wales.

Dalrymple. Between Ayr and Maybole in Ayrshire.

Glenrothes. A good course—north of Kirkcaldy in Fife.

Third Sunday—Drewsteignton, between Okehampton and Exeter in Devon.

Fourth Week—Glascoed, north-east of Pontypool in South Wales.

Fourth Saturday—Sudbrooke (1956), Lincoln. National-style layout with maltese cross at Barfield Lane Farm.

Three Lochs near Kirkcowan in Wigtownshire.

Fourth Sunday—Manorhamilton, east of Sligo in north-west of Ireland.

Thomastown in the Nore Valley in County Kilkenny, Eire.

Guilsborough, Northants. 250 yards fetch to National style between Rugby and Northampton.

Seale Hayne. 400 yards outrunning at the Agricultural College, Newton Abbot in Devon.

Spring Bank Holiday—Bamford (1943) on the recreation ground—trials of repute and quality competition in the High Peak of Derbyshire in the area of the Ladybower Reservoirs.

Cropredy & District Sheepdog Association (1948), Whitfield, near Brackley in Northamptonshire. Good 300 yards National-style course with Half-bred theaves on permanent grass land by A43 road.

Cwm-Du at the foot of the Black Mountains in the Vale of Rhiangoll between Talgarth and Crickhowell.

Tuesday—Wetherby Agricultural Society (1840), North Yorkshire. In Wetherby Grange Park adjoining main A1 road midway between Leeds and Harrogate.

Killerton Park, National Trust, near Exeter in Devon.

Fifth (or last) Saturday—Penton Discussion Society (1950),

Cumbria. Trials of long standing over sound course on Cumbria–Scottish borderland with keen competition from English and Scottish collies.

Barnard Castle, County Durham. Northern Sheepdog Association's trials over flat confined course at Demesne's Fields.

Cornwood. 200 yards outrun at Torre Farm, north-east of Plymouth in Devon.

Kingsland. Good National-style course over undulating ground at Shirleath Farm, Kingsland, Leominster.

Cardiff. A long narrow course at Ty-Du Farm, Nelson.

Kinross in Loch Levan country at Balado Home Farm.

Strathendrick Show, Drymen, by Loch Lomond.

Lesmahagow Farmers' Show in Border Country south-west of Lanark.

Crosby, Marown, Isle of Man. Opposite Crosby Hotel on A1 road to Peel, 3½ miles north-west of Douglas.

Whiligh at Wadhurst on The Weald.

Coagh between Cookstown and Lough Neagh in Tyrone.

Fifth (or last) Sunday—Letterkenny in Donegal.

June

First Week—Woburn Abbey. Two-day trials in the Parkland at the Duke of Bedford's stately home near Bletchley, with championship decider by the leading dogs.

Limavady by Lough Foyle, east of Londonderry.

First Saturday—Holme Sheepdog Trials Association (1959), Deerplay Hill, near Burnley, Lancashire. One of the toughest trials in the North Country with gather of hill ewes over 520 yards of rough bog moor, climbing through 260 feet to 1,450 feet lift.

Nebo, east of Betws-y-Coed on B5113 in Cambrian Mountains of North Wales.

Llannefydd. National-type course of 375 yards uphill fetch of Welsh Halfbreds on northern slopes of Clwydyn Valley with panoramic views of the North Wales coast.

Henryd and Llechwedd (1949). Three-day event with Welsh Mountain ewes over pastureland course near Groessfford village, 1½ miles from Conway.

Peebles Junior Agricultural Club. Long narrow tree-dotted course by the river in Hay Lodge Park, Peebles.

Carsphairn Pastoral & Horticultural Society in The Glenkens north of New Galloway in Kirkcudbright.

Luss—'45 men and their dogs' at Rossdu on the banks of Loch Lomond.

Culter Unionist Association in Coulter Village by Culterallers south of Biggar in East Lanarkshire.

Assynt. Cheviot hoggs by Loch Assynt in the west of Sutherland.

Pettigoe by Lough Erne near Irvinestown in County Fermanagh, Ireland.

First Sunday—Clonroche in County Wexford, Eire.

Second Week—Andreas, Isle of Man. 300 yards gather of Suffolk Halfbreds on the sports-field in the northern Sheading of Ayre.
Ballymena in Antrim, Ireland.
Second Saturday—Littleborough High School, near Rochdale, Lancashire. Lonk ewes over adequate National course on flat playing field.
Trawden Sheepdog Society, near Colne, Lancashire. National layout on high rough grassland above village in Forest of Trawden on the fringe of the Bronte country.
Roman Wall at Haltwhistle in Northumberland.
Lowgill, near Lancaster. Level 200 yards gather of Country-bred ewes over grass land to National-style at village show in Tatham Fells of North Lancashire.
Robertsbridge at McKays Fruit Farm north of Battle in Sussex.
Trefil. A searching National test with 650 yards gather on open moutain moorland just north of the Heads of the Valleys in Gwent, South Wales.
Bontuchel (1947), Ruthin. Leading Welsh competition in the Vale of Clwyd.
Monymusk Sheepdog Trials Association in the Don Valley, Aberdeen.
Gifford at Yester Main Farm by the Lammermuir Hills in East Lothian.
Lochgoilhead Sheep Dog Trials Association (1977). Gather of Blackface hoggs over 350 yards of undulating pasture at Drimsynie Park in the sea-loch country of Argyll.
Second Sunday—Northampton Y.F.C. at Castle Ashby. Big National-style course in fine setting of parkland off A428 Northampton–Bedford road.
Northern Sheepdog Association at Barningham Park on the Durham–North Yorkshire border.
Peebles invitation trials at Hay Lodge Park, Peebles.
Burnfoot, Mallow in County Cork, Eire.
Castlederg by the B72 road in County Tyrone, Northern Ireland.
Lifford, north-west of Strabane in Donegal.
Third Week—Moorcook. Renowned fellside test for a prestigious championship over open and rough course in the remote and beautiful moorlands of Upper Garsdale between Hawes in Wensleydale and Sedbergh in Lunesdale.
Hiraethog, Bryn Trillyn,.Welsh Mountain sheep over testing course in three fields at the Sportsmans Arms by A543 in Clwyd.
Kildonan at Brodick, Isle of Arran.
Machrie. Blackface gimmers on the west of Arran.
Third Saturday—Harden Moss Sheepdog Trials Association (1908). Famous Yorkshire trials held over high grassland above Holmfirth near Huddersfield to less than National size layout. Large spectator interest with attractions arranged to cater. Hill ewes often tricky.
Shap Hound Trailing Club, Shap, Cumbria. Testing conditions on rough open ground with uphill gather.

Alston Moor Sheepdog Trials Association (1945), Alston, Cumbria. Top North Country competition on flat playing fields land of 250 yards outrun among the fells.
Winton, Kirkby Stephen. Good trials on Swaledales at The Raines on the Cumbrian–Durham border.
Westward Sports Committee. Trials over 300 yards of uphill gather on Swaledale sheep as part of village sports day, by the Roman Fort of Olenacvm near Wigton in Cumbria.
Llanbedr-Dyffryn-Clwyd, Ruthin. Popular four classes of trials over Plas Isa farmland, with gymkhana attractions.
Kinlochard by Loch Ard west of Aberfoyle in the Trossachs.
City of Glasgow invitation trials between leading Scottish, English, and Welsh collies on Blackface hoggs in Bellahouston Park.
Tomatin. Blackfaces at Corrybrough in Strath Dearn, Inverness-shire.
Third Sunday—Allendale Agricultural Society. National-sized course over high ground by Allendale Common on Northumberland–Durham border. Northumberland League.
Arpinge on the North Downs near Folkestone.
Llanrhaeadr. Welsh crossbred sheep on a big sloping field near Denbigh in the Vale of Clwyd.
Leamybrien in County Waterford, Eire.
Mahon Bridge, Ireland.
Fourth Week—Orkney West Mainland Agricultural Society at Garson, Sandwich.
Fourth Saturday—Taunton Vale on Kingsmead School playing fields Wiveliscombe.
Oxton. Blackface hoggs on impressive braeface course in Lauderdale, Berwickshire.
West Renfrewshire on the edge of Knapps Loch outside Kilmalcolm.
Four Roads at Roscommon in the Central Plain of Ireland.
Fourth Sunday—Wheatley. North Berkshire Sheep Dog Trials Association in conjunction with Oxford Country Sports Fair on attractive course in Shot-over Park, Wheatley, Oxford.
Dromara by B7 road south-west of Ballynahinch in County Down.
Charleville in County Cork
Fifth (or last) Week—Rathdangan in County Wicklow.
Fifth (or last) Saturday—Lairg Sheepdog Trials Association (1967). Good testing National-style trials serving the Highland Region, with 250 yards gather, 300 yards drive of North Country Cheviot hoggs over a flat pasture park at Coloboll Farm by Loch Shin in Sutherland.
Lintrathen (1969) at Formal Farm west of Kirriemuir by Strathmore, Angus. Open layout of 350 yards gather and 150 yards drive of Blackface sheep over hill field.
Fifth (or last) Sunday—Braddan, Isle of Man, over the Manx National course at Port-e-chee Meadow near Quarter Bridge outside Douglas.

The North Berkshire Society's committee, Betty Corley, Ron Webb, Jimmy Ogston, Bill de-Grey, Bill Smith (Chairman), Barbara Houseman (Secretary—and the first lady ever to be elected to the directorate of the I.S.D.S. in 1980), and Alan Walters. The trials organised by this, and some other societies in the area of Wessex, are equal to any National event.

July

First Week—*Watten* county between Wick and Thurso in Caithness.

Atacal in County Down.

Killarney in the lovely countryside of County Kerry in the south-west of Eire.

First Saturday—*Shepherdswell,* north-west of Dover in Kent.

Llanerchymedd, a level course in central Anglesey.

Great Glen over rough ground at Spean Bridge, north of Fort William in Inverness.

Buchanan at Drymen by the shores of Loch Lomond.

Evanton. Good gather of Cheviot hoggs over a National-type course by Cromarty Firth in Ross-shire.

Smailholm between Earlston and Kelso in the Borders.

St Boswell's near Melrose in the Borders.

St John's, Isle of Man, on the sports field by the St John's to Foxdale road.

First Sunday—*Cambridge* on Huntingdon racecourse.

Yarcombe, Honiton in east Devon.

South Somerset open driving class at Royal Bath & West Showground at Shepton Mallett.

Tregony (1979) at Trewarthenick Estate as a feature of the village carnival week. A testing course of National standard with a 400 yards gather of polled Dorsets across a valley in beautiful wooded grounds east of Truro in Cornwall.

Seaton Ross (1980). Halfbred ewes on old airfield adjoining Agricultural Show in Humberside.

Nier at Ballymacarbry south of Clonmel in County Waterford, Eire.

Downhill in County Londonderry, Northern Ireland.

Second Week—*West Somerset Hunt* at Dunster in Somerset.

Lewis Trials at Shawbost on north-west coast of Isle of Lewis for Hebridean Cup.

Ness Trials at Lionel. Machair, Butt of Lewis for Hebridean Cup.

Skye Sheepdog Society (1976) at Drumuie by Portree. A 270 yards gather, 150 yards drive over a flat area of hill ground bordered by earthen dykes—Hebridean Cup.

Glan Gwana at Caethro near Caernarvon. Welsh Mountain sheep on 300 yards rising gather in Snowdonia.

Fort Belan Sheep Dog Trials Society at Dinas Dinlle, Llandwrog, near Caernarvon. 250 entries from Wales, England, Scotland over three eliminating National-type courses on flat airfield with finals on second day. Regularly televised by BBC Welsh programme.

Beddgelert below Snowdon in the National Park of beautiful scenery in North Wales.

Manx National Trials at Port-e-chee Meadow, near Quarter Bridge, outside Douglas. Isle of Man Championship which has been greatly responsible for improvement of the island collies since started in 1939. First-class trials with qualifying tests to National-style and Double-gather Championship. Brace Championship.

Hilltown, north-east of Newry by the Mourne Mountains in County Down.

Second Saturday—Liskeard Show, Cornwall. Small course adjacent to showground.

Launceston. Double 400 yards gather of crossbred sheep over flat open pastureland to the north of Bodmin Moor at Botathon in north Cornwall.

Ellwood Sports Club (1964), Gloucestershire. Delightful setting at Trowgreen Farm in the Royal Forest of Dean.

Butser Shepherds Society (1978). National-type trials with novice and four-counties team events on Half-bred sheep in a beautiful valley nestling into the western end of the South Downs at the Queen Elizabeth Country Park fair at Horndean, sixteen miles north of Portsmouth in Hampshire.

Stenton near Dunbar. North Country Cheviots on a hill course in East Lothian.

Aberfeldy & District J.A.C. Blackface hoggs midst the hills of Perthshire.

Poltalloch over Kilmartin's National course in Argyll.

Strathaven Agricultural Exposition (1979). A 500 yards outrun at Braehead Farm in the Southern Uplands. Site of the 1982 Scottish National.

North Uist (1980) at Hosta in the Outer Hebrides.

Westside trials on Shetland.

Kildalton and Oa Sheepdog Society on the Isle of Islay.

Sulby, Isle of Man. National style by the Sulby to Ramsey road.

Second Sunday—Brenzett on Romney Marsh in Kent.

Dundee. East of Scotland event at Camperdown Park, Dundee.

Bennettsbridge. A fine big course in the Nore Valley north of Thomastown in County Kilkenny, Eire.

Third Week—Cornwall Sheep Dog Society at Lower Tregale Farm, Liskeard.

Warkworth near Banbury, Oxon.

Sutton Agricultural Show, Thirsk, North Yorkshire. Flat grassland course adjoining the showground.

Royal Welsh Agricultural Society. Invitation trials on the hill by the Llanelwedd showground, Builth Wells, Powys.

Efailnewydd in Bodfal Bach field on the Lleyn Peninsular near Pwllheli.

Bute Sheepdog Trials Association (1928). Strong testing Blackface hoggs over a wide sloping pasture of 350 yards outrun at Eskeehraggan Farm—of fatstock fame—on the Isle of Bute. (First Wednesday after Glasgow Fair—variable.)

Third Saturday—Ewhurst Green near Robertsbridge in Sussex.

Eglingham Leek Club. A National-type test of the Northumberland League over pastureland north-west of Alnwick.

Ruardean Woodside Sheep Dog Trials Society (1945). National and South-Wales classes on medium size pasture, high on Ruardean Hill on the northern edge of the Royal Forest of Dean.

Guisborough. 400 yards rising gather of Masham ewes on pastureland by the Cleveland Hills.

Stamford on the Meadows by the River Welland in Lincolnshire.

Nocton (Lincoln). Halfbred ewes over flat grassland in Lincolnshire.

Mathon (1965). Good sized course over rising ground near Cradley at the foot of the Malvern Hills.

Mynyddislwyn Sheepdog Society (1900), near Blackwood, Monmouthshire. A trial of great repute over a large, testing and natural course of approx. 700 yards gather on the mountain at Toneiddon. South-Wales and National styles.

Llanrwst in the Vale of Conway, North Wales.

Dunvegan Sheepdog Society (1949) Blackface sheep on a 400 yards gather on sloping pasture to National style at Mrs Campbell's Croft on the Isle of Skye.

North Harris in the Hebridean Cup.

Inversnaid Sheepdog Society. Hill trial at Garison Farm in the beautiful country of the Trossachs. Open to counties of Perthshire, Argyll, Stirlingshire and Dunbartonshire.

Gairloch & District Sheep Dog Trials Association (1950). Blackface sheep over a large hill course by the coast at Achtercain, Wester Ross.

Aboyne. Blackfaces on the Castle Home Farm by the River Dee, Aberdeen.

North Mavine trials on Shetland.

Heriot (1948). A good National-style trial with 300 yards gather of Blackface hoggs over flat pasture-land at Corsehope Farm by McFie Hall in the Moorfoot Hills of Midlothian.

Third Sunday—Devon & Exmoor Sheep Dog Society between Bampton and Wiveliscombe on Devon–Somerset border.

Meyseyhampton (1979) east of Cirencester over large slightly rising field in conjuction with Vale of White Horse Hunt kennels open day. Halfbred sheep to National style.

Peterborough (1981). Qualifying and Double-gather Championship at Ferry Meadows.

Newcastleton invitation trials.

Johnstown by Freshford in County Kilkenny, Eire.

Castlewellan by the A25 Downpatrick to Newry road in County Down, Ireland.

Rushen, Isle of Man. Blackface sheep on National course by Shore Hotel by road from Castletown to Port St Mary in the south of the island.

Fourth (or last) Week—Porlock. Exmoor horn sheep on recreation ground in Somerset.

Ryedale & Pickering Agricultural Show. A wide flat course with 300 yards gather adjoining the show-field.

Royal Lancashire Agricultural Show. National-style course over undulating grassland at Witton Park, Blackburn. Three days of top North Country competition culminating in championship final.

Newquay, Cornwall. Popular trials on Suffolk cross-breds with 350 yards outrun, difficult driving on uphill course at Lower Treludderow Farm, near Newquay on the holiday coast.

Par. Good 400 yards gather of Poll Dorsets over undulating high ground overlooking St Austell Bay at Penpell Farm, Par, in Cornwall.

Sarn at Y Ddol near Abersoch, south of Lleyn Peninsular.

Aberdaron on the southern tip of the Lleyn Peninsular.

Llandudno Sheepdog Trials Society (1923) on the former International course of Maesdu Golf links, Llandudno, North Wales coast, with the Ty-Gwyn Championship stakes on National lines.

Cowal Sheep Dog Trials Association by Dunoon on the Firth of Clyde.

West Sandwick, Yell, Shetland.

Fourth (or last) Saturday—Bishop Wilton Show in the Yorkshire Wolds.

Norden & Bamford Agricultural Show, Rochdale, Lancashire. Small grassland course over undulating ground adjoining showfield.

Husthwaite Agricultural Show (1946) adjoining showfield at Acaster Hill in the Vale of York.

Lorton (Cockermouth). 250 yards level gather of Swaledales at Casshow in Lorton Vale, the valley of the River Cocker in Western Lakeland.

Penrith Agricultural Show. Good flat 350 yards pastureland course to National style adjoining showfield at Lowther Bridge, Penrith, in Cumbria.

Cleveland Agricultural Show. Small course by the showground in Stewart's Park at Darlington.

Vale of Evesham (1959). Open course to National style on various sites in the locality of Pershore.

Haggerston. Small course by the A1 inland from Holy Island in Northumberland.

Devon & Exmoor at Collacott Farm, Langtree, Torrington.

Huby and Sutton-on-Forest. Big National-style course of 350 yards gather in level Parkland by Sutton Hall in the Vale of York.

Sedlescombe at Lower Jacobs Farm north of Hastings in Sussex.

Belford. Testing trial over the pastures of the Northumberland League on the A1 road inland from Budle Bay.

Newent (1979) near Gloucester. Strong competition in Open and Brace trials with Double-gather Championship at Alderley's Farm, Newent in Gloucestershire.

Denbigh at Kilford Farm in the Vale of Clwyd.

Glamorgan and Gwent novice events at Alps Farm, Wenvoe, south of Cardiff.

Alma, Meidrim, north of St Clears, Carmarthen.

Trefeurig, Banc-y-Darren. Two open classes.

Rhesycae at Tyddyn Farm near Flint by the Dee Estuary.

Criccieth on Tremadoc Bay, Caernarvonshire.

Islay, Jura, and Colonsay Association at Islay.

Dougarie on Arran.

Nairn on the Moray Firth north-east of Inverness.

Doon Valley (1948). Hill trial with 350 yards gather, 240 yards drive of Blackface gimmers on the banks of the River Doon—made famous by Robbie Burns—at Dalmellington in the Southern Uplands of Ayrshire.

Edinburgh (1975). National style with 400 yards flat gather of Blackface hoggs at Mauricewood Mains Farm, Penicuik, south of Edinburgh in the Pentlands.

Fourth (or last) Sunday—Hornsea. A good and popular National test over 400 yards of flat pastureland at Frodingham in Holderness.

Bedfordshire Y.F.C. A strongly contested and popular event to National standard at Manor Farm, Wilstead, in Bedfordshire.

Lochgoilhead Sheep Dog Trials Association (1977). Confined (Cowal and Campbeltown areas) National-type trial on undulating pasture in Drimsynie Park.

Blairgowrie Tourist Association. Blackfaces at Rosemount in Strathmore, Perthshire.

August

First Week—Gwithian by St Ives Bay in Cornwall.

North Devon Agricultural Show at Bideford.

Simonsbath on Exmoor in Somerset.

Thornton Dale Agricultural Show in the Vale of Pickering in North Yorkshire.

Harewood Agricultural Society, trials in Harewood Park near Leeds in West Yorkshire.

Keswick. Mini-International with invited teams from England, Scotland, and Wales over the parkland.

Vale of Llangollen Sheep Dog Society (1890) at Plas-yn-Vivod, west of Llangollen. Prestigious Cambrian Stakes 'open to the world' on Vivod and Eirianallt fields with championship of leading dogs from each field.

South Wales Sheep Dog Trials Association at Llystyn Farm, Brechfa, Carmarthen.

New Cross (1973) south-east of Aberystwyth. Border–Leicester × Speckled-face sheep on 25 acres flat course.

Builth Wells, Powys.

Abergavenny (1950). A long flat course to National style at Great.

Lhoyngwyn at the foot of the Black Mountains in Gwent.

Aberaeron at Pengarreg Field near New Quay in Cardigan.

Lampeter. National and South-Wales trials in Cardigan.

Cwm Owen. South-Wales style on mountainside of Mynydd Eppynt between Builth Wells and Brecon.

Bennlech and District Sheep Dog Association at Cae Top Fields, Bryteg on Anglesey.

Llanllyfni at Bryngwydion Field on the A499 Caernarvon–Pwllheli road.

Talsarnau at Ty Cerrig Farm on A496 north of Harlech.

Conway and District Sheepdog Society (1922) by the Sychnant Pass road in North Wales.

Llanfairfechan on the coast of Conway Bay between Conway and Bangor.

Tignabruich. Ardlamont trials by the Kyles of Bute in Argyll.

Tallaght near Dublin City, Eire.

Ballycastle on the northern point of Antrim, Ireland.

First Saturday—Whitechurch and Sampford Spinney near Tavistock in Devon.

Macclesfield Sheepdog Trials Association (1947). Leading National-style trials with Double-gather Championship in Cheshire at Sutton near Macclesfield.

Husbands Bosworth and Theddingworth. A good National-style trial in the attractive parkland setting of Bosworth Hall Park between Market Harborough and Lutterworth in Leicestershire.

Osmotherley Horticultural & Agricultural Society. Limited competition on a small flat course by the showground on the western slopes of the Hambleton Hills to the east of Northallerton.

Boon Hill trials at the Saltersgate Hunt show and gymkhana in the picturesque area of Newton Dale on the North Yorkshire moors above Pickering.

Powburn. Northumberland League trials off A697 road south of Wooler.

Udimore at Road End Farm near Rye in Sussex.

Alma Meidrim at Waunolev Fawr Fields.

Trefeglwys. National style course by the Roman road to Caersws, west of Newton in Montgomeryshire.

Elan Valley. South-Wales style contest in the Cambrian Mountains by Rhayaden.

Trelech in Carmarthen. National and South-Wales styles.

Whitton Women's Institute (1931). National and South-Wales style trials organised by the Women's Institute over small flat course south of Knighton in Radnorshire.

Largs Agricultural Society. Popular event attracting large entries at Fairlie on the Firth of Clyde in Ayrshire.

Ardkinglas (1924) at Cairndow at the head of Loch Fyne in Argyll. One of the most prestigious and practical tests in Scotland with a double-gather

over 500 yards of steep hill side rising through 400 feet to lift.

Duns at the foot of the Lammermuirs in Berwickshire.

Keith Sheepdog Trials Association. National-style course at Braco Farm, Grange, Keith.

Aberdeen trials.

Creich & Kincardine. North Country Cheviots at Invercharron Mains by Kyle of Sutherland estuary to Dornoch Firth in the Highland Region.

Fintry in the Campsie Fells of Stirlingshire.

First Sunday—Bath and West Showground at Shepton Mallett in Somerset.

South Molton, South Cockerham in Devon.

Marple Bridge. Testing double-gather of hill ewes over the undulating grassland of the Cheshire–Derbyshire border.

Lilford Park south of Oundle in the Nene Valley of Northants.

Oldhamstocks. Good gather on the east of the Lammermuirs on the East Lothian–Berwickshire borderland.

Kilbeheny near Mitchelstown in County Cork.

Castlefinn in Donegal.

Rathkenny in County Antrim.

Second Week—Heighington. Large flat course north of Darlington in county Durham.

Hinderwell Agricultural Show on the north-east coast by Runswick Bay near Whitby in North Yorkshire.

Lake District Sheepdog Trials Association. A society founded in 1897 which has done much for working collies in an area where they are of vital importance. Top class test of working dogs whilst held over the famous fell course of Applethwaite Common. Venue changed to Ings between Windermere and Staveley.

Bala. The most historic of trials—the first-ever trials held in 1873—now held on the flat lands by the River Dee with two National-type courses on the first day and the leading six dogs from each contesting a Double-gather Championship of International standard on Welsh Mountain sheep on the second day.

Machynlleth on the Dovey Valley north-east of Aberystwyth in Powys.

Llanbedrog by A499 Abersoch to Pwllheli, Lleyn Peninsular.

Cardigan County at Cilpyll, Bwlchllan, Lampeter.

Caerwedros. Medium sized course near New Quay in Cardigan.

Doldowlod at Glangwy Ddole between Newbridge-on-Wye and Rhayader.

Abersoch & Llanengan. South of Pwllheli on the southern point of the Lleyn Peninsular.

Llwyngwril on Barmouth Bay.

Harlech in Merionethshire.

Trawsfynydd by the lake off A487 in Merioneth.

Second Saturday—Hastings at Alexander Park in Sussex.

Barbon. Sound workmanlike test on hill sheep over steep fellside grassland in the Manor Park on

Cumbria–Yorkshire border in Lunesdale. Top class demands and worthy test of stamina and intelligence. Open and novice classes and village sports.

Caton. Good hill course in Littledale near Lancaster in North Lancashire.

Hornby. An extensive course in the Lune Valley above Lancaster.

Lowgill at Parkhouse in Tatham Fells of North Lancashire.

Glanton. National style by the ancient Devil's Causeway off the A697 south of Powburn in Northumberland.

Llanwrtyd Wells. Beulah Speckled-face sheep on flat course over Abernant fields.

Newbridge-on-Wye at Penbont Field near Llandrindod Wells.

Gwynfe open National style.

Llangurig. National style in Cambrian Mountains south-west of Llanidloes.

Llanarmon-yn-Ial in the Clwydian Range south-east of Ruthin.

Trelech. National and South-Wales styles by B499 road north of St Clears in Carmarthen.

West Perthshire Sheepdog Society at Trean Farm, Callander by the Trossachs in the lovely Perthshire countryside.

Uyeasound (1950). The most northerly trials in Britain on testing Shetland–Cheviot crossbred sheep over a 450 yards gather which dips to the lift on the croft of Ronan in Uyeasound, Unst, Shetland.

Mull and Morvern.

Latheron. Open to Caithness and Sutherland on the coast south of Wick.

Amulree. A tough hill course in Strath Braan in Perthshire.

Kinlochbervie in the north-west by Loch Inchard in Sutherland.

Second Sunday—*Dulverton* in Somerset.

Lowick. A Northumberland League trial over National-style pasture a few miles inland from historic Holy Island.

Kinneff J.A.C. at Mineral Well Park, Stonehaven, on the Kincardine coast.

Hawick in the heart of Border sheep country in Roxburgh.

Carnwath in the Pentlands of the Borders.

Third Week—*Kilkhampton* at Herdacott Farm north of Stratton in Cornwall.

Vale of Rydal, Rydal Park near Ambleside. Lakeland's famous 'dog-day' with open and novice courses set in narrow adjoining valleys, undulating and testing with sheep often bad to manage. Hound-trails and hound-show included in programme.

Dovedale. Well established top class competition in the beautiful Derbyshire dale of the River Dove near Ilam, north-west of Ashbourne. Site of 1967 English National trials.

Northern Sheepdog Association at Denton near Darlington in County Durham. Testing double-gather course on Mule ewes by the Roman road of Dere Street.

Meltham Sheepdog Society, Huddersfield, West Yorkshire. National-style layout on big flat rough grassland at Blackmoorfoot near village of Meltham.

Threlkeld Sheepdog Trials Society. Keen competition of northern collies in Lakeland setting near Keswick, Cumbria, with hound-trails and show.

Glassonby. Level 300 yards course in the Eden Valley above Penrith in Cumbria.

Llangeitho at Goyallt Field west of Tregaron in Dyfed.

Llangwynfon, south of Aberystwyth.

Pentre-Ty-Gwyn near Llandovery.

Llanilar (1978) Flat parkland course with 350 yards gather south of Aberystwyth. National and South-Wales styles.

Rhiw. One of the oldest trials in Wales at Penarfynydd near Aberdaron on Lleyn Peninsular.

Llandrillo in the Berwyns east of Bala.

Llangower on the shores of Bala lake.

Kingussie Sheep Dog Trials Association on Speyside in Inverness-shire.

Nethy Bridge Sheepdog Association (1946). National style on flat field at Tomachrochar Farm in Strath Spey.

Watten Sheep Dog Trials Association at Bilbster Farm in Caithness.

Mey Sheep Dog Trials Association (1945). A 400 yards gather of North Country Cheviot ewes to National style over the most northerly trials course on the mainland at Barrogill Mains near Mey village in Caithness. Trials often attended by Her Majesty the Queen Mother whose rose-bowl is contested in the Open Championship.

Michael, Isle of Man. At Whitehouse Farm just north of Kirk Michael.

Third Saturday—*Ashwater Agricultural Show* near Beaworthy in Devon.

Brushford near Dulverton in Somerset.

Wingham in Goodnestone Park east of Canterbury in Kent.

Ravenstonedale Agricultural Show near Kirkby Stephen in Cumbria.

Ripley Agricultural Show near Harrogate, North Yorkshire.

Chatton Horticultural Society, Chatton, near Wooler in Northumberland.

Brampton Abbotts near Ross-on-Wye, Hereford. National style with 600 yards gather, with the championship decided on a double-fetch test. Magnificent view over Welsh hills.

Sutherland Sheep Dog Trials Association, Dunrobin, Golspie. A most testing trial on the site used for the Scottish National event.

Betws Garmon at Plas Isaf Farm in Snowdonia.

Llanuwchllyn off the A494 road south of Bala lake.

Llanrhaeadr ym Mochnant by B4580 on Denbigh–Montgomery border.

Betws yn Rhos on B5381 south of Colwyn Bay.

Llanwrda at Cwmargenau near Llandovery.

Lower Chapel (1965) north of Brecon in Honddu Valley. National and South-Wales tests over uneven pasture with a gather of crossbred sheep over 300 yards and 110 yards driving.

Llanddeusant at Nantgwinau Farm in the Black Mountain south of Llandovery.

New Cumnock (1893). Well established trials by the A76 between Cumnock and Sanquhar in Ayrshire.

Glenfarg Sheep Dog Trials Society (1966). A rising 300 yards gather of Blackface hoggs in the Ochil Hills of Perthshire.

Dumfries & Lockerbie Agricultural Society (1969). National-style trials on level ground at Drumlanrig Estate, Thornhill.

Appin Sheepdog Society at Greenfield Farm, Duror, in North Argyll.

Colmonell & Ballantrae Agricultural Society at Pinwherry in the Carrick District of Ayrshire.

Skipness by Kilbrannan Sound in North Kintyre.

Campbeltown in South Kintyre.

Glenealy by Wicklow in Eire.

Third Sunday—Warrenford by the A1 road between Belford and Alnwick in the coastal lands of Northumberland.

Gower. National and South-Wales styles at Penrice Castle.

Arbory, Isle of Man. 350 yards National gather of Halfbreds at Friary Farm, Ballabeg, off the Castletown to Colby road in the south of the island.

Kilcullen by the Liffey in County Kildare, Eire.

Glenariff (Waterfoot) on the north-east coast by the Red Bay in County Antrim. Northern Ireland.

Fourth (or last) Week—Reeth Agricultural Society near Richmond in Swaledale, North Yorkshire.

Egton Bridge Agricultural Show. Small course in the North Yorkshire moors inland from Whitby.

Hesket Newmarket. Swaledale ewes on a compact course near Caldbeck in north Cumbria.

Crosby Ravensworth in Westmorland fells east of Shap.

Monmouth Show. Suffolk crossbreds over a level course in South-Wales and National Styles.

Llandrillo. National type near Corwen.

Nantlle Vale at Talmignedd Isef, Drws-y-Coed, Nantle.

Llanwddyn south-east end of Lake Vyrnwy in Montgomery.

Caerwedros Y.F.C. at Blaenglowenfawr, Talgarreg. Sports and tug-o-war.

Atholl and Weem Sheepdog Trials Club (1927). National layout of 350 yards gather over a large and very picturesque tree-dotted flat field in The Target Park of Blair Castle by Blair-Athol in romantic Grampian country.

Fourth Saturday—Mountfield north of Battle in Sussex.

Chipping Agricultural Show in Bowland, Lancashire.

Good testing course with 400 yards uphill fetch of Swaledales.

Whittingham in the valley of the River Aln west of Alnwick in Northumberland.

Falstone in the North Tyne valley of Kielder Forest in Northumberland.

Hayfield. Small hill course by the side of the Grouse Inn between Hayfield and Glossop in North Derbyshire.

Downham. Rising course in two fields with wall and brook obstructions in the shadow of Pendle Hill of Lancashire witchcraft legend near Clitheroe.

Rhandirmwyn (1930). Long established trials in Tywi valley amid the Cambrian Mountains north of Llandovery.

Libanus. A flat 300 yards fetch at Lower Cwmclyn Farm, Libanus near Brecon.

Dolgellau. Open and novice National-style classes by the market town in Merioneth.

Ruthin in the Vale of Clwyd.

Llansannan by the A544 road in Denbighshire.

Llanfyllin by the A490 road in Montgomery.

Clova. North of Kirriemuir in Agnus.

Peel, Isle of Man. At Headlands Field off the Peel to Kirk Michael road in the west of the island.

Fourth Sunday—Brentor trials of the Devon & Exmoor Sheep Dog Society.

Kendal Lions Club (1975). Swaledales on undulating ground at Spitalfields at the start of Kendal Gathering week in south Cumbria.

Hawkshead, north of Esthwaite Water in the lovely Lake District country of Cumbria.

Kirknewton. Northumberland League trials at the foot of the Cheviots west of Wooler in the valley of the River Glen.

Hawes (1981) by the river in Wensleydale.

Northleach. North-east of Cirencester in Gloucestershire.

Three Lochs near Kirkcowan in Wigtownshire.

Fifth (or last) Saturday—Challacombe south of Lynton on Exmoor in North Devon.

Flimwell at Rosemary Farm on The Weald in Kent.

Lyme Sheepdog Trials Society. Good three-day programme with Double-gather Championship at Plattwood Farm in Lyme Park, Disley, near Stockport in Cheshire.

Abbeystead. Country-bred ewes over a good course in the valley of the Wyre in North Lancashire fell country.

Malham Agricultural Show. Small course by the showfield in lovely Dales country of Yorkshire.

Ullswater Sheepdog Society. 'Dog-day' at Patterdale amid the Lakeland fells in Cumbria with open competition on testing course of driving work for the Lonsdale Stakes. Hound-trails and show.

Stoke Climsland. A good 'old fashioned' Cornish trial in a welcoming country atmosphere with crossbred sheep not easy over a short course north of Callington on the Devon border.

Wensleydale Agricultural Show. Swaledale gimmers on

a testing drive at Leyburn in the Yorkshire Dales.
Coquetdale at Warton. Northumberland League trials near Rothbury.
Dufton. Good 300 yards gather of Swaledales on pastureland in the Eden Valley in Westmorland.
Withington (1980). Mule ewes over a large undulating Cotswold pasture south-east of Cheltenham in Gloucestershire.
Ceiriog Valley Sheepdog Society (1901) at Glyn Ceiriog near Chirk in Clwyd. A strongly contested championship—'open to the world'—with collies worked in two eliminating trials on the slopes of the valley before the top dogs meet in the final. National style with 500 yards gather of Welsh Mountain sheep on the hillside. Sheep show and gymkhana.
Penybont Fawr off B4396 road north-west of Llanfyllin.
Llangwm off A5 west of Corwen in Denbigh.
Senni. National and South-Wales styles in the Usk Valley west of Brecon.
Westruther Sheepdog Trials (1949) and sheep show at Westruther Mains in the Lammermuirs of Berwickshire.
Carrick Sheepdog Society at Knockgerran Farm, Girvan, in the Carrick district of south west Ayrshire.
Alva, north of Alloa in Clackmannanshire.
Fifth (or last) Sunday—Kirkley Hall, Northumberland College of Agriculture. By the River Blyth between Ponteland and Belsay, north-west of Newcastle.
Romney Marsh at Burmarsh, south of Hythe, Kent. 350 yards gather, 450 yards drive of Romney sheep on flat marsh land.
Strathkinness, by St Andrews in Fife.
Springkell Sheepdog Society (1976). Blackface ewes on 350 yards gather over tree-dotted parkland at Springkell House, Eaglesfield, Lockerbie.
Burncourt near Clogheen in County Tipperary.
August Bank Holiday—Garstang on the fringe of the Bowland Fells in Lancashire.
North Berkshire Sheep Dog Trials Association (1968). Quality trials of testing National style held on the legendary Blowing Stone Field in White Horse country near Wantage.
Hope Valley Agricultural Show, Hope, Derbyshire. The highest competition from leading collies in the sheep country of the High Peak and the beauty of the North Derbyshire Dales.
Wolsingham in Weardale west of Crook and Tow Law in Durham.
Great Draynes, Liskeard, Cornwall. Driving and maltese-cross tests on a downhill gather of Poll Dorsets in a pleasant Country Fair setting.
Wooler. National-style trial at the market town of the Cheviots in Northumberland.
Llanwonno. National and South-Wales styles in Carmarthenshire.
Maelienydd. National course on the open hill near Knighton in Radnor.

Pontardulais adjoining showfield north-east of Llanelli.
Llanedwen on Llwyn Onn fields near Llanfair PG, Anglesey. 400 yards rising gather on National-type course.
Pistyll Rhaeadr near Oswestry.
Llansilin by the B4580 west of Oswestry.
Garndolbenmaen by the A4085 Caernarvon to Portmadoc.
Llanbrynmair in the Cambrian Mountains by A489 west of Newtown.
Newcastleton. Good double-gather trials in Liddesdale in the Cheviots.
Sutherland Sheep Dog Trials Association at Dunrobin.

September
First Week— Lunesdale Agricultural Show near Sedbergh.
Longshow (1898), Grindleford, near Sheffield. Three days of top quality work in an ideal moorland setting from collies of England and Wales, and often from Scotland, over one of the most famous courses in Britain, culminating in the Longshaw Championship which is a coveted and prestigious honour in the sheepdog world.
Upper Wharfedale Agricultural Show Popular event at Kilnsey by the River Wharfe.
Llanarthne. 400 yards gather with rising ground and natural obstructions at Wernbongam Farm east of Carmarthen.
Pennal in the Dovey Valley west of Machynlleth.
Caethro in Snowdonia.
Ladyhill in Antrim.
First Saturday—Kildale Agricultural Show in the Cleveland Hills.
Dent. Open work on Swaledale ewes at Hill Top Farm near Sedbergh.
Devon County & West of England Championship at Halsanger, Newton Abbot.
Otterburn Border Sheepdog Society, Northumberland. Two days of the strongest trials competition from English and Scottish collies at Brownchesters in the Redesdale country of sheepdog origins.
Northern Sheepdog Association at Wynyard Park, Wolviston, north of Stockton on Teeside in Cleveland.
Hodder Valley Agricultural Show. Held at either Newton or Slaidburn in Forest of Bowland, Lancashire, of sound testing proportions on grassland course.
South Somerset Preservation Society at Curry Rivel, Langport, Somerset.
Harbottle. Hill trial in the historic centre of the medieval Middle March in Coquetdale, Northumberland.
Bodmin. Cornwall Sheep Dog Society Championship trials deep in the beautiful Cornish countryside surrounded by woodland and hill at Burlorne Tregoose.
Northleach (1978). Large sloping course near the

village by the Foss Way north of Cirencester in the Cotswolds.

Gladestry. National and South-Wales classes by the Hergest Ridge on the Radnor–Hereford border west of Kington.

Llandderfed by the B4402 road near Bala.

Pontrhydfendigaid north-east of Tregaron near Strata Florida Abbey.

Tregaron. National and South-Wales classes at Penybont Field.

Hundred House. National and South-Wales styles.

Rhayader on flat course by the River Wye in Radnorshire.

Brechfa Agricultural Society (1912) at Llystyn Farm, Brechfa on the edge of the beautiful Cothi Valley north-east of Carmarthen. National and South-Wales styles with 300 yards rising gather of Black and Speckled-face ewes.

Laggan (1954), near Newtonmore, Inverness-shire. 400 yards gather of Blackface sheep, 200 yards driving, on flat land at Gaskbeg Farm in Badenoch.

Glendevon and District Sheepdog Trials Association. A testing course in the Ochil Hills east of Dunblane.

Argyll County at Bridgend on central Islay.

Rosehall in Strath Oykel south-west of Lairg.

Rogart, west of Golspie in the Highland Region.

Lockerbie Sheep Dog Society (1951) at Broomhouses Farm, Lockerbie.

First Sunday—Egton in the North Yorkshire Moors near Whitby.

Thanet Sheepdog Society (1959). Championships on Isle of Sheppey. Mule sheep on 400 yards gather, 450 yards drive on undulating downland.

West Anstey, Hawkridge, Dulverton in Somerset.

Carnlough on the east coast of County Antrim by the A2 road in Ireland.

Second Week—Cwmdauddwr. National and South-Wales styles on rising ground.

Cairncastle Sheepdog Society (1936). Good trials with 300 yards gather, 250 yards drive of Blackface sheep from the Antrim Hills on Cockermaine Farm pasture by the village of Cairncastle, four miles from Larne in County Antrim.

Second Saturday—Ivybridge at Stowfold Farm in Devon.

Otterburn, by Hellifield in Ribblesdale. A large level course with testing drives.

Beulah in the Irfon Valley near Llanwrtyd Wells.

Efail Isaf at Berth Llwyd Farm, Pen-y-Coedcae, Pontypridd.

Llangynidr in Brecknock.

Llanarmon Dyffryn Ceiriog, south of Glyn Ceiriog in Denbigh.

Pandy at Cefn Clytha Farm, Grosmont.

Vale of Usk (1855) in Monmouthshire. South-Wales and National styles with Suffolk crossbreds on a steep hillside adjoining Usk Show.

Acharacle at Strontian, eastern end of Loch Sunart in Argyllshire.

Strathnaver at Syre Farm in Sutherland.

Borthwick Water at Roberton west of Hawick in the Borders.

Yarrow Show.

Second Sunday—Exford on Exmoor in Somerset.

Sussex Sheepdog Society (1962). Championship of 350 yards gather, 450 yards drive of Mule sheep at Birling Manor on the South Downs near Eastbourne.

Llangeitho, National and South-Wales styles.

Jedforest in the sheep lands of the Borders.

Skye double-lift hill trials at Ostaig by the Sound of Sleat, Isle of Skye.

Kildorrey. Small course north-west of Fermoy in County Cork.

Third Saturday—Whitworth between Bacup and Rochdale in East Lancashire.

Northern Sheepdog Association at Sough Hill, Caldwell, on Durham–North Yorkshire border. Halfbreds on stubble.

Ousby. An uphill gather of Swaledale ewes in the Northern Pennines, north-east of Penrith in Cumbria.

Hayfield. Strong competition for the Peak District Championship over a double-gather course at Spray House Farm above the village in North Derbyshire.

Meon Valley (1976). National, gently sloping open course in Corhampton Park, on A32 near Winchester, on the South Downs in Hampshire.

Slaggyford, Northumberland. In the valley of the South Tyne on the Cumbrian border.

Whitley Chapel. Northumberland League trials south of Hexham.

Launceston. Devon and Cornwall Championships on driving and maltese cross courses at Bothathon Farm in North Cornwall.

Penmachno by the B4406 south of Betws-y-Coed.

Llanafan Fawr (1885) A 500 yards gather of Beulah Speckled-face ewes to South-Wales style in one of oldest trials in Wales between Newbridge-on-Wye and Beulah.

Cefn Coch. A small flat course on Speckled-face sheep near Welshpool.

Stirling Sheep Dog Society at Kildean.

Strathaven. 500 yards gather over the 1982 Scottish National site at Braehead Farm.

Saline at Cadgerford Farm by the B913 north-west of Dunfermline in Fife.

Teviothead between Hawick and Langholm by the A7 in Roxburghshire.

Cairnryan & District Sheep Dog Trials Association on the shores of Loch Ryan north of Stranraer in Wigtownshire.

Third Sunday—Kildovery in County Cork.

Fourth (or last) Week—Nidderdale Agricultural Show at Pateley Bridge in Yorkshire.

Kentmere in the Kent Valley north-east of Windermere in Westmorland.

Senni. A big rising course near Brecon in South Wales.

Moniaive (1918). Long standing trials of good

reputation with Blackface ewes over slightly hilly terrain at Crechan Farm in Dumfriesshire.

Fourth (Or last) Saturday—Stoke Bliss near Tenbury Wells.

Brampton near Appleby, Cumbria. Open and local classes which are always well supported by top class collies.

Crosthwaite. Work on Rough Fell ewes in the Lyth Valley east of Lake Windermere in Cumbria.

Rochester in the historic sheepdog country of Redesdale in Northumberland where in 1876 the first English trials were held at nearby Byrness.

Holme Sheepdog Trials Association (1959). National-style 300 yards gather across stream on undulating grassland at entrance to Cliviger Gorge in conjunction with the ancient Sheep Fair of Holme-in-Cliviger near Burnley in Lancashire.

Escleyside at Vowchurch in the Golden Valley between Hay-on-Wye and Pontrilas in Hereford shire.

Penybont. South-Wales and National styles on flat land by the river in the Ithon valley near Cross Gates, Llandrindod Wells, Powys.

Ysbyty Ifan in the Conway Valley.

Caerwys off the B5122 in the Clwydian Range.

Abington and District Sheep Dog Society near Crawford in the Southern Uplands of Lanark.

Newton Stewart and Kirkcowan at Boreland Farm, Kirkcowan, south-west of Newton Stewart in Galloway.

Elmford near Duns in the Borders.

Tomatin hill trial with double-gather off the A9 in Inverness-shire.

Strathlochlan in Argyll.

Drakemyre near Dalry north-east of Ardrossan.

Glenkens Collie Dog Trials Club at Newfield Farm, Dalry on A737 south of Paisley.

Fourth (or last) Sunday—Devon & Exmoor novice trials at Downes Crediton.

Chatton Sandyfords, Chathill. National-type course with Blackface sheep over the Chatton moors in Northumberland.

Hoo between Thames and Medway near Rochester in Kent.

October

First week—Cashel in the Golden Vale of County Tipperary.

First Saturday—East Guildeford at Salts Farm near Rye in Sussex.

Northern Sheepdog Association at Carkin Field, East Layton on Durham–North Yorkshire border. 350 yards gather of Masham ewes over National-type layout of long drives on stubble flats.

Cockermouth in Western Lakeland, Cumbria.

Wormside. National style on large flat course at Webton Court, Kingstone, near Hereford.

Kirkconnell & Sanquhar. South Country Cheviots by the A76 in Nithsdale in the Southern Uplands.

New Luce. Big outrun over hill-type course in Wigtownshire east of Stranraer.

Yetholm in the borderland of the Cheviots.

Sorn Sheepdog Trials Association (1946) popular trials with 400 yards gather of four Blackface ewes over steep green field at Blindburn Farm in Ayrshire.

First Sunday—North Newbald Good gather of Masham ewes on stubble course south of Market Weighton in the Yorkshire Wolds.

Portadown south of Lough Neagh, South-west of Belfast in County Armagh.

Second week—Cornwall County Championship on Suffolk cross sheep at Burydown near Liskeard.

Gatehouse. Confined to handlers from Galloway.

Second Saturday—Alwinton in Coquetdale in the Cheviots, Northumberland.

Northern Sheepdog Association at Howe Hills, Great Stainton, County Durham.

Manmoel on the mountain between the Ebbw and Sirhowy valleys in South Wales.

Crosshill. Popular trial south of Maybole in Ayrshire.

Manor Water south of Peebles in the famed Border sheep country.

Second Sunday—Humbie. Blackface ewes on a double outrun over undulating stubble ground in the Borders.

Third Saturday—Painscastle. Beulah Speckled-face ewes over an interesting course on undulating ground by the village between Builth Wells and Hay-on-Wye in south Radnor.

Third Sunday—Cardiff. National-type course on Ty Du Farm, Nelson.

Bannow. A good course by the south coast near Bridgetown in County Wexford.

Fourth (or last) Saturday—Weobley. Long gather of Halfbreds over a narrow National-type course at Twyford Farm, Pembridge in Herefordshire.

Clun Y.F.C. (1981). Speckled-face ewes over a National course on a sloping field at Llanhedric Farm, Bicton, off the A488 road between Clun and Bishops Castle.

Bargrennan. A good testing hill course at the southern edge of Glentrool Forest by the A714 Girvan to Newton Stewart road in Galloway.

Barr. Double-lift at Knockeen Farm by the B734 road east of Girvan in Carrick.

Dalmellington. Local trials at Minnivey Farm in the valley of the Doon River by the A713 road in Ayrshire.

Indexes

Where a topic or dog is referred to on numerous occasions (as in breeding details) the main references only are included.